On Weak-Phases

An Extension of Feature-Inheritance

Tomonori Otsuka

Kyushu University Press

Kyushu University Press
3–8–34–305, Momochihama Sawara-ku, Fukuoka-shi 814–0001, Japan

ISBN 978–4–7985–0197–0

Printed in Japan

Table of Contents

Acknowledgments

This book is a revised version of my doctoral dissertation, which investigated the nature of weak-phases in the Minimalist Program's Phase Theory. The focus of this book is an examination of a theoretical problem with Chomsky's (2008) Feature-Inheritance framework, which was the basis for the development of the Minimalist Program to a large extent, the first draft of which appeared in 2005. The central idea of this book was first presented at the 65th general meeting of the Kyushu branch of the English Literary Society of Japan held at Kyushu Sangyo University in 2012 and was then presented at some other conferences, including the 6th ELSJ International Spring Forum held at Tokyo University, the 66th general meeting of the Kyushu branch of the English Literary Society of Japan held at the International University of Kagoshima, and the 31st and 32nd general meetings of the English Linguistic Society of Japan (ELSJ) held at Fukuoka University and Gakushuin University, respectively. The main part of these discussions was published as Otsuka (2014) and, finally, all the discussions were gathered and reorganized into this book (also, a summarized version of the whole discussion was presented at the meeting of the Fukuoka Linguistic Circle (FLC) held at Fukuoka University in 2015).

While I was writing the original version of this book and then revising it, I have been supported by so many people that it seems almost impossible to fully express my gratitude here, although I would definitely like to try. Moreover, it is pity that because of the requirement of my Sensorimoter system, I have to thank them in a linear order. Let me emphasize that the order is a purely phonological matter and my gratitude is equally deep for all the people related to this book.

No matter what I write here, I cannot thank Nobuaki Nishioka enough. He supervised me at Kyushu University and taught me not only about generative grammar, but also inspired in me the pleasure to research languages. He is truly earnest in his research but has a warm and friendly personality, which is probably the reason why I enjoyed the research I undertook under his supervision. He read the first draft of Otsuka (2014) and gave me invaluable suggestions, even though he was intensively busy as Secretary General of ELSJ, lacking the time to sleep. Even after I had finished my studies at Kyushu University, he still offered me the chance to keep in touch with the graduates and graduate students. The meetings held there are a jewel box, where insights, ideas, and suggestions are gathered. With no doubt, without his sincere support, I could not have come this far.

I also want to express my special thanks to Toshiaki Inada, who taught profound knowledge in various fields of linguistics including syntax at Kyushu University. His class was filled with his passion for linguistics which impressed me deeply. Even after retirement, he still teaches us on various occasions, such as at some meetings, or even at cafes and restaurants, which is a great joy to me.

I would also like to give thanks to the other members of the dissertation committee. Hiroshi Ohashi taught me a lot of intriguing linguistic phenomena from the point of view of cognitive linguistics. Tomoyuki Kubo offered me some insightful comments as well as stylistic suggestions concerning phonetic transcription. Moreover, I am sincerely grateful to Tsutomu Sakamoto, who should have been a member of my committee, for having taught me how to enjoy research in various ways.

Apart from the committee, I am truly indebted to Hisatsugu Kitahara, who helped me understand the theoretical framework behind the generative grammar through his intensive lectures at Kyushu University in 2015. During the lectures, he gave us time for discussion even after the classes, which was a great opportunity for me to connect with the latest theories. I am also obliged to Shigeyuki Fujimoto, who taught us studies related to argument structure over two semesters in 2013 and 2014 at Kyushu University. In addition, I sincerely appreciate the dedication of Carey Benom. He read whole parts of the original version of my thesis, pointed out the grammatical errors, and offered me stylistic suggestions, even though he was very busy. He also gave me constructive comments about the discussions in the original version of this book from a different perspective, which broadened my viewpoint. My thanks also go to Stephen Laker and Jenifer Larson-Hall, who not only taught me at Kyushu University but also gave me grammatical judgments on many examples as well as writing style suggestions. Moreover, I am grateful to the literature teachers at the English department of Kyushu University, Kazuhiko Murai, Nobumitsu Ukai, and Yasushi Takano.

I am also thankful to two anonymous reviewers at Kyushu University Press. Their comments and suggestions helped to deepen my views on various topics. I also thank two anonymous reviewers at ELSJ for their invaluable suggestions and advice. Additionally, I am indebted to the chairs at the 31st and 32nd general meetings of ELSJ and 65th and 66th meetings of Kyushu branch of English Literary Society of Japan; Fumikazu Niinuma, Yoshiki Ogawa, Yoshihiro Munemasa, and Yubun Suzuki. I also appreciated the comments from the floor at all the meetings above and the FLC meeting in 2015. Of these, Miki Obata, Nobu Goto and Shin-Ichi Tanigawa gave me especially fruitful comments. I sincerely thank them, again.

I express my deep gratitude to the graduates and graduate students at the English department of Kyushu University. Above all, I am genuinely thankful to Hiroyoshi Tanaka, who has offered me a great deal of advice since I was writing Otsuka (2014). Without doubt, I could not have completed that paper and the original version of this book, were it not for his help.

I would also like to thank Takayoshi Kurogi, who is my co-worker (and, also partly my superior). He helped me in my first year as lecturer at Kyushu Kyoritsu University when I was nervous in the new environment. In addition to conversations about work, we sometimes talked about our research, which got me back to the enjoyment of the study of the generative grammar. Thanks to his support, I could barely find the time to revise my dissertation for publication.

Furthermore, I am genuinely grateful to Masako Maeda, who read the dissertation draft and offered me particularly valuable comments and suggestions, even when she was very busy with publishing her book. Her ideas were always insightful and improved the depth of my thinking.

My thanks also go to Megumi Nishimura, Shoji Yamamoto, Masahiko Dansako, Sho Shimokariya, Kento Nagatsugu, Rumi Takaki, Takashi Kayashima, Riichi Yoshimura, Hiroshi Yanagimoto, Kiyoko Takaba, Yoichiro Yamamoto, and Norimasa Hayashi, who have supported me, encouraged me, and, above all, offered me inspiration concerning research.

I would also like to express my thanks to the editorial staff of Kyushu

University Press, especially to Mari Ichinose and Rie Oishi, as well as my sincere apologies for repeatedly delaying the submission of the draft of acknowledgement (which indicates how hard it was for me to put my feelings of thankfulness into a few pages). Moreover, this book was published as one title of *Studies in the Humanities* thanks to financial support from the Faculty of Humanities, Kyushu University.

Finally, let me devote just a little space to my personal acknowledgements. I am grateful to all of my friends and the alumni at Kyushu University (including Takuro Mizukami, Shuhei Yasumatsu, and Shingo Kanasaki) and to all the people involved in Yamakasa, who heartened me through their enjoyable conversations over uncountable glasses of beer. I am also thankful to Junko Saitsu for her untiring support. She has always cheered me on since writing the original version and relieved me when I had problems with my research. She also read the whole original version and gave me helpful comments. Lastly, I would like to say thanks to my family. Firstly, thanks to my grandmother Hideko, who had gone to the better place when I was writing the revised version; my great regret is that I could not show her my book. Furthermore, I thank my brother Kazuhiro and my parents, Shigeki and Atsuko, who understand me and have always supported my research and the writing of this book.

Again, thank you to all the people who have supported me. All of you have made me what I am.

On Weak-Phases: An Extension of Feature-Inheritance

1

Introduction

Generative grammar has been pursuing explanatory adequacy in research on human languages since its outset in the 1950s. Researchers have attempted not only to describe the grammar of human languages, but also to explain why it is what it is. The enterprise of generative grammar once achieved a level of analysis which is to some extent satisfying in the GB era. However, the framework in the GB era, which presupposes an extremely rich UG including a lot of apparatuses, rules, and filters, raises a doubt in terms of Darwin's problem (see Hornstein (2009)); can human beings have learned such a complicated grammar in "the blink of an evolutionary eye (Hornstein (2009: 5))?" The Minimalist Program (the MP) was initiated by Chomsky (1995) to answer such a question.

In the MP, researchers' attention is therefore shifted from proposing new rules and restrictions for linguistic phenomena to reducing them to more principled factors (as is shortly touched on in 2.1). In this way, UG, which was once assumed to be truly complex, has been simplified and, hopefully, discussions in generative grammar are becoming more and more convincing.

With such a tendency, Chomsky (2000) has proposed one interesting concept; phases. Under the Phase Theory, a sentence is considered to be constructed separately in multiple small units called phases. Therefore, syntactic derivations occur phase by phase in the new framework unlike the former framework, where a sentence as a whole is constructed in one fell swoop. The introduction of phases enables us to reduce the computational burden to a large extent since the computation can *forget* the syntactic operations within earlier phases. Thus, phases contribute to a further theoretical development of the framework in generative grammar.

In Chomsky (2000) and his subsequent works (2001, 2007, 2008, 2013, 2015), it is suggested that CP and *v*P form phases and this assumption is widely adopted today.[1] However, there is one question which is not answered completely: whether *v*P always forms a phase or not. Interestingly, Chomsky (2001) assumes that *v*P phases are subdivided into strong-phases (represented as "*v**P") and weak-phases (expressed as "*v*P" without "*"). As summed up in (1), the strong-phase *v**P can assign the accusative case to an object, introduce an external argument, and trigger transfer, while the weak-phase *v* loses all of these abilities.

(1) Differences between *v**P and *v*P

	*v**P	*v*P
a. Case Assignment	Yes	No
b. External Argument	Yes	No
c. Transfer of Complement	Yes	No

In his following papers, however, Chomsky has not discussed the detailed

1 Of course, there are other approaches. For instance, Epstain and Seely (2002) and Abels (2003) argue that every XP may constitute a phase. However, Chomsky's assumption seems to me to be empirically and theoretically preferable and thus I will follow his assumption in this book.

In addition, Chomsky (2015) proposes the latest framework, which is sometimes referred to as POP+. POP+ radically develops the Phase Theory based on the assumptions that internal/external merge is freely available when a phase is formed (Free Merger), phase-head-ness is inherited by the complement-head, and the transfer domain shifts. Although this latest framework is fascinating and may bring about a drastic development of the Phase Theory, I claim that it raises some empirical and theoretical problems that should be solved. The first problem and probably the most serious one is that under the free merger-based framework, superiority, which is captured in the former framework (namely Chomsky (2008)) based on an Agree operation and intervention effect, cannot be formulated any longer because any movement operation should be allowed as long as it produces a labelable constituent under the assumption of free merger. Of course, we can make some additional assumption based on representational relations such as "this type of movement beyond this element is banned." However, such an assumption is, needless to say, ad hoc and theoretically dis-preferred. Furthermore, as is touched on in footnote 6 and 8, respectively, the framework of POP+ raises the simultaneity problem and it cannot formulate A/A-bar distinction and the ban on Improper Movement based on transfer domains without additional assumptions. Hence, POP+ still requires a great deal of theoretical debates concerning its validity and it is too early to move on to a wide range of empirical analysis based on it. Because of this reason, discussions within the framework of POP+ are left for future studies and this book adopts Chomsky's (2008) version of the Phase Theory with Feature-Inheritance-based simultaneous operations (although Chomsky's (2013) Labeling Algorithm is discussed in Chapter 6).

status of the weak-phase *v*P anymore. While some researchers have even attempted to eliminate *v*P by assimilating it into the strong-phase *v**P (see Legate (2003) and Richards (2012)), in the other research, to my best knowledge, discussions on weak-phases have been ignored even when verbal phases are referred to.

The aim of this book is, therefore, to shed light on this unclear and also unwelcome concept of weak-phases. Importantly, we cannot ignore the weak-phase *v*P once we assume verbal phases. Let us briefly see the main point of this discussion.

(2) a. John was hit *t*. (passive)

b. John arrived *t*. (unaccusative)

In (2), the subject *John* moves from the complement of VP to Spec-TP. Putting aside details of the relevant discussions (see chapter 2 for the details), a phase is assumed to serve as a boundary for movement operations under the recent version of the Phase Theory (see especially Chomsky (2007, 2008)). For A-movement, a phase boundary acts as a barrier, whereas it serves as a host for an intermediate landing site for A-bar movement. That is, A-movement cannot occur beyond phase boundaries, while A-bar movement is capable of passing the boundaries by moving successive-cyclically from one phase edge to another. Therefore, if we eliminate weak-phases, the examples in (2) should be taken as indicating that such *v*P does not constitute a phase.

On the other hand, the following examples suggest the opposite.

(3) a. [At which of the parties that he_i invited $Mary_j$ $to]_k$ was every man_i t_k' introduced to her_j t_k?

b.* [At which of the parties that he_i invited $Mary_j$ $to]_k$ was she_j t_k introduced to every man_i t_k?

(Legate (2003: 2))

According to Legate (2003), the examples in (3) imply that the Spec of *v*P in passive and unaccusative examples is available for reconstruction so as for the bound pronoun *he* and the pronoun *her/she* to be interpreted properly (see 3.1.2 for more detail). Now, given that the reconstruction operation requires a trace (or a copy) under normal assumptions, the examples in (3) indicate that the A-bar element is moved via the Spec of *v*P. This, in turn, suggests that *v*P in passive and unaccusative examples constitutes a phase.

Now, we face a contradiction if we do not assume weak-phases; on the one hand, the examples in (2) suggest that *v*P in passive and unaccusative sentences *must not be a phase* in order for the subject DP to be moved to Spec-TP, but on the other hand, the examples in (3) indicate that *v*P in passive and unaccusative examples *can act as a phase* so as for the *wh*-element to be moved via the Spec of *v*P. The situation can be summed up as in (4) as *the paradox of weak-phases*.

(4) The paradox of weak-phases
  a. Concerning A-movement, a weak-phase serves **as a non-phase**.
  b. Concerning A-bar movement, a weak-phase serves **as a phase**.

It is worth noting that the paradox in (4) has been ignored in previous research. However, if we sincerely tackle the status of *v*P, (4) raises the serious problem for the present Phase Theory.

In this book, I attempt to contribute to the development of the present Phase Theory by solving the paradox in (4). I demonstrate that the paradox of weak-phases is solved by assuming that weak-phases actually exist and suggesting a solution in (5). Moreover, book proposes the operation called Feature-Transcription as in (6) to derive (5). In (6), *S-Ph-H* and *W-Ph-H* stand for *strong-phase head* and *weak-phase head*, and *EF* and *AF* represent *Edge Feature* and *Agree Feature*, respectively.

(5) A solution to the paradox of weak-phases:
  The operations in a weak-phase must occur **at the next strong-phase level**.

(6) Feature-Transcription

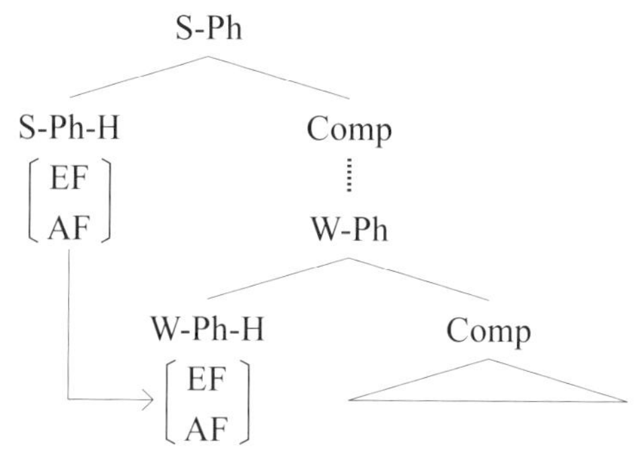

Feature-Transcription in (6) is an activation operation from a strong-phase head to a weak-phase head. I claim that based on this assumption, the paradox of weak-phases is readily solved.

Moreover, the claim in this book has an interesting theoretical consequence. The assumption in (6) can derive "optionality" in syntactic operations. Probably, it is fair to say that optionality is one of the most difficult concepts to derive in the MP. Because derivations or operations are evaluated in terms of "economy" in the MP, optionality is not usually obtained in the present framework in the Phase Theory.[2] However, optionality is derived as a consequence of two kinds of equally legitimate derivations in (7) in the framework of this book:

(7) a. Simultaneous-derivation:
The syntactic operations in a weak-phase occur simultaneously with those in a strong-phase above it.

b. Individual-derivation:
The syntactic operations in a weak-phase occur independently from those in a strong-phase above it.

It is also argued that these two possibilities in (7) derive optionality in case

2 Interestingly, as anonymous reviewers point out, optionality is readily derived under Chomsky's (2015) framework based on "free merger." However, as is discussed in footnote 1, the new framework raises some empirical and theoretical problems. Thus, this paper pursues a possible way to derive the optionality within Chomsky's (2007, 2008) framework, without adopting free merger.

manifestation patterns in tandem with the transfer-based case assignment mechanism in (8).

(8) A phase head determines a DP's case within its domain, when it triggers Transfer.

Thus, another contribution of this book is to explain optional phenomena. As can be witnessed below, there are many phenomena related to optionality in human languages. Notice that the following examples are difficult to accommodate within the present framework in the MP.

(9) The nominative/accusative case conversion in Japanese (see 4.3)

a. Taro-ga migime-o tsumur-e-ru (koto).
Taro-Nom migime-Acc close-can-Prs (the fact)

b. Taro-ga migime-ga tsumur-e-ru (koto).
Taro-Nom migime-Nom close-can-Prs (the fact)
'(the fact that) Taro can close his right eye.'

(10) The Raising-to-Object Construction in Japanese (see 5.2)

a. Taro-wa Yuki-o [baka da to] omot-teiru.
Taro-Top Yuki-Acc [stupid COP COMP] think-Prog
'Taro thinks that Yuki is stupid.'

b. Taro-wa [Yuki-ga baka da to] omot-teiru.
Taro-Top [Yuki-Nom stupid COP COMP] think-Prog
'Taro thinks that Yuki is stupid.'

(Takeuchi (2010: 101))

(11) Preposition-stranding/pied-piping in English (see 6.3)

a. Who did you give the book to?

b. To whom did you give the book?

I argue that the Feature-Transcription framework can explicate the problems of optionality observed above.

Therefore, the main claim in this book is that a serious consideration on the status of weak-phases not only sorts out tangles in the recent Phase Theory, but also increases an explanatory power of the Phase Theory by accounting for optional phenomena.

This book is largely divided into the two parts. The first half of the book mainly includes theoretical discussions on weak-phases. In chapter 2, I will provide background assumptions of the discussion, namely, uninterpretable feature checking, the Phase Theory, Feature-Inheritance, and A/A-bar distinctions. Based on the background, we will move to the paradox of weak-phases in chapter 3. After introducing the paradox, I will propose the main claim of this book, namely, Feature-Transcription.

Then, the discussion moves to explanations of empirical problems in the latter half of this book. Firstly, in chapter 4, we will investigate verbal weak-phases. This chapter includes phenomena related to passives; the inflection-movement connection in passives in some Scandinavian languages and Icelandic, which are discussed by Holmberg (2002), Richards (2012), and so forth, and Thematization/Extraction in English, which is suggested by Chomsky (2001). In addition, this chapter deals with the Japanese nominative/accusative case conversion as is discussed by Koizumi (1994), Tada (1992), Ura (1996), and Takahashi (2011). The last part of this chapter is dedicated to the Double Object Construction in English, which has attracted the attention of a large number of researchers (e.g. Barss and Lasnik (1986), Larson (1988), Oba (2005), and Bruening (2010a, b)) but unsolved problems still remain.

In chapter 5, we move to clausal weak-phases. Kanno (2008) points out that some CP layers do not constitute phases. Taking such a non-phase CP as a weak-phase version of CP, I will account for phenomena related to Quantifier Floating in *wh*-questions in an Irish dialect of English (see McCloskey (2000)) and the nominative/accusative case conversion in the Japanese Raising-to-Object Construction (see e.g. Saito (1985), Oka (1988), Sakai (1998), Hiraiwa (2005), Ura (2007), and Takeuchi (2010)). Following that, I explicate Complementizer Agreement in West Flemish pointed out by Haegeman and Koppen (2012) based on the concept of weak-phases.

Chapter 6 deals with phenomena related to prepositional phrases, namely, *p*P weak-phases. The main topic in this chapter is closely related to adjunct islands. In this chapter, I will pursue an explanatory possibility of Chomsky's (2013) Labeling Algorithm regarding adjunct islands. Following the discussion on adjunct islands, I claim that the Feature-Transcription framework can derive the optionality of preposition-stranding and preposition-pied-piping in English. In addition, I also address a problem of obligatory preposition-pied-piping in rightward movement in this chapter, as pointed out by Drummond et al. (2010).

Finally, I will conclude this book in Chapter 7.

2

Theoretical Background

In this chapter, I will give an overview of the theoretical background of this book, namely, the assumptions of uninterpretable feature checking, the Phase Theory, Feature-Inheritance, and the A/A-bar distinction. In 2.1, we will take a look at the concept of uninterpretable features, which are triggers for syntactic operations in the MP. In 2.2, we move to the Phase Theory, which has been a focus of research for more than a decade in the MP. These discussions about uninterpretable features and the Phase Theory lead us to the assumption of Feature-Inheritance suggested by Chomsky (2008), which is shown in 2.3. Finally, we turn to a brief history of the A/A-bar distinctions in 2.4.

2.1 Uninterpretable Features and Syntactic Operations

After the Government and Binding (GB) era finished, a lot of changes were made with the dawning of the MP era. One of the most influential changes is that "economy" is considered to be the most important factor in the MP. That is to say, the more economical a certain operation is, the more highly it is evaluated in the MP.

Note that in the GB era, syntactic operations were freely applied as Move-α, and quite a few mechanisms (such as indexes and traces) and restrictions (e.g. case filter, Empty Category Principle and so forth) were suggested to rule out unwelcome outcomes. Based on the concept of "economy" in the MP, however, such mechanisms cannot be adopted due to the Inclusiveness Condition and the restrictions should be derived from more fundamental principles with sufficient motivation.[3] Moreover, in the MP, no syntactic

3 However, these terms, such as indexes and traces, may be used in what follows only for explanatory purposes.

operations are available without compelling factors. That is to say, some triggers for syntactic operations should exist.

A question is, then, what the trigger for syntactic operations is. As was already mentioned, we cannot add new apparatuses without a theoretical or empirical requirement in the MP. Nevertheless, even if we abandon all of the additional mechanisms, features on lexical items remain irreducible. For example, the word *John* necessarily possesses features such as "third person" and "singular." Since a lexical items cannot be interpreted at the Conceptual-Intentional (C-I) Interface without such features, the existence of features is necessarily motivated. Therefore, Chomsky (1995) focuses on investigation of the nature and roles of features.

While the features *John* owns are interpretable, we can easily find features which seem to lack interpretations, e.g. φ-features on T, which are realized as inflection. Ideally, such uninterpretable features should not exist because they seem to play no role since they do not make any contribution to interpretations at the C-I Interface; Chomsky (2000) refers to this as an "imperfection" of human languages. However, the empirical fact that inflection appears in many languages indicates that such uninterpretable features actually exist. Given this fact, we have to assume that such uninterpretable features have to be removed from the derivation before they reach the C-I Interface; otherwise, they cause the derivation to crash for they violate the full interpretation principle in the MP. Based on this consideration, it is suggested that syntactic operations occur in order to deal with these uninterpretable features (see Chomsky (1995)). In other words, syntax has to check uninterpretable features to remove them before they are sent to the C-I Interface, and most of the syntactic operations occur through this feature checking. Therefore, these uninterpretable features are now considered to be triggers for syntactic operations in the MP.

Although it used to be argued that feature checking occurs in Spec-Head relations at the beginning of the MP era (e.g. in Chomsky (1995)), Chomsky (2001) proposes that feature checking occurs through an Agree operation: When a certain head is merged into the derivation, an uninterpretable feature (Probe) on the head starts to search its c-command domain in order to find its matching Goal and the uninterpretable feature is checked, as is schematically expressed in (12). Thus, it is now agreed that most of the syntactic operations (e.g. movement and agreement) occur through an Agree operation in (12).

(12) Agree

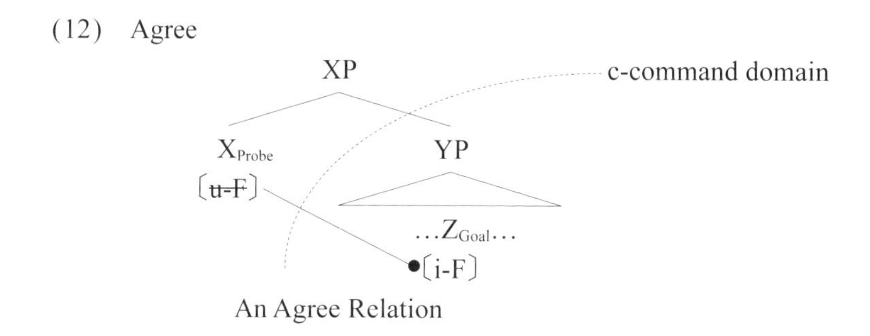

2.2 The Phase Theory

Although the assumption that syntactic operations occur based on Agree operations is more economical than the former assumption of Move-α, it should be noted that an Agree operation in itself can establish a relationship not limited by distance with the matching Goal as is expressed in (13).

(13)

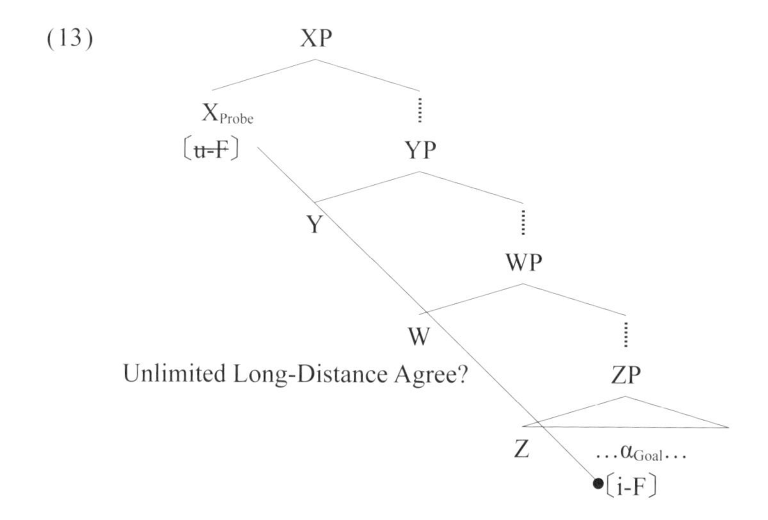

This still imposes quite a heavy burden on the human language computation and thus the mechanism is not economical enough. It is preferable that Agree operations should be limited locally somehow.

Concerning the theoretical inadequacy, Chomsky (2000) introduces the concept of phases, which prohibits this unlimited Agree operation. A phase is defined as a chunk of meaning and pronunciation, and is also argued to be a unit of syntactic operations.[4] Under the Phase Theory, a sentence is not constructed in one fell swoop, but is generated separately phase by phase. Each phase includes its sub-numeration, or lexical sub-array, which is collected from the lexicon. A phase starts its derivation based on its sub-array and when the sub-array is exhausted, the syntactic operations in the phase finish and phase head transfers its complement to the C-I Interface and the SensoriMotor (SM) Interface.[5]

(14) Phase

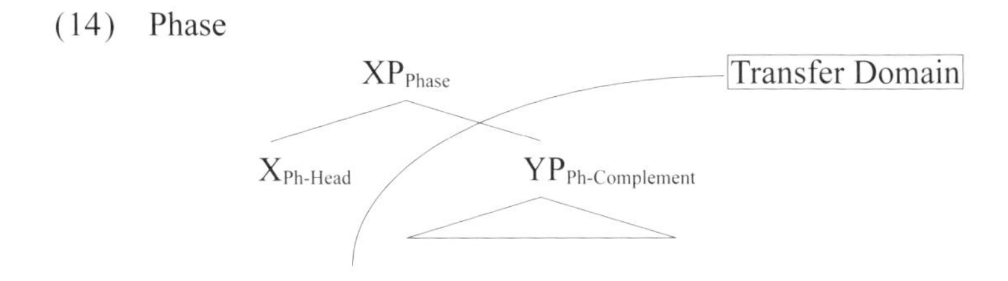

Moreover, syntactic operations in a phase cannot access an element within the complement of another lower phase, since the complement is already transferred to the interfaces. The ban on accesses into the complement of another lower phase is named the Phase Impenetrability Condition (the PIC). Note that when transfer occurs, the phase head and its Spec, which are called a phase edge, remain un-transferred. Therefore, an element has to move via the phase edge if it moves into the next phase, so as to circumvent a PIC violation. Thus, the PIC bans unlimited long-distance Agree operations as in (15), holding the locality of syntactic operations.

4 As a chunk of meaning, CP represents discourse-related interpretation and *v**P holds a full θ-role interpretation, as is touched on below. Moreover, Legate (2003) proposes a test for phaseness based on the Nuclear Stress Rule, which is related to pronunciation.

5 Chomsky (2001) assumes a different version of the PIC in terms of a different timing of transfer, namely, transfer in a phase is triggered when the next phase is completed. In this book, nevertheless, I follow Chomsky's (2000, 2007, 2008) version of the PIC in that the complement of a phase is transferred once the phase is completed.

(15) The PIC

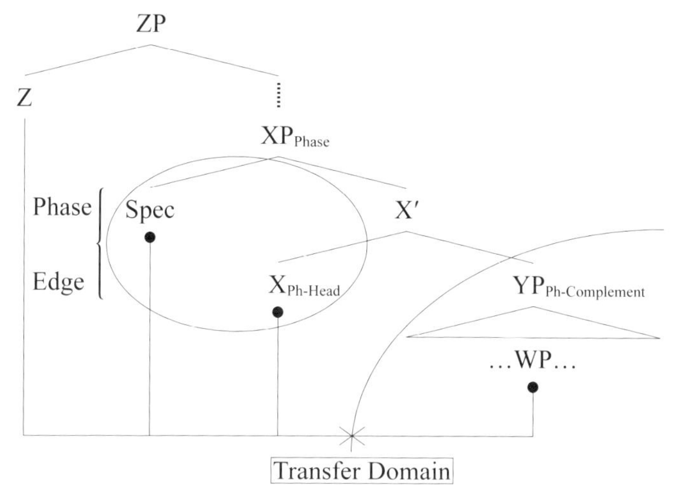

The introduction of phases enables us to reduce computational burdens as well as to rule out the unlimited long-distance Agree operations. The computation can forget the operations in the "past" phases because they are already transferred, which reduces the burden on computational memory. Moreover, multiple cycles which used to be suggested during the GB era, namely, operations in DS, SS, and LF/PF, are reduced into a single cycle within a phase. Thus, quite a large theoretical development is accomplished by the introduction of phases.

After the introduction of phases, research topics have moved to establishing the definition of phases. Chomsky (2000) argues that a phase represents a proposition. After theoretical and empirical discussions, Chomsky (2000) concluded that transitive *v*P (which is called *v**P), which represents a full theta-role relation, and CP, which represents a discourse-related interpretation such as interrogative and focus, form phases.

(16) a. CP Phase

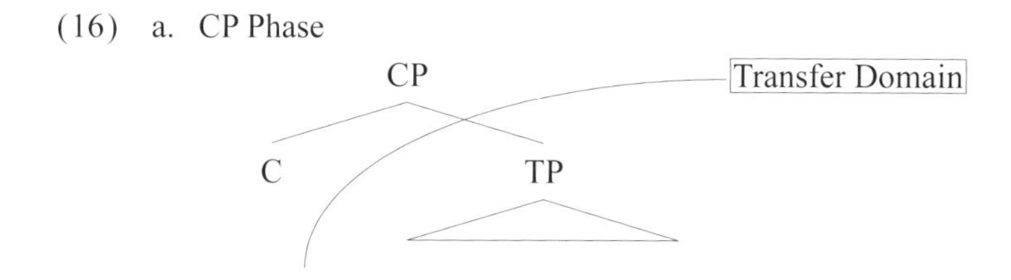

b. *v**P Phase

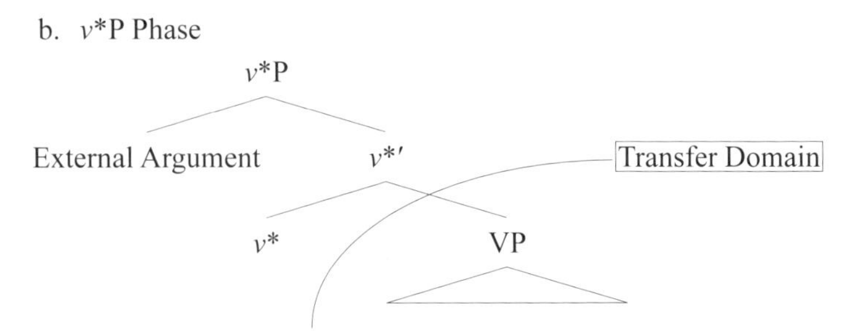

2.3 Feature-Inheritance

In this section, we take a look at a sequence of discussions between Epstein et al. and Chomsky concerning phases and uninterpretable features. Their discussions result in introducing concepts of syntactic values and Feature-Inheritance.

2.3.1 Uninterpretable Features and Syntactic Values

As was discussed in 2.1, uninterpretable features are considered to be triggers for syntactic operations in the MP. However, Epstein et al. (1998) cast a doubt on this feature checking approach. The most serious problem they point out is the following theoretical one: how can syntax know whether a relevant feature is interpretable or not before it is sent to the interfaces? Note that an uninterpretable feature is defined as a feature which is not interpreted at the C-I Interface. That is to say, the "uninterpretability" of the uninterpretable feature cannot be conceived of until it reaches the C-I Interface as is schematically expressed in (17).

(17)

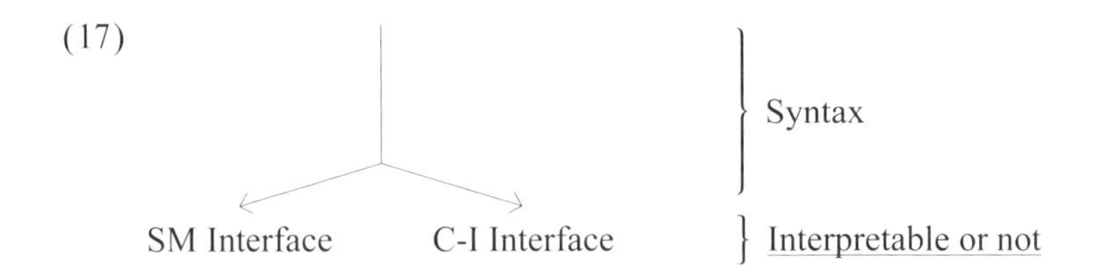

Therefore, if syntax has to distinguish uninterpretable features from interpretable ones in order to check them, syntax needs to look ahead so as to know what will happen at the C-I Interface. However, this "look ahead" is an unwelcome concept in the MP and should be avoided. Epstein et al. (1998)

refer to this problem as an "absolutely fundamental question." In sum, the original feature checking assumption contained a theoretical problem.

However, Chomsky (2001) introduces a concept of syntactic "values." Under this assumption, an uninterpretable feature is analyzed as a feature which lacks a syntactic value and an interpretable feature is a feature which has a syntactic value. *U-features* and *I-features* in (18) stand for *uninterpretable features* and *interpretable features*, respectively.

(18)		At Syntax	At the C-I Interface
	a. U-features	no value	uninterpretable
	b. I-features	value	interpretable

Owing to the introduction of syntactic values, syntax need not "look ahead" to know whether a feature is interpretable or not; it only has to see whether the feature has a syntactic value or not. Epstein and Seely (2002) use the following metaphor to explain this assumption: "Spell Out is analogous to a device that is designed to detect color (say, red vs. blue); but can in no way detect heat (say, hot from cold). But imagine that red is always hot and blue is always cold. In that case, we, as observers outside the device, can say that since it can distinguish red from blue, then it can effectively sort hot from cold without in fact being heat sensitive. Unvalued features are always PF- and LF-uninterpretable; and syntactically valued features are always LF-uninterpretable. So we can say that Spell Out can distinguish LF-interpretable from LF-uninterpretable without being 'semantically-sensitive' (Epstein and Seely (2002: 74))."

Moreover, there is another theoretical advantage concerning the introduction of syntactic values. They can also solve a problem of redundancy of "deletion" and "erasure" of features, which is another "architectural paradox" of a feature checking framework, as Chomsky (2001) touches on. Before the introduction of syntactic values, uninterpretable features are "deleted" through checking by their interpretable counterparts. However, some uninterpretable features have influences at the SM Interface. For instance, uninterpretable φ-features on T can be realized as "-es" at the SM Interface when they hold an Agree relation with interpretable φ-features with third person, singular values on a DP. On the other hand, the uninterpretable φ-features on T must not reach the C-I Interface, otherwise they will cause the derivation to crash since they are uninterpretable. Then, a question is what checking operations (or "deletion") can do to uninterpretable features. If checking completely eliminates uninterpretable features from the derivation at syntax, the features cannot reach the SM Interface. However, if they are not eliminated at all, the derivation crashes at the C-I Interface. Thus, redundant double operations used to be assumed: the uninterpretable features are checked (this is a "deletion" operation) but remain in the later derivation, and another operation "erasure" completely eliminates them from the derivation (at the timing of Spell-Out). Then, uninterpretable features can correctly be delivered to the SM Interface but removed before the C-I Interface.

(19)

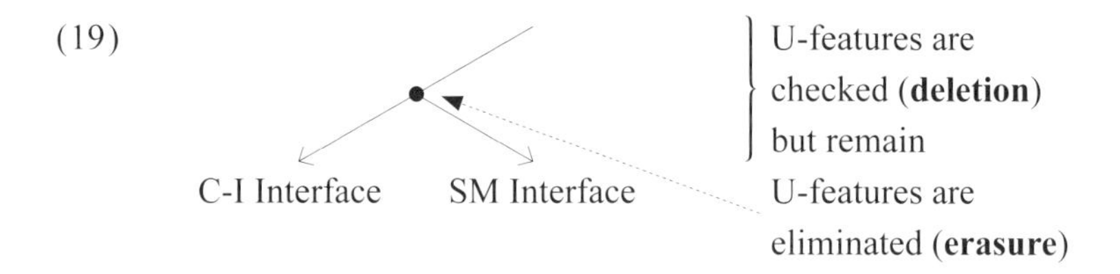

But, under the deletion-erasure assumption, the nature of checking becomes quite unclear; why should uninterpretable features be checked? Do they really have to be checked (or "deleted") if we have another operation "erasure," which can eliminate them? Obviously the two operations of "deletion" and "erasure" are superfluous.

Syntactic values offer us a solution to this problem. Feature checking is not "deletion" of an uninterpretable feature but is reframed as a copy operation of a syntactic value from an interpretable feature to its uninterpretable counterpart. Therefore, even after being checked, uninterpretable features exist in the derivation and can correctly be sent to the SM Interface. Moreover, if they have not been given syntactic values, their phonetic realization forms are not determined and they cannot be assigned proper pronunciation forms at the SM Interface. Therefore, the existence of feature checking (the former "deletion" operation), namely, copying operations of syntactic values, is theoretically motivated. On the other hand, the checked uninterpretable features have to be removed before reaching the C-I Interface. Thus, Spell-Out finally needs to get rid of them to prevent them from being delivered to the C-I Interface. Thus, the former "erasure" operation, namely Spell-Out, is also required. To sum up, the architectural paradox in the former feature checking mechanism is solved by the introduction of syntactic values.

2.3.2 A Simultaneity Problem

As we saw in the last subsection, syntactic values now play an important role in the feature checking mechanism. However, Epstein and Seely (2002) again point out a theoretical problem with this mechanism. If uninterpretable features are features without syntactic values and feature checking is a copy operation of a syntactic value, how can syntax distinguish uninterpretable features from interpretable ones after feature checking?

(20)		At Syntax	At the C-I Interface
	a. U-features	no value	uninterpretable
	b. I-features	value	interpretable
	c. Checked U-features	value	uninterpretable

As can be seen in (20), checked uninterpretable features have values and seem equivalent to interpretable features at syntax. However, since they are uninterpretable at the C-I Interface in essence, syntax needs to distinguish them from interpretable ones and prevent them from being delivered to the C-I Interface.

Chomsky (2001) realizes this problem and tries to deal with it. He claims that "Spell-Out must therefore apply *shortly* after the uninterpretable features have been assigned values (Chomsky (2001: 5))." However, Epstein and Seely (2002) claim that this is too late. They argue that uninterpretable features have to be transferred to the interfaces *at the same time* with checking. This is because even if they are sent to the interfaces *shortly* after checking, syntax still has to refer to their derivational histories so as to distinguish them from interpretable ones. That is to say, since checked uninterpretable features already have syntactic values, syntax needs to see whether or not the relevant features used to lack values in order to know whether they are interpretable or not. Nevertheless, this "look back" is not economical and thus dispreferred in the MP. Therefore, assumption (21) is suggested.

(21) Feature checking and transfer must occur simultaneously.

2.3.3 Richards (2007) and Feature-Inheritance

This simultaneity problem has remained unsolved. However, Richards (2007) offers an elegant solution to this problem based on Feature-Inheritance. Let us examine his solution in this subsection.

Chomsky (2008) proposes the Feature-Inheritance operation. But this assumption used to have nothing to do with the simultaneity problem in (21). Chomsky (2008) tries to derive two kinds of T, that is, φ-complete T, which is selected by C, and defective T, which is not selected by C, from a more principled perspective. Chomsky (2001) assumes independent items for them, namely, T and $T_{\text{-def}}$. However, if we assume that φ-completeness of T is derived from C, we need not assume the two kinds of T. That is, under this assumption, T itself has no uninterpretable φ-features but when C is merged with T, T inherits the φ-features on C.

(22) Feature-Inheritance

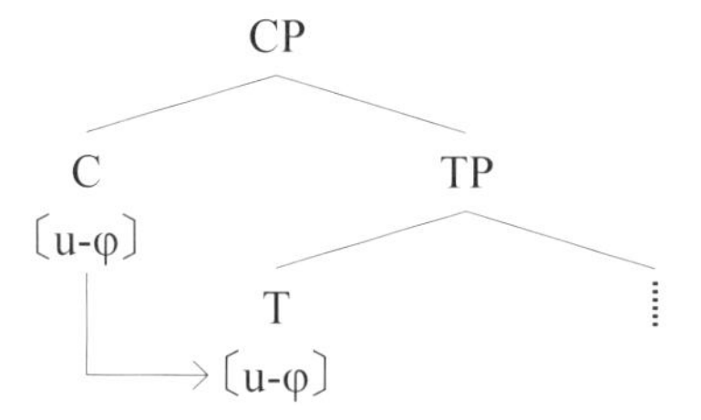

Moreover, Chomsky (2008) suggests that Feature-Inheritance occurs not only from C to T, but from a phase head to its complement head (or the label of the complement) in general. A phase head originally possesses uninterpretable features and its complement inherits them, triggering syntactic operations. Based on this mechanism, syntactic operations occur only after a phase head is merged since uninterpretable features do not exist within the complement of the phase head before Feature-Inheritance occurs. Therefore, a strict cyclicity in phases is derived. However, even though it contributes to quite an interesting theoretical development, Feature-Inheritance was a mere stipulation at that moment and the reason why this occurs remained unclear.

Richards (2007) offers both a theoretical backup to Feature-Inheritance and an explanation for the simultaneity problem noted in the last subsection, at once. Recall that under the normal assumptions in the MP, a phase head transfers only its complement, except for the head itself and its specifier (namely a phase edge). Then, if uninterpretable features originally exist on a phase head, they cannot be transferred when they are checked as in (23a). On the other hand, if we assume that these features are transmitted to the complement when syntactic operations occur, they can be transferred simultaneously with checking as in (23b). Thus, in order for uninterpretable features to be transferred simultaneously with checking, they have to be transmitted to the complement of a phase. This indicates that Feature-Inheritance is not a mere stipulation but it gains strong theoretical support; it has to occur to posit uninterpretable features in the transfer domain of a phase so as for the uninterpretable features to be transferred simultaneously with checking. Hence, a theoretical backup and a solution for the simultaneity problem in (21) are presented simultaneously.[6] In (23), *u-F* stands for *uninterpretable-feature*.

(23) a. The checked u-F is not transferred without Feature-Inheritance.

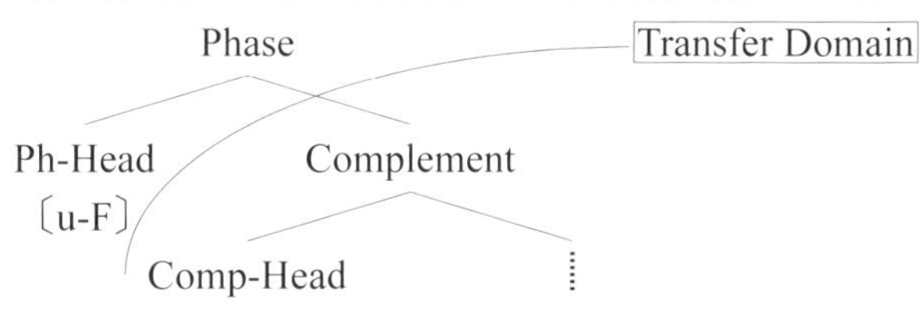

b. The checked u-F is transferred with Feature-Inheritance.

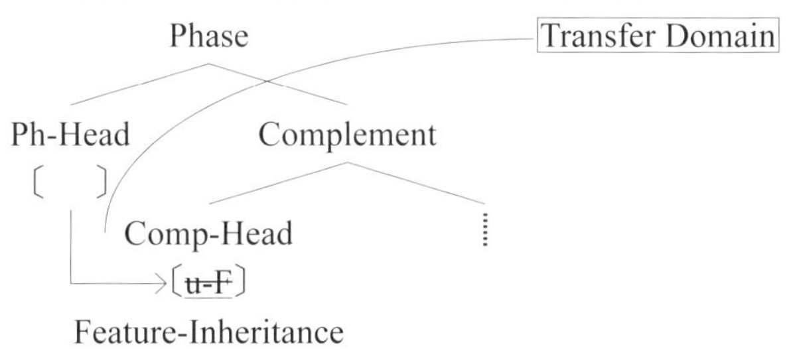

6 Obviously, the discussions in 2.3.2 and 2.3.3 are not carried over to Chomsky's (2015) latest framework, where the timings of Feature-Inheritance and Transfer are separated. Therefore, the theoretical problem noted in 2.3.2 arises within the new framework. Although Chomsky (2015) assumes "phase-based memory" and the simultaneity problem may be solved by this, it would be theoretically preferable if we can get rid of this assumption, as in Chomsky's (2007, 2008) framework.

2.4 A/A-bar Distinctions

Let us turn to a brief history of A/A-bar distinctions. Nowadays, syntactic movement operations are divided into two groups, namely A-movement and A-bar movement. A-movement is movement related to arguments and A-bar movement is concerned with operators. Representatives of A-movement are DP movement in passives, in the raising construction, and so on. On the other hand, examples of A-bar movement include *wh*-movement, focus movement, and so forth.

(24) a. John was hit *t*. A-movement (passive movement)

b. Who did you hit *t*? A-bar movement (*wh*-movement)

The A/A-bar distinction noted above was traditionally based on movement landing sites. Namely, A-movement is a movement operation into A-position and A-bar movement is that into an A-bar position. A-position is considered as a position where θ-role assignment and case assignment may occur. On the other hand, A-bar position is not related with θ-role or case but is a position for creating operator-variable relations. Thus, a movement operation into Spec-TP in (24a) is A-movement because Spec-TP is A-position related to nominative case assignment, whereas a movement operation into Spec-CP in (24b) is A-bar movement since Spec-CP is an A-bar position as it is an operator position.

However, based on the current assumption of feature checking, such a position distinction disappears. A DP is assigned the nominative case not because it moves into Spec-TP but because its interpretable φ-features establish an Agree relation with uninterpretable φ-features on T (see also 3.5.2). Thus, the movement operation of the DP to Spec-TP is a mere secondary product of the Agree relation and Spec-TP is not a case position any longer. Then, how can we define A/A-bar distinctions? Of course, we can assume that movement operations related to certain features (for instance, φ and case features) are A-movement and those related to others (say, *wh*/Foc/Top features) are A-bar movement. Nevertheless, such a definition is nothing more than ad hoc. As Chomsky (2004) even tries to abandon the A/A-bar distinction, the status of the A/A-bar distinction became quite unclear in the early MP.

However, note that strong empirical evidence for the existence of the A/A-bar distinction is found in (25).

(25) a. [A man seems to *t* be in the room]

b.* A man seems [that *t* is in the room]

c. [What do you like *t*]

d. What do you think [Mary believes [John likes *t*]]

In general, it is agreed that A-movement occurs within a local area to some extent, whereas A-bar movement can be applied beyond clauses almost without limit. Thus, although (25a), where *a man* undergoes A-movement within the clause, is grammatical, (25b), where the element moves beyond the finite clause, is ungrammatical. On the other hand, when it comes to A-bar movement, the element can move beyond clause boundaries as (25d) exemplifies.

Therefore, the existence of the A/A-bar distinction is empirically supported; clearly, the two groups exhibit different behaviors. Thus, if we lack the definition of the distinction, we are doomed to lose quite a significant explanatory power.

Importantly, the A/A-bar distinction can be redefined in the Feature-Inheritance framework without relying on syntactic positions such as Spec-XP, or features involved in the movement operation. Under the Feature-Inheritance framework, A-movement is analyzed as movement operations within the transfer domain of a phase which is triggered by an Agree Feature (a set of φ-features) that the complement inherits.[7] On the other hand, A-bar movement is a term for movement operations beyond the transfer domain of a phase and it is triggered by an Edge Feature on the phase head.[8] *AF* and

7 In what follows, I use the term *Agree Feature* instead of *φ-feature* following Chomsky (2008).

8 The A/A-bar formulation based on a transfer domain cannot be utilized in Chomsky's (2015) framework, since it assumes that a transfer domain shifts when a phase head is deactivated (or deleted). Thus, the new framework needs to explore another way to capture the A/A-bar distinction. Moreover, since the explanation of Improper Movement is strongly related to the A/A-bar distinction, Chomsky's (2015) framework also has to find a new way to rule out Improper Movement.

EF in (26) stand for *Agree Feature* and *Edge Feature*, respectively.

(26)

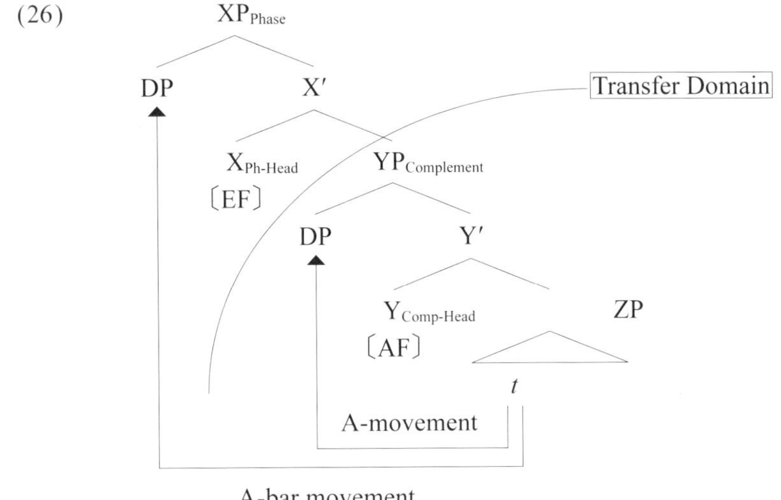

Based on this assumption, the A/A-bar distinction exemplified in (25) can readily be captured. Since A-movement is a movement operation within the transfer domain of a phase as is shown in (26), if the element is moved further, the PIC will be violated. However, since A-bar movement is movement outside the transfer domain of a phase, the element can be moved further without violating the PIC. In addition, if A-movement occurs via a phase edge (namely the Spec of a phase), this is considered to be Improper Movement as in (27) since the movement to the phase edge is A-bar movement. Note that, as May (1979) argues, Improper Movement is prohibited because A-bar movement gives rise to an operator and a variable, the latter of which is considered to be an R-expression, and if the DP undergoes A-movement further, the variable is c-commanded by its co-referential DP, which violates Condition C (also see Fukui (1993) for another approach to Improper Movement based on Chain Uniformity and Obata and Epstein (2008) and Obata (2010, 2012), based on feature-splitting). Therefore, example (25b) is ruled out even if the subject *A man* is moved via the Spec of the CP phase in order to circumvent the PIC violation as is shown in (28).

(27)

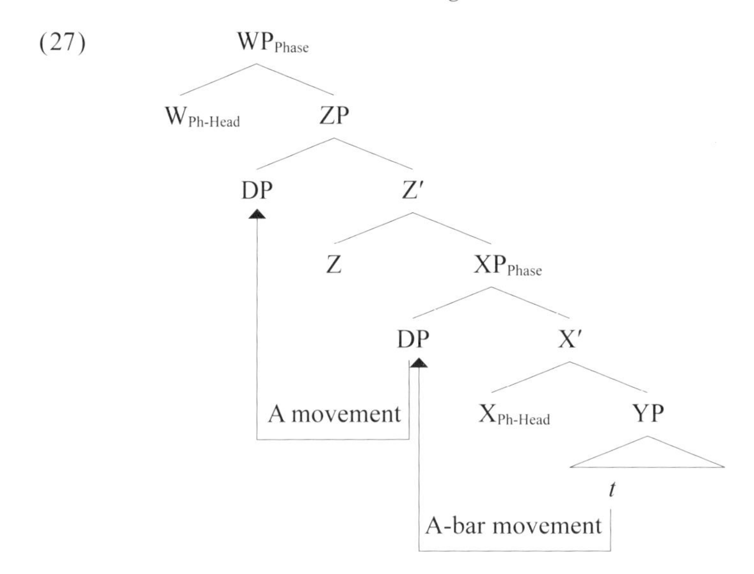

*Improper Movement

(28) *A man seems *t* that *t* is in the room.

2.5 Summary

In this chapter, we have briefly observed the theoretical background of this book, namely, the assumptions of the feature checking mechanism in the MP, the Phase Theory, and Feature-Inheritance. Following that, we have witnessed how the A/A-bar distinction can be reframed under the Feature-Inheritance framework after having shown a brief history of A/A-bar distinctions.

However, the A/A-bar distinction we saw in 2.4 raises a paradox when it comes to weak-phases, which is the main topic of the first half of this book. In the next chapter, let us turn to the paradox and search the way to solve the problem.

3

A Proposal

In this chapter, I will claim that weak-phases must exist by pointing out a paradox of weak-phases in 3.1, which is the main problem discussed in this book. After observing the problem, we will look at previous analyses on weak-phases and witness their problems in 3.2. In 3.2.1, Chomsky (2001) is shown and then we move to the other candidate, Richards (2012), in 3.2.2. Having discussed that neither position can solve the paradox of weak-phases, I will propose another approach to solve the paradox in 3.3. This approach leads us to an assumption of some sort of activation from a strong-phase head to weak-phase heads, and I suggest that Feature-Transcription, namely an extended version of Feature-Inheritance between strong/weak-phase heads, serves as the activation operation, in 3.4. Finally, in 3.5, we observe that the assumption of Feature-Transcription derives a theoretical consequence that weak-phases include two possibilities of derivational patterns. The two possibilities derive optionality in derivations in tandem with a new case assignment mechanism.

3.1 The Paradox of Weak-Phases

3.1.1 The Existence of a Strong/Weak Distinction in Phases

In this section, the paradox of weak-phases, which is the main topic in the former half of this book, is presented. Notice that Chomsky (2001) suggests that there are two subclasses in phases, namely, strong-phases and weak-phases. Strong-phases are normal phases and the characteristics discussed in chapter 2 concerning phases (namely, PIC, Feature-Inheritance, transfer, and so on) hold in them. However, Chomsky (2001) argues that although *v*P in transitive sentences form strong-phases (they are represented as "*v**P"), *v*P in passives and unaccusative sentences constitute weak-phases (expressed as "*v*P" without "*"), and the discussion about phases in chapter 2 is not applicable to weak-phases. Let us exemplify weak-phases with the following *v*P instances in (29).

(29) a. [$_{TP}$ John was [$_{vP}$ hit *t*]] (passive)

b. [$_{TP}$ John [$_{vP}$ arrived *t*]] (unaccusative)

Under the widely-accepted assumption about passive and unaccusative sentences, the examples in (29) include A-movement from the complement position of V to Spec-TP (concerning a different possibility, see Kitada (2013)). Note that as was argued in 2.4, A-movement is analyzed as movement operations within the transfer domain of a phase. That is to say, if *v*P in (29) is a strong-phase, the A-movement operation of *John* should be impossible since it occurs beyond a phase boundary.

In his following works, however, Chomsky has not discussed weak-phases. Moreover, discussions on the nature of weak-phases have been ignored in most of the previous analyses dealing with passive and unaccusative sentences, with the only exception to my knowledge being Richards (2012). Nevertheless, I claim that the existence of weak-phases is empirically motivated and if we abandon the concept of weak-phases, we will face serious problems.

3.1.2 The Paradox

In order to argue that the Phase Theory does not work without the assumption of weak-phases, let us tentatively assume that weak-phases do not exist and consider possible problems under the assumption. Without the concept of weak-phases, we have to choose either of the following two positions.

(30) To abandon weak-phases:
a. Treat a weak-phase as a non-phase
b. Treat a weak-phase as a phase

However, as we saw in (29) in the last subsection, the most prominent difference of weak-phases from strong-phases is that weak-phases permit A-movement operations beyond their domain. Therefore, if we take the position of (30b), this fact cannot be explained since under (30b), a subject

DP has to undergo A-movement beyond the phase boundary in order to reach Spec-TP (thus, causing a PIC violation or Improper Movement). Hence, (30b) is problematic.

However, Legate (2003) points out quite an interesting but complicated fact.

(31) a. [At which of the parties that he_i invited Mary_j $\text{to}]_k$ was every man_i t_k' introduced to her_j t_k?
b.* [At which of the parties that he_i invited Mary_j $\text{to}]_k$ was she_j t_k introduced to every man_i t_k? (Legate (2003: 2))

The examples in (31) show that Spec-*v*P serves as an intermediate landing site for A-bar movement. In (31a), under the normal assumption, *he* in the *wh*-phrase has to be c-commanded by *every man* so as to be interpreted properly as a bound pronoun. At the same time, *Mary* cannot be c-commanded by *her* in order to circumvent a Condition C violation. Therefore, the *wh*-phrase has to be interpreted at the position of t_k'. Notice that (31b) is ruled out because it does not include a position to ensure the desired c-command relation. In sum, the examples in (31) indicate that the Spec-*v*P position can be utilized as an intermediate trace position and this implies that A-bar movement has to occur via Spec-*v*P so as to create a reconstruction site.

Legate (2003) presents other two pieces of evidence to support the argument that A-bar movement has to occur making a brief visit to the Spec of *v*P.

(32) a. Mary wasn't $[_{\text{VP1}}$ introduced to $[_{\text{DP}}$ anyone you were $[_{\text{VP2}}$ e]]].
b. The road didn't $[_{\text{VP1}}$ go by $[_{\text{DP}}$ any of the scenic spots you expected it to $[_{\text{VP2}}$ e]]].
(Legate (2003: 509–510))

(33) a.? Which house did John buy [Op [before we could demolish t_{Op}]]?
b.? Which house was John sold [Op [before we could demolish t_{Op}]]?
c.? Whose name did John forget [Op [before he wrote t_{Op} down]]?
d.? Whose name escaped John [Op [before he wrote t_{Op} down]]?
(Legate (2003: 511))

Following Chomsky and Lasnik (1993), Fox (1995), and others, Legate (2003) claims that DPs in Antecedent-Contained Deletion have to undergo Quantifier Raising (QR) and that the examples in (32) indicate that the landing site of the QR operation should be Spec-*v*P in order for *anyone* and *any* to establish a local relation with *not* so as to be licensed as negative polarity items. Moreover, based on Nissenbaum's (1998) assumption, the examples of Parasitic Gaps in (33) imply that the *wh*-element has to be moved to Spec-*v*P for reasons of interpretation. Therefore, Legate (2003) argues that both (32) and (33) also serve as empirical support for the claim that Spec-*v*P should be considered as an intermediate landing site for A-bar movement.

The examples in (31)–(33) show that A-bar movement does not ignore Spec-*v*P boundaries. Note that under the A/A-bar distinction shown in 2.4, the intermediate landing site for A-bar movement is considered to be an edge of a phase. Therefore, the examples in (31)–(33) force us to treat weak-phases as phases, when it comes to A-bar movement. Thus, in order to capture the examples in (31)–(33), we have to take the position of (30b), in turn, repeated as (34b) below.

(34) To abandon weak-phases: (=(30))
  a. Treat a weak-phase as a non-phase
  b. Treat a weak-phase as a phase

Here, we face a paradox. Recall the discussion concerning the examples in (29) above. On the one hand, the A-movement examples in (29) prevent us from assuming (34b), but on the other hand, we cannot choose the position of (34a) based on the A-bar movement examples in (31)–(33). Thus, neither position in (34), which are based on the no weak-phase approach, can explain *v*P's behavior. Therefore, the existence of an inherently defective subclass in phases, that is, weak-phases, is required. The fact can be summed up as the paradox of weak-phases in (35).

(35) The paradox of weak-phases
  a. Concerning A-movement, a weak-phase serves **as a non-phase**. (=(29))

b. Concerning A-bar movement, a weak-phase serves **as a phase**. (=(31), (32) and (33))

Therefore, we can conclude that without the concept of weak-phases, the paradox in (35) occurs and the Phase Theory does not work. Moreover, the paradox of weak-phases in (35) gives rise to a complicated theoretical puzzle, though it will be considered later (in 3.3), after reviewing previous analyses on weak-phases.

3.2 Previous Analyses

Now that I have shown the evidence for the existence of weak-phases in the last section, let us observe how weak-phases have been analyzed in previous research. In this section, we will take a look at Chomsky (2001) and Richards (2012) and their problems in sequence. I claim that neither of them can solve the paradox of weak-phases in (35).

3.2.1 Chomsky (2001)

As was already discussed in 3.1.1, Chomsky (2001) proposes the strong/weak distinction in phases. However, Chomsky (2001) only claims that a weak-phase *v*P is a defective phase, arguing that it includes defective uninterpretable φ-features and it does not trigger transfer. In this way, Chomsky's (2001) approach is almost equivalent to the position in (34a) shown above, where a weak-phase is treated as a non-phase. Thus, his approach suffers from a similar problem to that in (34a). Let us see a brief overview of Chomsky (2001) and his problems in what follows.

3.2.1.1 A Weak-Phase without Transfer

As has already been noted, Chomsky (2001) considers that weak-phase heads possess defective uninterpretable φ-features. Therefore, they lack a status as a case assigner. Let us observe the details.

(36) John was hit. (passive)

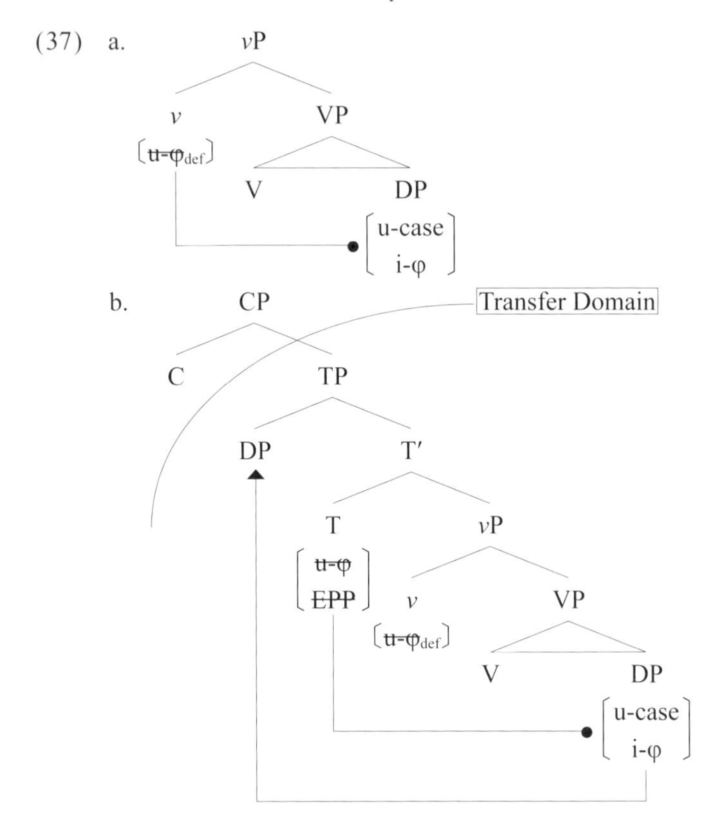

As is shown in (37), the *v* head has defective uninterpretable φ-features (represented as u-$\varphi_{\text{-def}}$).[9] When *v*P is formed as can be seen in (37a), the defective φ-features start an Agree operation and find the interpretable counterpart on the DP.[10] Although an Agree relation holds here, the uninterpretable case-feature on the DP cannot be checked since the uninterpretable φ-features on *v* are defective.

---

9 It should be noted that Chomsky's (2001) approach is simplified here for expository purposes. For instance, Chomsky (2001) assumes passive participles include a *Prt* head (paraphrased as *v* here), which is adjectival and is assigned case by T, and claims that there are included triple Agree relations between features on Expletive-T, T-DP, and T-Prt. However, these details are not related to the main point here; the most important point is that he assumes an Agree operation by defective φ-features which do not assign case to a DP, and weak-phase heads do not trigger transfer.

10 Notice that Feature-Inheritance has not been proposed yet in Chomsky (2001). Thus, a syntactic operation is triggered when a head possessing an uninterpretable feature is merged.

The derivation continues by the merger operation of T. When the T head is merged into the derivation, complete uninterpretable φ-features on T start to probe down to search out the interpretable φ-features on the DP (see footnote 10). When this occurs, in turn, the u-case on the DP is checked since the uninterpretable φ-features on T are φ-complete. Moreover, since the T head possesses an EPP feature, which attracts a DP to its Spec, the DP is moved to Spec-TP. When the C head is merged, a phase is completed and its complement is transferred.[11]

In this derivation, A-movement of the DP out of *v*P is accepted without violating the PIC since the complement of *v*P is not transferred when the movement is triggered. Therefore, the paradox of weak-phases in (35a) (repeated as (38a) below) is captured. Moreover, because in Chomsky's (2001) framework we can assume EPP features if they have effects later in the derivation, (38b) is also captured once we assume an EPP feature on *v* in general.

(38) The paradox of weak-phases (=(35))
   a. Concerning A-movement, a weak-phase serves **as a non-phase**.
   b. Concerning A-bar movement, a weak-phase serves **as a phase**.

3.2.1.2 Problems with Chomsky (2001)

However, note that Chomsky's (2001) approach is based on the former framework. Since the theoretical framework has shifted, in order to discuss weak-phases' nature, we have to reanalyze them in the recent one, namely, Chomsky's (2008) Feature-Inheritance framework (otherwise the simultaneity problem discussed in 2.3.3, namely the distinction problem of valued interpretable/uninterpretable features, occurs). Note that under Chomsky's (2008) framework, uninterpretable features always have to be transferred when checked, whether or not they are defective. Thus, if defective uninterpretable φ-features on *v* in (37a) are checked by their interpretable counterparts on the DP, they have to undergo Feature-Inheritance and to be transferred in order to avoid the look back problem noted in 2.3.2 (namely, otherwise

11 Strictly speaking, under Chomsky's (2001) version of PIC, the complement of a strong-phase is transferred when the next strong-phase is completed (see footnote 5). Also note that since the simultaneity problem is not considered at that time, checking and transfer are assumed to be able to occur separately.

the computation needs to look back at the history of the valued uninterpretable features in order to know whether they are uninterpretable or not). Therefore, if we try to reanalyze Chomsky's (2001) approach on weak-phases under the Feature-Inheritance framework, we need to assume that no uninterpretable features (even defective) exist on a *v* head, since otherwise a transfer operation is necessary.

Here, Chomsky's (2001) approach faces problems. Firstly, the reframed version of Chomsky's (2001) approach cannot account for the latter half of the paradoxes of weak-phases, seen above in (38b). Notice that Chomsky (2008) rephrases EPP features as Edge Features. In addition, A-bar movement is triggered by an Edge Feature on a phase head, which attracts discourse-related elements to the edge of the phase, namely to the left periphery, considered to be a position for scope-discourse interpretation, such as topic and focus.[12] However, since weak-phase heads in Chomsky's (2001) approach do not behave as strong-phase heads without causing transfer, it is questionable whether such a weak-phase head may also own a discourse-related Edge Feature, which only strong-phase heads possess. Thus, it seems at least to me that Chomsky's (2001) framework cannot offer a theoretically well-motivated explanation for (38b).

Moreover, Chomsky's (2001) analysis faces another serious problem. As can be seen in (39), there is strong empirical evidence for the existence of uninterpretable φ-features on a *v* head.

(39)	Les	chaises	ont	été	repaintées.
	the	chairs-F-Pl	have-Pl	been	repainted-F-Pl
	'The chairs were repainted.'				(Boeckx (2008: 33))

As (39) indicates, French passive verbs (namely, participles) show agreement based on the φ-features on subject DPs. Under the feature checking framework in the MP, the agreement is analyzed as a realization of checked unin-

12 Chomsky (2008) assumes that an Edge Feature simply ensures that a relevant item can be merged. Thus, every merged item possesses an Edge Feature and it might in essence trigger every kind of merger operations (whether or not internal/external merge in Chomsky's (2008) sense). However, I claim that an Edge Feature a phase head possesses is different from Edge Features lexical heads own triggering external merge. Although I do not offer the details here, see 6.5 for theoretical considerations on the status of Edge Features.

terpretable φ-features. Therefore, example (39) cannot be explained under the reanalyzed version of Chomsky's (2001) approach, since if the uninterpretable features exist in *v*P, they have to be transferred in order to circumvent the simultaneity problem.[13]

In sum, although the shift from Chomsky's (2001) framework to Chomsky's (2008) contributes to a lot of theoretical developments, unfortunately, we are doomed to lose the explanation for weak-phases under the newer framework. It is concluded that although Chomsky's (2001) approach successfully explains one part of the paradox of weak-phases, namely the assumption that A-movement can pass weak-phase boundaries, the other part of the paradox, related to A-bar movement, remains uncaptured. Moreover, his approach contains the problem with the explanation of the existence of agreement on passive participles as well. In the next subsection, we will take a brief look at Richards (2012), who takes a different approach to weak-phases, and I will describe problems under this analysis.

3.2.2 Richards (2012)

Although Chomsky (2001) treats weak-phases in almost the same fashion as non-phases in that they do not trigger transfer and thus allow A-movement to occur beyond their domains, there are some researchers who attempt to assimilate weak-phases into normal strong-phases. Crucially, as we already saw in 3.1.2, Legate (2003) shows empirical evidence for this assumption and claims that weak-phases are equivalent to strong-phases. Legate (2003) herself does not propose a detailed mechanism of the behavior of weak-phases. However, Richards (2012) takes almost the same position as Legate (2003) and constructs a full-fledged mechanism to capture the behavior of weak-phases. Thus, in this subsection, we will take a brief look at Richards' (2012) discussion and point out a theoretical problem (for problems in his empirical discussions, see 4.1.2.2 and 4.2.2). Although his approach is quite interesting and theoretically well-motivated, I claim that his analysis is doomed to suffer from the same sort of problems as in (34b) under the no weak-phase approach in 3.1.2, where a weak-phase is treated as a phase.

13 To make matters worse, Chomsky (2001) himself also refers to the existence of inflection on participles in passives in Scandinavian languages and Icelandic. As we have seen, they cannot be captured by the reframed version of his approach and need another explanation.

3.2.2.1 A Weak-Phase with Transfer

Richards' (2012) starting point is to recapture weak-phases in the Feature-Inheritance framework. He realizes Chomsky's (2001) problem shown in the last subsection, namely that uninterpretable features cannot exist on weak-phase heads under the current framework if they do not trigger transfer. Richards (2012) takes the opposite position to Chomsky (2001) and proposes that even a weak-phase head can trigger transfer if there is an uninterpretable feature on the head, whether or not it is defective. In this sense, his approach treats weak-phases as normal strong-phases, with the only difference being whether or not they have an ability to assign case to a DP. Under his approach, a sentence including a weak-phase *v*P is generated as follows:[14]

(40) John was hit. (passive)

(41) a.

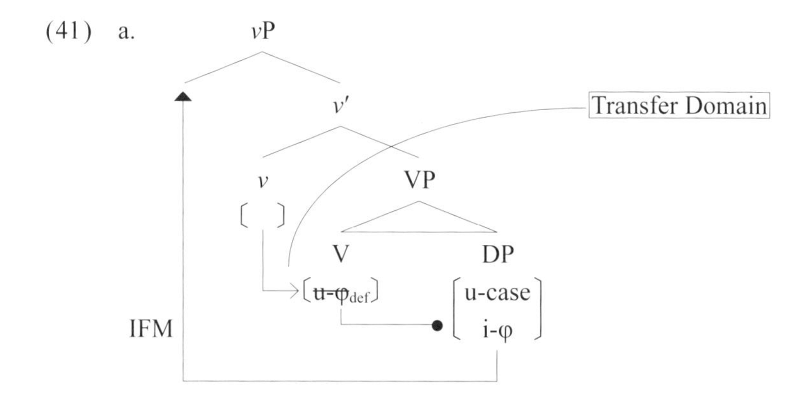

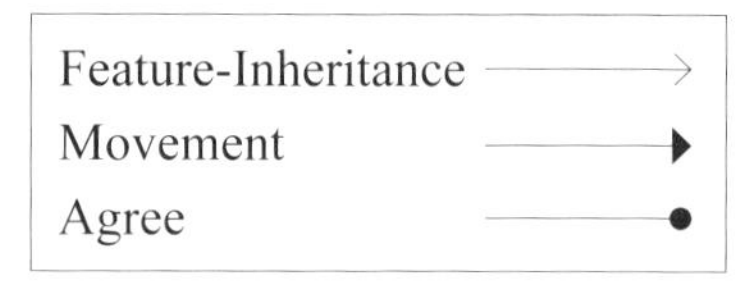

14 Based on the Feature-Inheritance framework, the checked DP here should be moved to Spec-VP as well as Spec-*v*P via IFM. This is omitted here for notational simplicity.

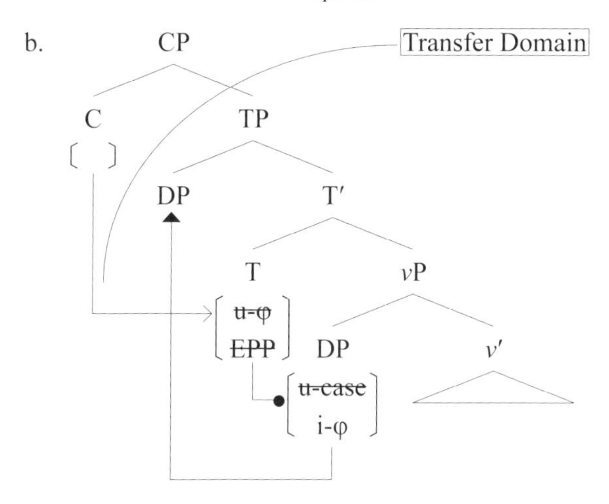

In his analysis, although *v* is a weak-phase head (strictly speaking a "partially-defective" head in his term as is discussed in 4.1.2), it serves as a strong-phase head in that it triggers Feature-Inheritance and transfer. As is shown in (41a), when the weak-phase *v*P is formed, a full set of syntactic operations occurs. The *v* head transmits its uninterpretable φ-features to the V head (Feature-Inheritance) and the uninterpretable φ-features hold an Agree relation with their interpretable counterparts on the DP. In this case, however, the uninterpretable case feature on the DP is not checked because he assumes that the φ-features are defective, following Chomsky (2001). Here, note that the DP is moved out of the domain of *v*P in order to avoid the crash by the unchecked u-case feature on the DP. Richards (2012) calls this operation Indirectly Feature-Driven Movement (IFM), to which we will return later. Thus, the DP is moved to Spec-*v*P via IFM and then the complement VP is transferred.

The derivation continues by the merger operations of T and C successively. When C is merged into the derivation, another phase is formed and syntactic operations are triggered as in (41b). The C head passes its uninterpretable φ-features on the T head and an Agree relation holds between the u-φ on T and their interpretable counterparts on the DP in Spec-*v*P. Notice that the u-case feature on the DP remains unchecked. Thus, when the Agree relation is established, u-φ on T are checked by i-φ on the DP and its u-case is checked at the same time since the uninterpretable φ-features on T are φ-complete in this case. Through these checking processes, the DP moves to Spec-TP.

Finally, C transfers its complement TP and the derivation converges.

Note that in Richards' (2012) analysis, weak-phase heads can possess uninterpretable features and check them, since weak-phase heads trigger transfer under his analysis. Therefore, he can account for the fact that inflection appears on V in passive sentences, unlike Chomsky (2001) in 3.2.1. Moreover, his approach can readily explain Legate's (2003) theoretical conclusion that A-bar movement occurs via Spec-*v*P, because weak-phase heads can own uninterpretable features and A-bar movement is successfully triggered by an Edge Feature on *v*.

3.2.2.2 A Theoretical Problem in Richards (2012)

However, his approach also has problems. Although I will point out his empirical problems in detail in 4.1.2.2 and 4.2.2, one crucial theoretical problem should be noted here. On the one hand, as we have just witnessed, the second part of the paradox of weak-phases (again repeated in (42b)) is explained without any problem in his analysis.

(42) The paradox of weak-phases
  a. Concerning A-movement, a weak-phase serves **as a non-phase**.
  b. Concerning A-bar movement, a weak-phase serves **as a phase**.

On the other hand, however, notice that his account needs to assume IFM in order to capture (42a), since every weak-phase head (strictly speaking every head possessing uninterpretable features) triggers transfer and thus some additional mechanisms are necessary to allow A-movement beyond weak-phase boundaries somehow. However, the nature of IFM is quite controversial. He claims that IFM is triggered to save the derivation from a crash caused by remaining unchecked uninterpretable features. But as was shown in 2.4, movement operations out of the transfer domain of phases are considered to be A-bar movement and therefore, A-movement after IFM should be count as Improper Movement, as is shown in (43a). Of course, direct extraction of the DP out of the *v*P domain is also impossible due to the PIC as in (43b) given that Richards (2012) assumes *v* triggers transfer. Therefore, following the A/A-bar distinction under Chomsky's (2008) Feature-Inheritance framework witnessed in 2.4, which is based on transfer domains, his analysis does not work out since A-movement out of *v*P is ruled out either as a case of Improper Movement or as a PIC violation.

(43) a.

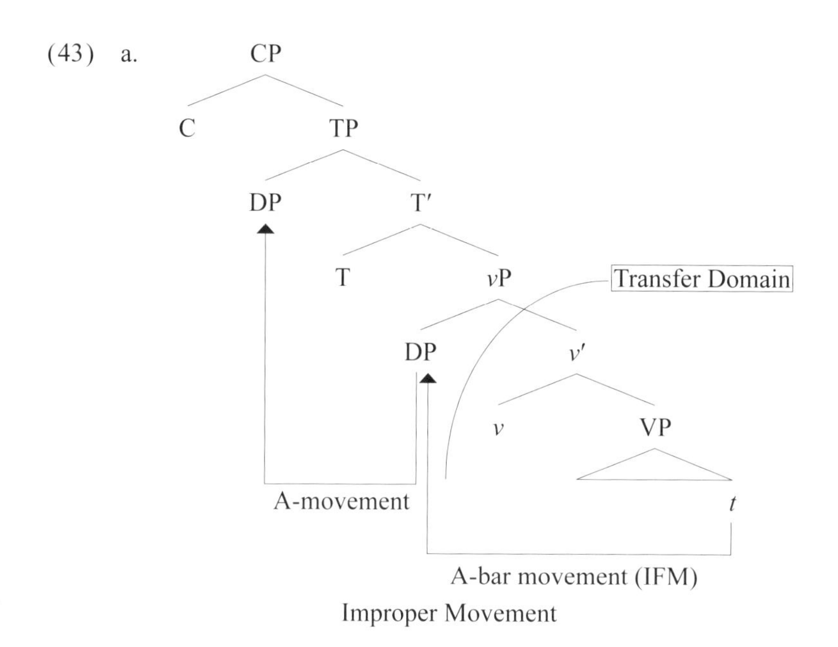

Improper Movement

b.

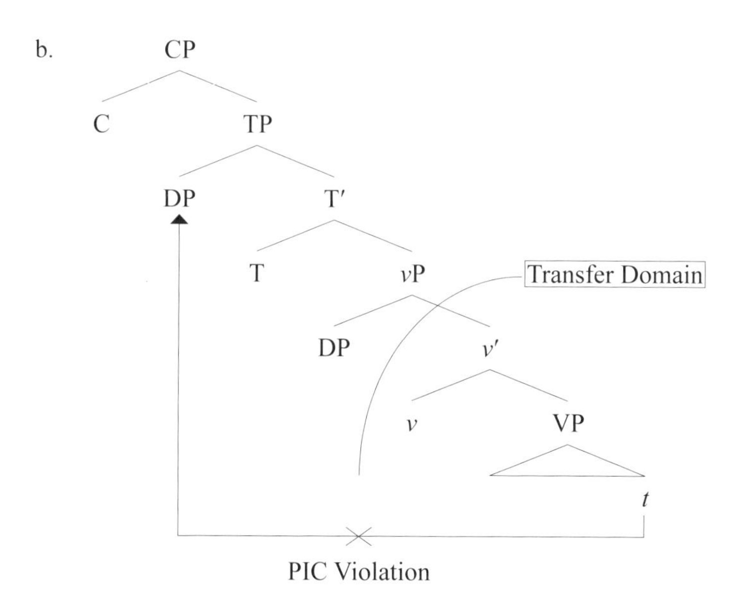

PIC Violation

In addition, recall that Edge Features on phase heads generally serve to attract discourse-related elements to the left periphery of the phases (see also discussions in 6.5.4). Now, why can Edge Features attract DPs without any discourse force in the first place? If Edge Features move DPs so as to prevent the future crash presumably caused by unchecked uninterpretable features on them, the process includes "look ahead," which is unwelcome in the MP as we saw in 2.3.1. Therefore, even if we ignore the theoretical consequence that his IFM is a case of Improper Movement, such movement as A-bar movement to Spec-*v*P cannot be permitted from the beginning due to "look ahead."

In sum, although Richards' (2012) account is theoretically interesting and should be valued in that he tries to deal with important problems in Chomsky's (2001) approach, there still remains a theoretical inadequacy concerning IFM in his approach.

3.3 A Solution to the Paradox of Weak-Phases

We have witnessed so far that although Chomsky (2001) and Richards (2012) try to derive the nature of weak-phases from different perspectives, the paradox of weak-phases remains unsolved. Shortly put, if we treat a weak-phase in a non-phase fashion without transfer, we lack an explanation of A-bar traces on the Specs of weak-phases, whereas if we regard a weak-phase as a case of a normal strong-phase triggering transfer, we cannot account for A-movement out of its domain. In this section, I claim that the paradox is solved by assuming an activation operation from a strong-phase head to weak-phase heads, after offering a theoretical consideration which leads us to this conclusion.

3.3.1 A Logical Conclusion of the Paradox of Weak-Phases

The paradox of weak-phases discussed thus far not only holds an obvious contradiction, but also provides us with a complicated theoretical puzzle when we consider it closely. On the one hand, as we know, the former part of the paradox forces us to allow A-movement out of the domains of weak-phases. This means that the domain of a weak-phase is not transferred, since if it were transferred, such an A-movement operation would violate the PIC or produce Improper Movement.

(44) Concerning A-movement, a weak-phase serves as a non-phase. (=(42a))
⇒ the domain of a weak-phase **cannot be** transferred.

On the other hand, notice that when it comes to the latter part of the paradox, we have to assume that an Edge Feature has to exist on a weak-phase head. Moreover, as example (39) in 3.2.1.2 indicated, an Agree Feature is also found in the weak-phase. Then, given that these uninterpretable features are checked within the weak-phase, the simultaneity problem discussed in 2.3.2 forces us to assume that the full set of syntactic operations in (45) has to be triggered. In other words, when feature checking occurs, Feature-Inheritance and transfer as well have to be triggered simultaneously.

(45) The full set of syntactic operations in a phase
a. Feature-Inheritance
b. Feature checking
c. Transfer

Therefore, when we consider the latter half of the paradox of weak-phases, we have to assume that the domain of a weak-phase has to be transferred.

(46) Concerning A-bar movement, a weak-phase serves as a phase. (=(42b))
⇒ the domain of a weak-phase **must be** transferred.

The discussion thus far can be summed up in (47).

(47) A Logical Conclusion of the Paradox of Weak-Phases
a. The domain of a weak-phase **cannot be** transferred.
b. The domain of a weak-phase **must be** transferred.

Here, we face another stronger contradiction. Nevertheless, if we can solve the contradiction in (47), the paradox of weak-phases is automatically settled as well because this is the core part in the paradox.

3.3.2 An Answer: Everything at a Strong-Phase Level

Now we are facing a serious contradiction in (47). Nevertheless, I claim that we only need to modify it slightly to solve the problem. At first glance, the propositions in (47) seem to be completely inconsistent. However, notice that the two propositions need not hold at the same time. In other words, it is possible that (47a) holds at a certain point in the derivation and (47b) is satisfied at another, different point. If we take a case of A-movement out of *v*P to Spec-TP, it should be noted that the A-movement operation to Spec-TP out of a weak-phase *v*P is applied *at the next strong-phase level*, namely at the CP level. Generalizing this fact, let us modify (47) into (48).

(48) a. The domain of a weak-phase cannot be transferred **before the next strong-phase level**.
b. The domain of a weak-phase must be transferred **at the next strong-phase level**.

Importantly, (48), a modified version of (47) does not contain a contradiction. Thus, based on (48), we can solve the paradox of weak-phases above. That is, we can explain the paradox of weak-phases by assuming that *every operation in weak-phases occurs at the next strong-phase level*.

(49) A solution to the paradox of weak-phases:
The operations in a weak-phase must occur **at the next strong-phase level**.

Now, let us exemplify (49) with a schematic structure to show how this assumption settles the paradox of weak-phases.

(50) a.

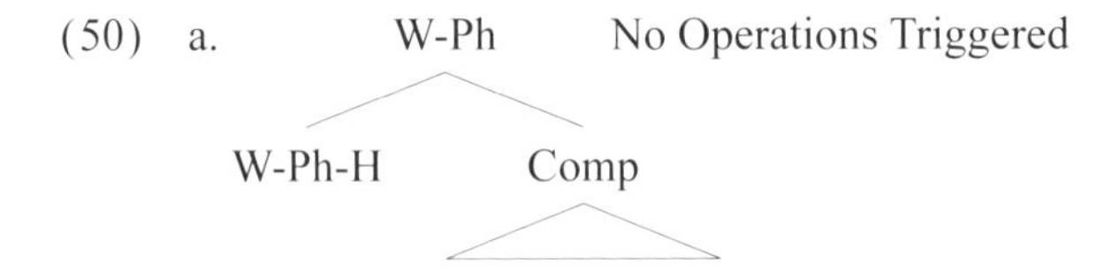

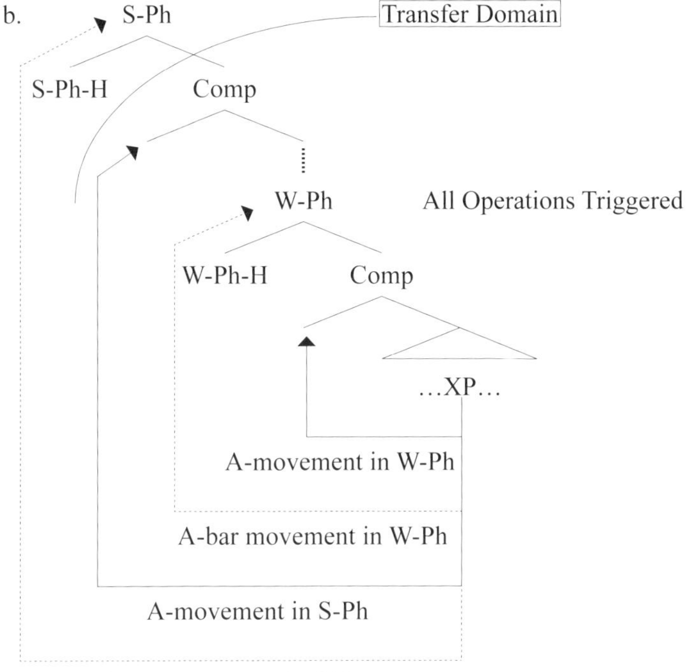

Based on (49), when the weak-phase is formed in (50a), no operation is triggered, with the complement of the weak-phase un-transferred. As is shown in (50b), when the strong-phase is completed, operations in the weak-phase as well as those in the strong-phase are triggered. Concerning the weak-phase, the XP can undergo A-movement within the complement of the weak-phase and is moved as A-bar movement up to the Spec of the weak-phase (expressed by a broken line). In a similar vein, regarding the strong-phase, A-movement of the XP can occur within the complement of the strong-phase including the un-transferred complement of the weak-phase, whereas the XP can undergo A-bar movement to the Spec of the strong-phase (also represented by a broken line). Hence in this derivation, the XP holds a multiple relations with the Edge Features on C/*v* and the Agree Features on T/V. Note that this is unproblematic since all of the relations are held simultaneously (cf. Hiraiwa (2005) for Multiple Agree). Therefore, the paradox of weak-phases repeated as (51) can readily be solved based on (49); A-movement out of the domain of a weak-phase is possible since the complement of the weak-phase is not transferred until a strong-phase is completed, whereas A-bar movement is triggered by an Edge Feature on the weak-phase head at the next strong-phase level.

(51) The paradox of weak-phases (=(42))
  a. Concerning A-movement, a weak-phase serves **as a non-phase**.
    ⇒ because the weak-phase head does not trigger its syntactic operations at the weak-phase level.
  b. Concerning A-bar movement, a weak-phase serves **as a phase**.
    ⇒ because the weak-phase head triggers its syntactic operations at the next strong-phase level.

In this section, I have shown that the paradox of weak-phases is solved by assuming (49). In the next subsection, I will propose an activation operation to derive (49) from a more fundamental mechanism.

3.4 A Proposal: Feature-Transcription

3.4.1 A Remaining Theoretical Question

In the last section, I presented an answer to the paradox of weak-phases. My answer was shown in (49), repeated below as (52).

(52) A solution to the paradox of weak-phases: (=(49))
  The operations in a weak-phase must occur **at the next strong-phase level**.

However, notice that in order for (52) to be enacted, we need the following assumption.

(53) A weak-phase head has to **put off** its operations until the next strong-phase is formed.

Here, another question arises: why can weak-phase heads *put off* their operations? Of course, this postponement needs some motivation. If we assume that the computation senses the future crash of the derivation in a weak-phase and keeps it from starting its syntactic operations, the process must include "look ahead," which Epstein et al. (1998) consider to be uneconomical, and therefore dis-preferred (see 2.3.1). Although the assumption in (53) can solve the paradox of weak-phases, there still remains a theoretical why-question as is shown in (54).

(54) Why can weak-phases put off their syntactic operations?

3.4.2 Activation: Feature-Transcription

The easiest answer to the why-question in (54) is this: it is because a weak-phase head is defective in that it cannot start its syntactic operations independently from a strong-phase. Thus, based on the theoretical consideration thus far, I conclude that a weak-phase itself cannot start its operations and there exists a certain activation operation from a strong-phase head onto the weak-phase head. That is to say, a weak-phase head cannot begin its work until its boss, namely, a strong-phase head, gives it a green light.

(55)

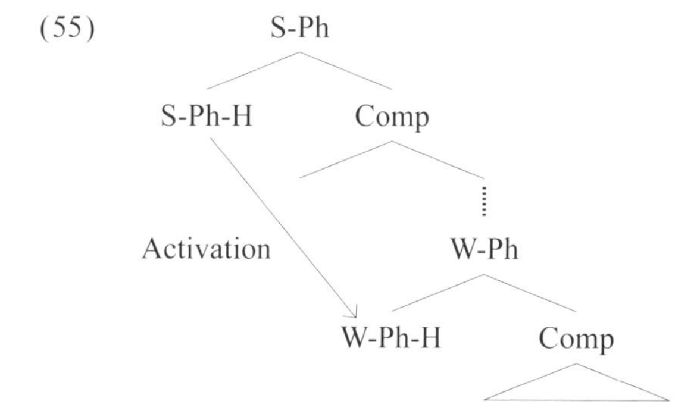

Finally, we need to consider the nature of this activation process. As we assume that most syntactic operations are triggered by uninterpretable features in the MP, then, if weak-phases cannot trigger their syntactic operations, a straightforward conclusion is that weak-phases do not possess uninterpretable features. Therefore, in this book, I assume that weak-phase heads do not own uninterpretable features originally, and feature transmission from a strong-phase head to the weak-phase heads serves as the activation. I claim that this is an extended version of Feature-Inheritance seen in 2.3.3, and I call this extended Feature-Inheritance between strong/weak-phase heads *Feature-Transcription* for explanatory purposes.

(56) Feature-Transcription

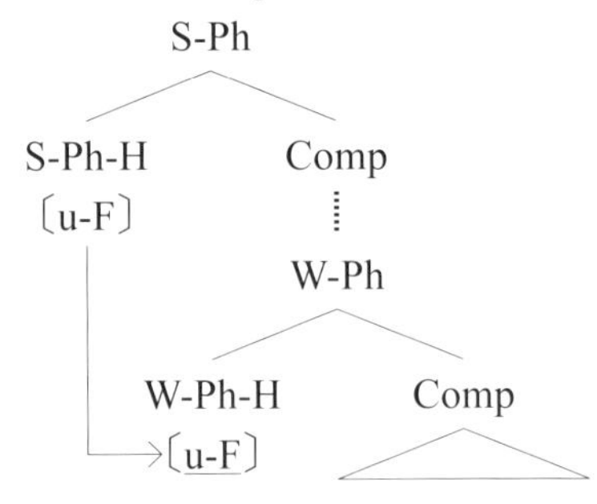

I assume that Feature-Transcription necessarily occurs when a weak-phase exists. Moreover, I claim that if multiple weak-phases are included within a strong-phase, Feature-Transcription occurs to every weak-phase head which the strong-phase head c-commands. In the following section, I will pursue the theoretical consequences of Feature-Transcription.

Of course, although I am assuming that Feature-Transcription is an extended version of Feature-Inheritance, there are obvious differences between them. As Chomsky (2013) notes, Feature-Inheritance is based on a direct relation between a (strong-)phase head and the label of its complement. On the other hand, Feature-Transcription occurs from a strong-phase head to a weak-phase head beyond other projections between them. Moreover, Feature-Transcription even occurs from a single strong-phase head to multiple weak-phase heads in its c-command domain. Therefore, Feature-Transcription seems to be more an Agree-like long distance operation than a direct transmission of features. Thus, I call this Feature-*Transcription*, which indicates uninterpretable features are transcribed on weak-phase heads within the domain of a strong-phase head. While I will briefly return to this point in chapter 7, the true nature of Feature-Transcription needs more serious considerations.

3.5 Theoretical Consequences

3.5.1 Two Possibilities of Derivations

In the last section, I proposed Feature-Transcription in order to solve the paradox of weak-phases. Now, let us explore theoretical consequences of the assumption. In this subsection, I claim that the Feature-Transcription mechanism produces two possibilities of derivations. Let us see the details.

Since Feature-Transcription is an activation operation from a strong-phase head to weak-phase heads, after Feature-Transcription, a situation where the weak-phases exist within the strong-phase level is yielded. Notice that a weak-phase head is equivalent to a strong-phase head in this approach once it receives the uninterpretable features on a strong-phase head. Hence, when one weak-phase is involved in the derivation, the resulting situation from Feature-Transcription is, as it were, that the two strong-phase heads exist at one phase level. When there are two candidates to start tasks, the two may start their tasks simultaneously or one of them may start before the other. Therefore, if a weak-phase is involved in the derivation, Feature-Transcription derives the following three logical possibilities (although I will claim that the last one is always invalid in what follows). Let us examine the possibilities one by one.

(57) Logical Possibilities

a.	Weak-Ph	=	Strong-Ph	Simultaneous
b.	Weak-Ph	>	Strong-Ph	Weak-Ph starts first
c.	Weak-Ph	<	Strong-Ph	Strong-Ph starts first

Firstly, the situation in (57a) is schematically expressed in (58). Notice that the derivation in (50) in the last section, which I have utilized to explain the paradox of weak-phases, is exactly this case. Thus, importantly, the derivation in (50) is nothing but one possibility derived from Feature-Transcription. In this book, I refer to a situation in which both (strong/weak-) phase heads start their operations simultaneously as *simultaneous-derivation* for expository purposes.

(58) Simultaneous-derivation

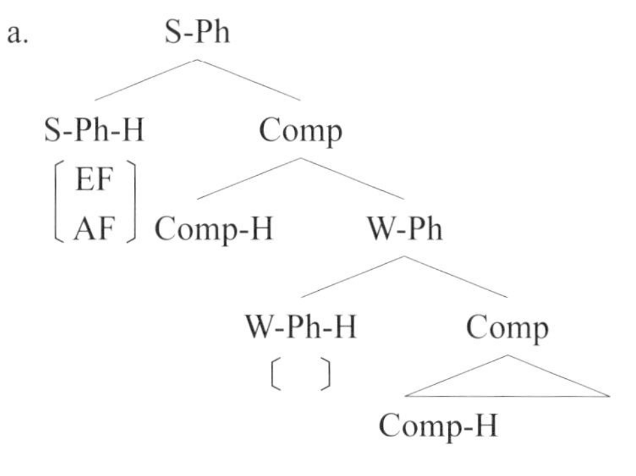

b.

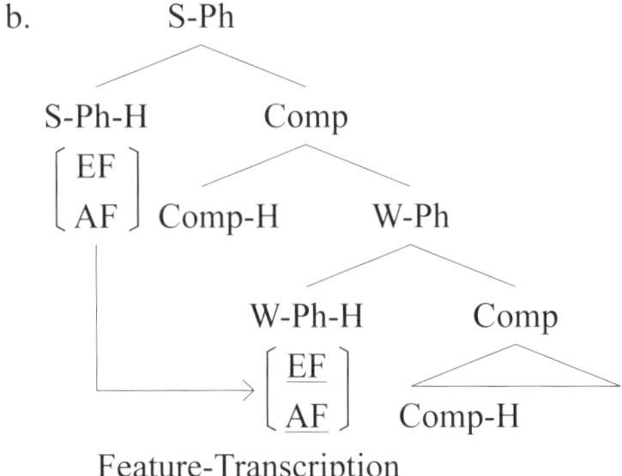

Feature-Transcription

c.

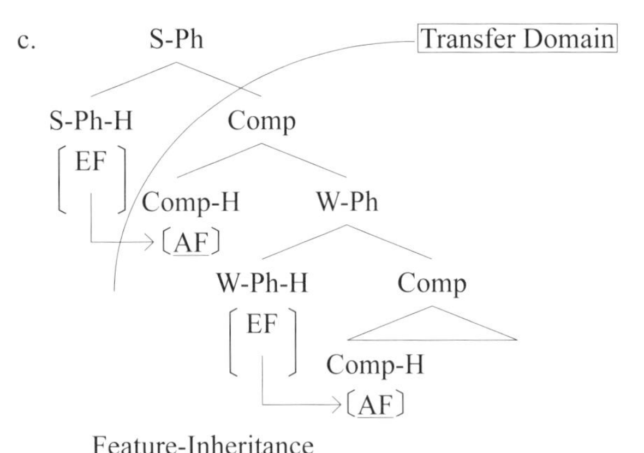

Feature-Inheritance

Under simultaneous-derivation, as was shown in (50) in the last section, a derivation which exhibits typical characteristics of weak-phases is generated. That is to say, A-movement out of the complement of the weak-phase is possible since the complement of the weak-phase remains un-transferred when the strong-phase starts its syntactic operations and therefore the operations in the strong-phase can access elements within the weak-phase.

Secondly, let us look into the situation in (57b), where the weak-phase head starts its operation independently. This is schematized in (59) and I name this version of derivation *individual-derivation*.

(59) Individual-derivation

a.

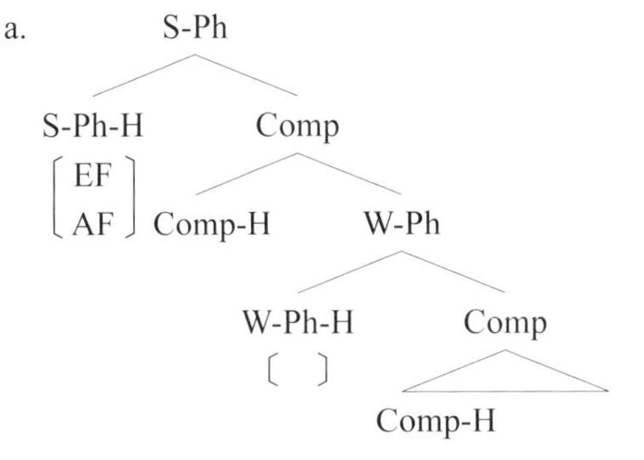

b.

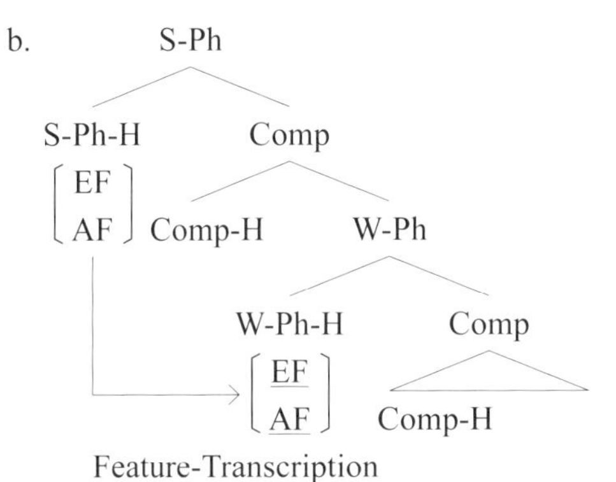

c.

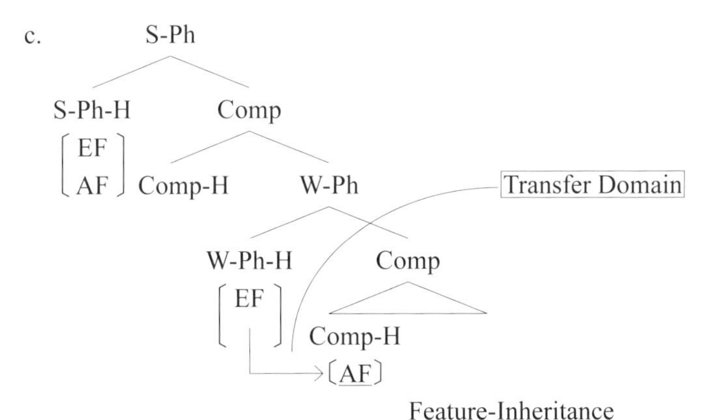

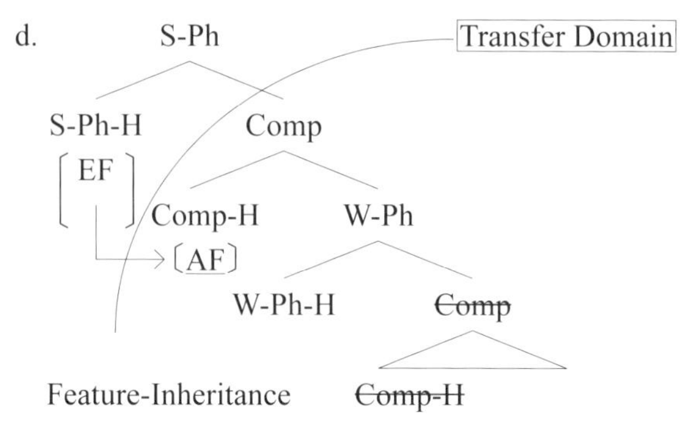

When individual-derivation occurs, the resulting situation is almost equivalent to a circumstance where two layers of strong-phases are formed.[15] As is shown in (59), when the strong-phase is completed, Feature-Transcription is triggered. In this case, however, before the strong-phase head starts its syntactic operations, the weak-phase head starts its operations. Therefore, the complement of the weak-phase is transferred separately from that of the strong-phase. Following that, the strong-phase head starts its operations. Thus, in this case, A-movement out of the complement of the weak-phase is impossible since the domain of the weak-phase is already transferred when the strong-phase head starts its syntactic operations.

Finally, let us test the third possibility in (57c). This is another version of individual-derivation in that the two (strong/weak-)phase heads start their operations independently. Unlike in (59), however, the strong-phase head starts its operations before the weak-phase in this case.

15 However, the situation in (59) is different from that derived from two strong-phase layers in that both the operations in the weak-phase and in the strong-phase occur *at the strong-phase level* in (59). Thus, the two possibilities in derivations can be compared at the strong-phase level without global computation (see footnote 16). Or, it may be helpful to describe individual-derivation as "including one *inherently* strong-phase head and one *derivationally* strong-phase head." I would like to thank an anonymous reviewer for offering this point of view, which I have not realized.

(60) Another Version of Individual-Derivation

a.

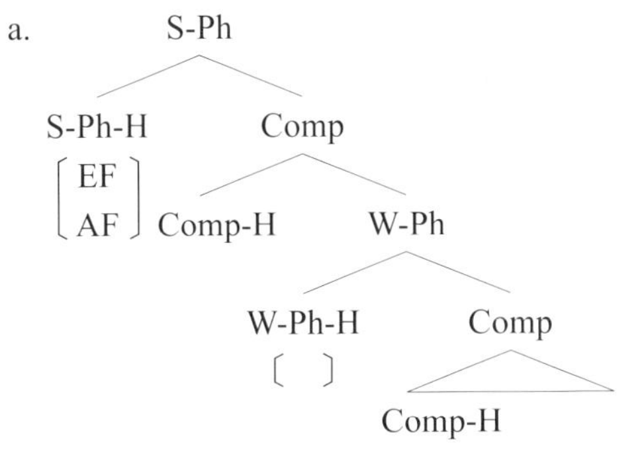

b.

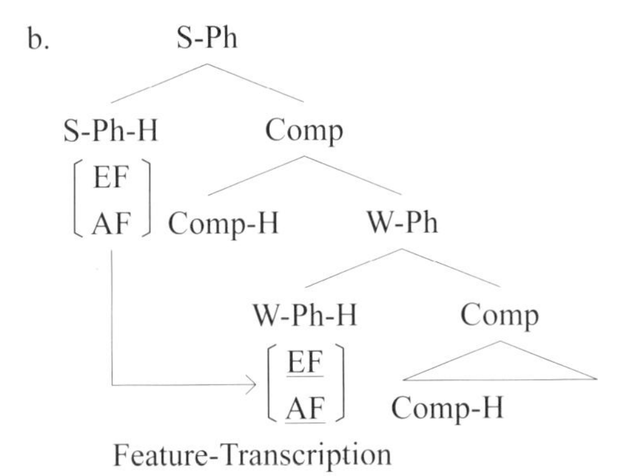

c.

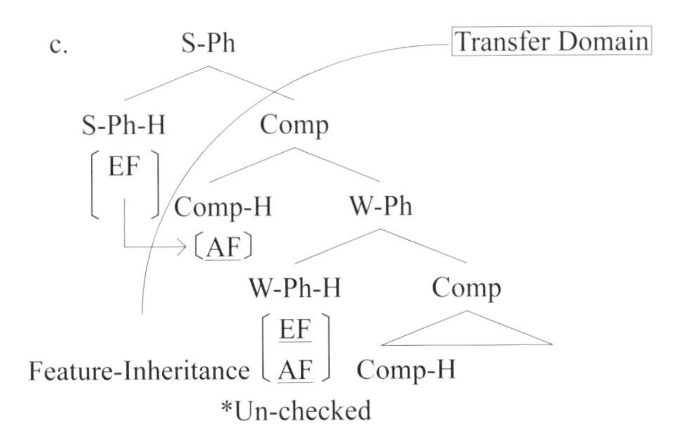

In this case, as is shown in (60), the transcribed uninterpretable features on the weak-phase head remain unchecked and thus the derivation crashes. Hence, this logical possibility is excluded. In conclusion, only the two of the logical possibilities in (57) survive as is shown in (61).

(61) Tenable Logical Possibilities
 a. Weak-Ph = Strong-Ph (=(58)) simultaneous-derivation
 b. Weak-Ph > Strong-Ph (=(59)) individual-derivation
 c.* Weak-Ph < Strong-Ph (=(60)) the derivation crashes

Before closing this subsection, concerning the two tenable possibilities (namely, (61a, b)), a question may occur. As was shown in 2.1, economy is considered to be the most important concept in the MP. Thus, if there are two possibilities, we usually have to choose the more economical one over the less economical one. Then, should we choose either of (61a, b) in terms of economy?

Here, I claim that both the possibilities are equally economical and thus they are always selectable as an option for derivations. The reasoning is simple; the number of transfer operations and the domain of transfer operations counterbalance each other. Note that in simultaneous-derivation in (58), only the strong-phase head triggers transfer. However, since the strong-phase head transfers its complement including the weak-phase in one fell swoop, the domain of the transfer operation increases. On the other hand, when it comes to individual-derivation in (59), the domains of the transfer operations decrease since they are transferred separately by the weak-phase head and the strong-phase head. Nevertheless, the number of the transfer operations, in turn, increases. Now, which derivation is more economical? One may argue that they are even because on the one hand, simultaneous-derivation is superior with respect to the number of transfer, but, on the other hand, individual-derivation is superior regarding the size of the domain of transfer. Namely, they result in a 1–1 draw. Or, it might be claimed that the number and the domain are such different measures that we cannot decide which is better. At any rate, the computation cannot choose one over the other and thus the two possibilities remain as an option.[16]

16 The discussion here seems to presuppose global computation, where two possible derivations are compared after they are generated. Such a global computation in essence needs "look

(62) Economy?

	The number of transfer	The domain of transfer
a. Simultaneous-derivation	decrease	**increase**
b. Individual-derivation	**increase**	decrease

To sum up, in this subsection, we have observed that we can elicit the two logical possibilities of derivations under the Feature-Transcription framework. In the next subsection, I claim that the current case assignment mechanism is not only incompatible with this framework, but it also has theoretical problems and therefore I propose an alternative case assignment mechanism based on transfer.

3.5.2 An Assumption on a Case Assignment Mechanism

Under the Feature-Transcription framework, not only is the paradox of weak-phases solved, but also optional derivations result. However, if we continue to explore further possibilities of Feature-Transcription, we need to consider a case assignment mechanism. Notice that in simultaneous-derivation under the Feature-Transcription assumption, a single element holds an Agree relation with multiple elements as we have witnessed in 3.3.2. Let us exemplify this with an example of passive.

(63) John was hit *t*.

(64) a.

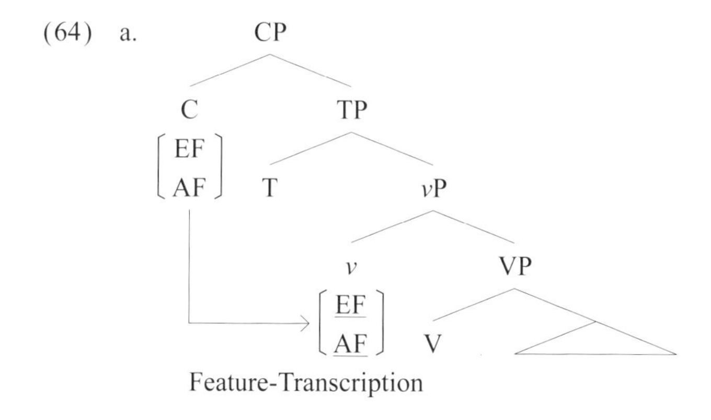

ahead" and thus is dis-preferred in MP. However, note that in this case, these two possibilities occur at a strong-phase level and can be evaluated within the level, as was already argued (see footnote 15). Hence, we need not assume global computation or "look ahead" here.

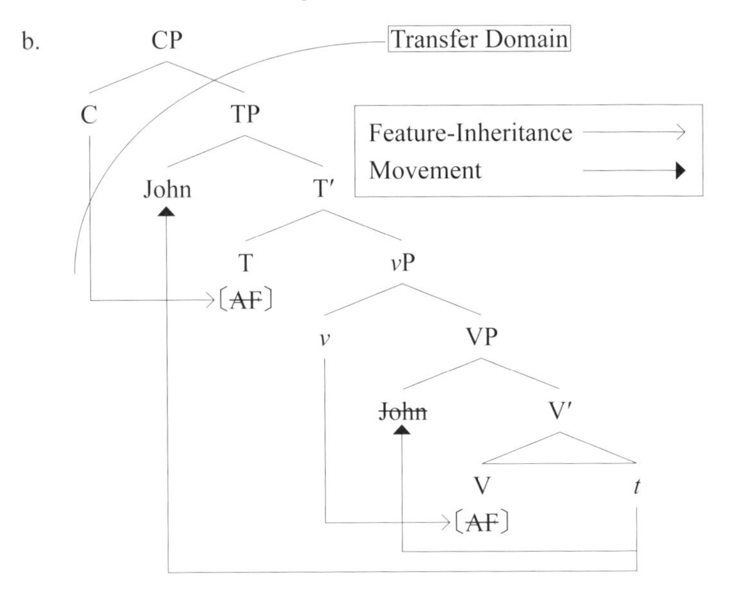

Note that in (64b), the uninterpretable Agree Features on T and V hold an Agree relation with the DP *John*. Then, what case is the DP assigned here?

Recall that under the normal assumption in the MP, case assignment is rephrased as u-case feature valuing by its case assigner. When uninterpretable φ-features on T hold an Agree relation with a DP, the φ-features on T are valued and at the same time, the u-case feature on the DP is valued as the nominative. In a similar vein, if uninterpretable φ-features on V hold a relation with a DP, the u-case feature on the DP is valued as accusative.

(65) a. [T[~~u-φ~~] …DP[i-φ, ~~u-case~~$_{\text{Nom}}$]…]

b. [V[~~u-φ~~] …DP[i-φ, ~~u-case~~$_{\text{ACC}}$]…]

Therefore, when we apply this mechanism to the derivation in (64), the DP receives values for its u-case feature from both T and V and hence is double-valued. Note that we cannot assume that the V head cannot assign case to the DP because the uninterpretable φ-features on it are defective. This assumption is invalid under the Feature-Transcription framework since we suggest that it is uninterpretable features on C that are transcribed on *v* via Feature-Transcription, and thus these uninterpretable features are equivalent, namely, both are non-defective.

However, the current mechanism concerning case assignment is not free from problems. Some researchers cast doubt on case assignment as a part of an agree operation by pointing out there are languages where agreement and case assignment do not necessarily occur together (see Sigurðsson (2006), Baker (2012), and so forth). Moreover, there is a serious theoretical question; given that uninterpretable feature checking requires its interpretable counterpart, what is an interpretable case feature? Importantly, although uninterpretable φ-features are checked (valued) by interpretable φ-features on a DP, an uninterpretable case feature lacks an interpretable counterpart, as can be seen in (65). Then, how is the uninterpretable case feature valued? In the current mechanism, thus, the checking of a u-case feature includes unclear, controversial points.

In this book, instead of assuming ad hoc stipulations to rescue the double-case-valued situation in (64b), I propose a brand new mechanism for case assignment.

(66) A phase head determines a DP's case within its domain, when it triggers Transfer.

(67) a. Transfer by C:

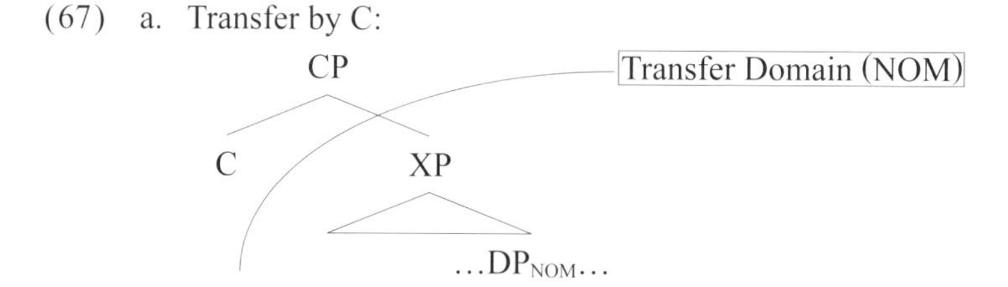

b. Transfer by *v*(*):

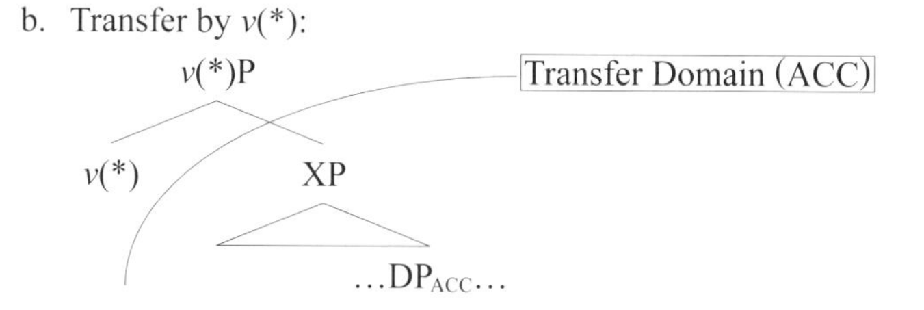

I assume that u-case checking does not include a one-to-one Agree relation with its interpretable counterpart, but rather its value is determined when it is transferred. Therefore, if a DP is transferred by C, the DP is marked as the nominative as in (67a), in order to ensure that it has been dealt with in a CP phase. On the other hand, if a DP is transferred by *v*(*), its case is defined as the accusative as is shown in (67b), which indicates the DP is *v*P phase-related.[17]

Thus, based on (66), the DP *John* in (64b) (repeated in (68)) receives the nominative value since it is transferred by C.

(68)

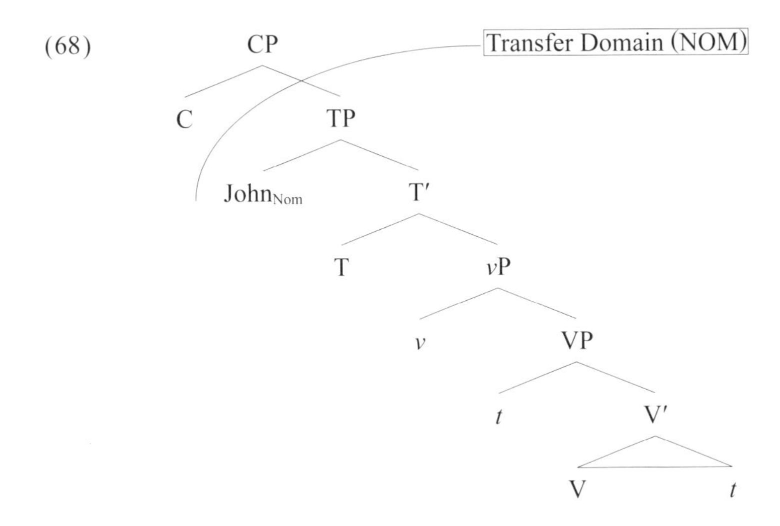

3.6 Summary

In this chapter, I have pointed out the paradox of weak-phases, which is derived based on the A/A-bar distinction in 2.4. In order to solve the paradox, I have proposed Feature-Transcription, the main proposal of this book. Following that, theoretical consequences involving two derivational possibilities and an assumption about case assignment have been proposed. Now, we are

17 The assumption here expects that there exist as many phase heads as case manifestation patterns. For instance, as for the oblique case, a phase head *p** has to value this (see chapter 6). Moreover, the genitive case may have something to do with a phase head D or n*, which Chomsky (2007) refers to, though I will not deal with problems related to nominal phases in this book.

ready to explore the explanatory potential of this framework in order to gain empirical backup for Feature-Transcription. This is the topic of the following chapters.

4

Verbal Weak-Phases

In the following three chapters, I will present empirical support for Feature-Transcription by offering explanations, based on the Feature-Transcription framework, for various problems which have not been fully accounted for in previous research. In this chapter, we witness problems related to verbal projections. Firstly, we observe inflection-related matters on verbal phrases in passives cross-linguistically. Then, we move to the optionality of case manifestations in Japanese discussed by Tada (1992), Koizumi (1994), Ura (1996), Takahashi (2011), and so forth. After showing that their approaches hold problems, I provide an explanation based on the two possibilities of derivations in 3.5.1. Finally, we investigate an explanatory possibility of Feature-Transcription concerning the Double Object Construction (the DOC), which has attracted quite a lot of researchers (for instance, Barss and Lasnik (1986), Larson (1988), Oba (2005), Bresnan et al. (2007), Bresnan and Nikitina (2010), Bruening (2010a, b)) but has still retained problems that have not been adequately resolved.

4.1 Inflection on Passive Participles

In this section, we will observe inflection-related phenomena in various languages and I will offer a solution to the problems that arise based on the Feature-Transcription mechanism. After showing relevant examples, I cite Richards' (2012) analysis based on his framework of weak-phases. Following that, I point out problems under his approach and provide an alternative account.

4.1.1 Inflection and Movement

Traditionally, it has been agreed that there is a connection between inflection and movement. As is exemplified in (69), when A-movement is observed, inflection is also found on passive participles, whereas when movement is not seen, it is not.

(69) Swedish

a. Det har blivit skrivet/*skrivna tre
Expl have been written-Nom-Sg/written-Pl three
böcher.
books

b. Det har blivit tre böcher *skrivet/
Expl have been three books written-Nom-Sg/
skrivna.
written-Pl

c. Tre böcher har blev *skrivet/skrivna.
three books have been written-Nom-Sg/written-Pl
(Richards (2012: 205))

(70) Norwegian

a. Det er kome/*komne nokre gjester.
Expl is come-Nom-Sg/come-Pl some guests

b. Det har vorte mange bøker *skrive/skrivne.
Expl has been many books written-Sg/written-Pl

c. Nokre gjester er *kome/komne.
some guests is come-Nom-Sg/come-Pl
(Richards (2012: 205))

(71) French

a. Il a été mangé/*mangées trois pommes.
Expl has been eaten-M-Sg/eaten-F-Pl three apples

b. Trois pommes ont été *mangé/mangées
three apples have been eaten-M-Sg/eaten-F-Pl
(Richards (2012: 206))

As can be seen in (69)–(71), when inflection is observed on a passive participle, the movement of the element holding an Agree relation with it is witnessed as well.[18] This fact seems to be widely found in Scandinavian languages cross-linguistically. This can be schematized as in (72).

(72) a. [...*Prt_{-infl}/$Prt_{-\varphi}$...XP...]
b. [...XP...Prt_{-infl}/*$Prt_{-\varphi}$...*t*...]

Originally, this is a reason why researchers in the early MP used to believe that feature checking occurs based on a Spec-Head relation, which was briefly touched on in 2.1. More specifically, under the previous framework, the XP in (72a) cannot be included in a feature checking relation with the Participle head (*Prt*) (I assume *Prt* corresponds to a V head within *v*P in this book) and thus inflection is not gained. On the other hand, in (72b), the XP occupies the Spec of *Prt* at one time, holding a Spec-Head relation with *Prt*, whether or not it is moved further. This implies that the XP can be in a feature checking relation with *Prt* when it is in the Spec of *Prt*, and the inflection is derived.

However, as was already mentioned in 2.1, the assumption of feature checking based on a Spec-Head relation is replaced by feature checking via an Agree operation, which is simply based on a c-command relation. This indicates that we have now lost the explanation for the inflection-movement connection based on a Spec-Head relation, and thus an alternative explanation is necessary. In the next subsection, we briefly observe Richards' (2012) analysis as a representative of such alternatives.

4.1.2 A Previous Analysis: Richards (2012)

4.1.2.1 Richards' (2012) Analysis

Richards (2012), who was already introduced in 3.2.2, is a recent representative who attempts to explain the inflection-movement connection in Chomsky's (2008) Feature-Inheritance framework. Although I claimed that his analysis is based on the assumption of Indirectly Feature-Driven Movement (IFM), which I claim is a case of Improper Movement and thus problematic, in 3.2.2, let us put aside the theoretical problem of IFM here and quickly review the main point of his approach in this subsection.

As was already noted in 3.2.2, he assumes that weak-phases (although he does not use the term *weak-phase*) should behave similarly to strong-phases

18 Although (70a) and (70c) are examples of unaccusative sentences (not passives), this difference is not relevant to the explanation here, since it is assumed that both passive and unaccusative verbs include a weak-phase *v*P.

triggering transfer, as long as they show inflection. To be more specific, he assumes that weak-phase *v* heads projecting above passive participles (namely, above V heads) are subdivided into two independent categories: "partially" defective *v* heads and "completely" defective *v* heads. A "partially" defective *v* head contains defective uninterpretable φ-features and holds an Agree relation with a DP to produce inflection. Moreover, since it possesses the uninterpretable features, it triggers transfer based on the simultaneity problem of checking and transfer as was discussed in 2.3.2. On the other hand, a "completely" defective *v* head is a completely vacant head without any uninterpretable features. Thus, no inflection is observed on its complement, nor does it trigger transfer.

Thus, Based on his analysis, the fact schematized in (72) is explained as follows:

(73) "Partially" Defective *v*P

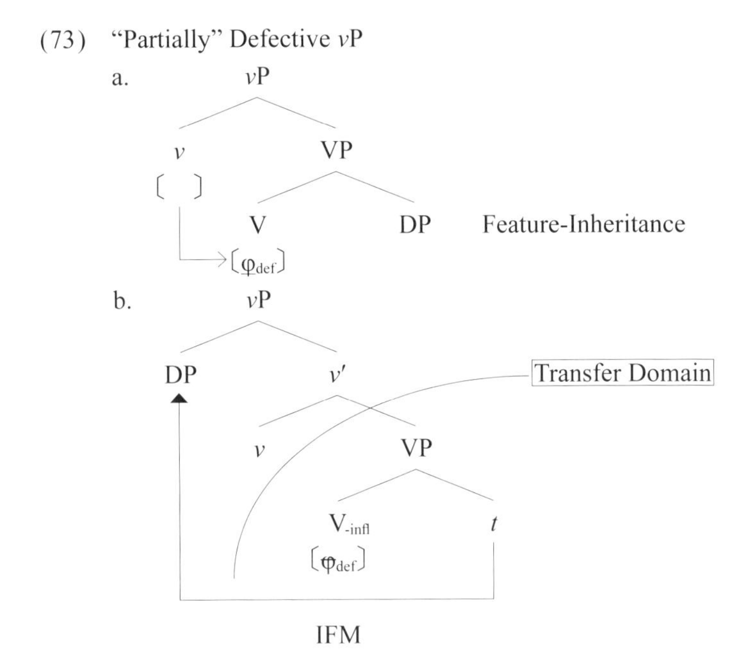

As is schematically shown in (73), when inflection is observed on a passive participle, a "partially" defective *v* head is included in the derivation. Since the "partially" defective *v* head possesses uninterpretable φ-features, Feature-Inheritance from the *v* head to the V head occurs. Moreover, since the uninterpretable features have to be transferred simultaneously with checking, the *v* head transfers its complement VP when the φ-features are checked by their counterparts on the DP (and then the DP is moved to Spec-VP, although this is omitted in (73)). Since the uninterpretable φ-features are defective, however, the u-case feature on the DP cannot be checked at this moment and it has to be moved to the edge of *v*P via IFM in order to circumvent a crash of the derivation due to its unchecked u-case feature (also see 3.2.2, concerning the process). Although omitted here, the u-case feature is checked later at the CP phase level. Thus, when inflection is found on a participle, the DP which holds an Agree relation with the participle has to be moved leftward because of IFM in Richards' (2012) framework.

On the other hand, when inflection is not observed, a sentence is derived as is shown below.

(74) "Completely" Defective *v*P

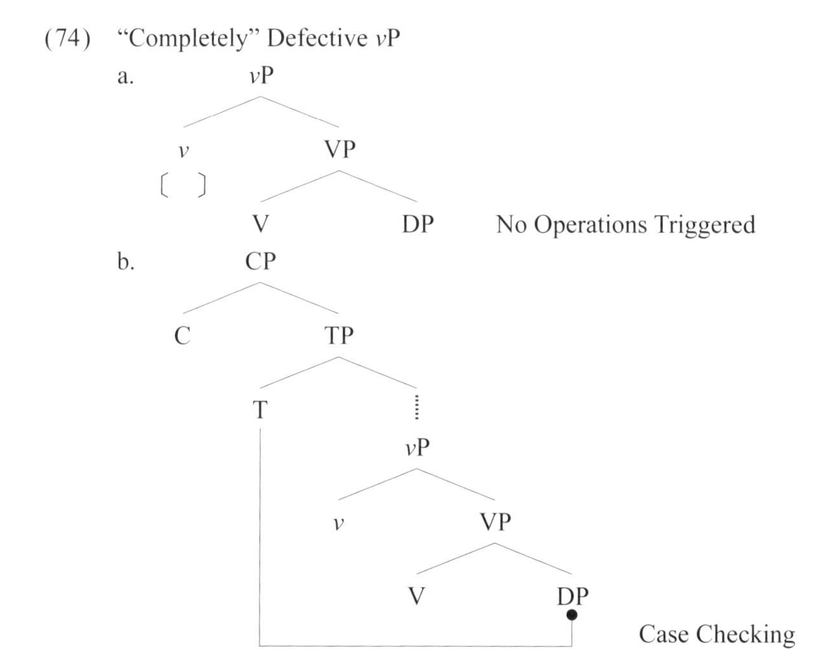

Since this derivation includes a "completely" defective *v* head, even when *v*P is formed, no syntactic operations are triggered. In this derivation, the T head inheriting uninterpretable features on the C head can access the DP within *v*P, since its complement VP is not transferred yet when the uninterpretable φ-features on T start the Agree operation. Because the uninterpretable φ-features on T are complete (not defective) in this case, they can check the u-case feature on the DP and the derivation converges. Hence, neither inflection nor movement is observed.

In sum, Richards (2012) attempts to derive the connection between inflection and movement based on the "partially/completely" distinction in *v* heads and IFM. In the next subsection, however, I claim that his approach raises empirical problems.

4.1.2.2 Problems in Richards (2012)

Although Richards' (2012) approach is theoretically well-motivated and elegant, it raises problems unless he assumes some stipulations. For one thing, the derivation in (74) by itself cannot capture the examples in (69)–(71) completely. Note that the schemata in (72) are too simplified. That is to say, I claim that we need to consider not only the inflection-movement connection but also the distribution of the expletives as well. Thus, the schematized structures in (72) should be modified as (75) below.

(75) a. [...Expl...*$\text{Prt}_{\text{-infl}}$/$\text{Prt}_{\text{-}\varphi}$...XP...] (=(69a), (70a), and (71a))
 b. [...Expl...XP...$\text{Prt}_{\text{-infl}}$/*$\text{Prt}_{\text{-}\varphi}$...*t*...] (=(69b) and (70b))
 c. [...XP...$\text{Prt}_{\text{-infl}}$/*$\text{Prt}_{\text{-}\varphi}$...*t*...] (=(69c), (70c), and (71b))

Given (75), it should be noted that the derivation in (74) in Richards (2012) wrongly generates (75c) without inflection, as is shown in (76).

(76)
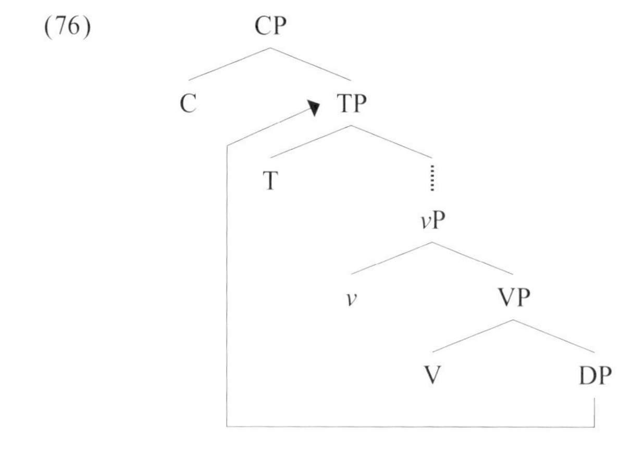

As can be seen in (76), the "completely" defective *v* head does not prevent the DP inside to be moved to Spec-TP since it does not trigger transfer. If an expletive exists at a higher position than the DP, no problem occurs, as is discussed below in (77). However, if there is no expletive in the structure, the DP can be moved to Spec-TP without causing any problems. Then, given that the "completely" defective *v* head does not show inflection, the derivation in (76) leads us to expect that the passive example without an expletive or inflection can be generated, going against (75c).

Richards' (2012) solution to this problem is to assume that all of the "completely" defective *v* heads have to include an expletive in their Specs. In this case, since the expletive c-commands the DP and thus it is closer to T, the superiority effect bans the movement of the DP to Spec-TP as in (77).

(77) Richards' (2012) solution

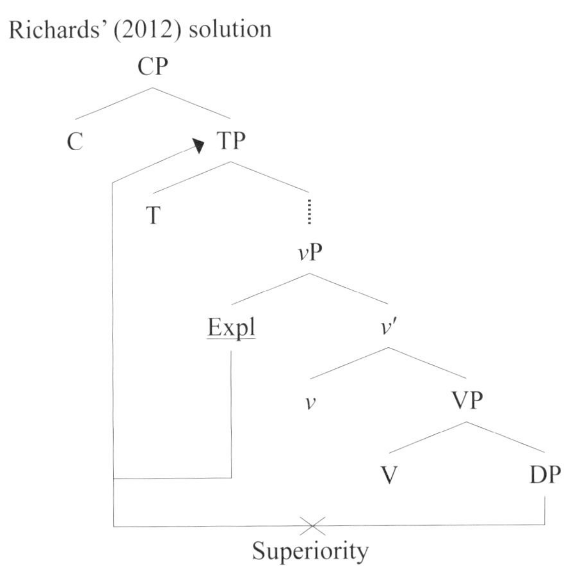

However, there is no denying this assumption is an ad hoc stipulation without motivation.

Moreover, Richards' (2012) assumption derives too strong a theoretical consequence; when inflection appears, no DP can remain within the *v*P domain. The reasoning is as follows: Firstly, if inflection appears, this indicates that a "partially" defective *v* head possessing uninterpretable features is included. Hence, once checking of the uninterpretable features is involved, the *v* head must transfer its complement VP due to the simultaneity problem. Then, given that the DP within VP has a u-case feature to be checked, the DP cannot remain within the transfer domain of *v*, namely within VP, so as to prevent the unchecked u-case feature on the DP from causing the derivation to crash. Then, keeping this in mind, let us take a look at the Icelandic examples below.

(78) a. Það hafa verið *skrifað/skrifaðar Þrjár bækur
Expl have been written-Sg/written-Pl three books
um Þetta
about this
b.* Það hafa verið Þrjár bækur skrifað/skrifaðar
Expl have been three books written-Sg/written-Pl
um Þetta
about this

(Richards (2012: 218))

As can be observed in (78a), in Icelandic, even if a DP is in the in-situ position, inflection has to appear. Moreover, whether inflection appears or not, the DP cannot be moved to the left of V in the first place, as can be seen in (78b). Therefore, the examples in (78) tell us that Icelandic realizes the very situation Richards' (2012) approach expects not to exist. This is a strong counter-example against his approach. Although he tries to capture this by introducing some assumptions, the assumptions seem to be mere stipulations lacking sufficient motivation.

In sum, I conclude that although Richards' (2012) approach to the connection between inflection and movement looks quite elegant and insightful, not only does it have the theoretical problem of IFM, which we have ignored so far, but also retains strong empirical problems as we have observed. In the next subsection, I will present an alternative account for the inflection-movement connection and for his empirical problems as well, under the Feature-Transcription framework.

4.1.3 An Alternative Account

4.1.3.1 An Explanation of the Inflection-Movement Connection

Let us briefly review the main problem of the discussion thus far as summarized in (79).

(79) a. [...Expl...*Prt_{-infl}/$Prt_{-\varphi}$...XP...] (=(69a), (70a), and (71a))
b. [...Expl...XP...Prt_{-infl}/*$Prt_{-\varphi}$...*t*...] (=(69b) and (70b))
c. [...XP...Prt_{-infl}/*$Prt_{-\varphi}$...*t*...] (=(69c), (70c), and (71b))

As the schematized structures in (79) show, when an XP is moved leftward beyond a participle, inflection is observed, whereas if it is not moved, inflection is not seen.

Recall that Richards (2012) assumes that there are two kinds of *v* heads in order to capture (79); a "partially" defective *v* head, which produces inflection triggering transfer and a "completely" defective *v* head, which is without inflection or transfer. Under the Feature-Transcription framework, these are rephrased as a *v* head to which Feature-Transcription is applied and a *v* head to which Feature-Transcription cannot be applied, respectively.

(80)

		Richards (2012)		F-T framework
a.	Prt_{-infl}	$v_{\text{-"Partially" def}}$	=	*v* involved in F-T
b.	$Prt_{-\varphi}$	$v_{\text{-"completely" def}}$	=	*v* not involved in F-T

Based on the assumptions in this book, a weak-phase head is a vacant phase head and if Feature-Transcription occurs to it, it can receive uninterpretable φ-features and inflection occurs. This results in the same situation as Richards' (2012) "partially" defective *v* head produces. On the other hand, without Feature-Transcription, the weak-phase head does not possess uninterpretable φ-features and no inflection occurs. This is the situation which Richards' (2012) "completely" defective *v* head derives. Of course, since I assume that Feature-Transcription is necessarily applied to every weak-phase head within the c-command domain of a strong-phase head, in order to derive (80b), we need some factors to prevent Feature-Transcription.

Here, I propose the following assumption.

(81) If a DP exists in the Spec of a weak-phase, the weak-phase head cannot be involved in Feature-Transcription.

This assumption gains theoretical support. This can be derived because a weak-phase head is mistaken as a strong-phase head, with a DP in its Spec. Note that Feature-Transcription is only applied from a strong-phase head to every weak-phase head it c-commands. It does not occur between strong-phase heads, however. Thus, I claim that if a weak-phase head possesses a DP in its Spec, the strong-phase head wrongly treats the weak-phase head as another strong-phase head and Feature-Transcription skips the weak-phase head with a DP in the Spec.

Let us, in turn, consider how (81) can derive (79). Note that the examples that we are dealing with include multiple verb layers. I repeat the Swedish examples here as (82). The Swedish examples in (82) at least include two verb layers, namely a participle layer (*skrivet/skrivna*) and a *be*-verb layer (blivit).[19]

(82) Swedish (=(69))
a. Det har blivit skrivet/*skrivna tre
there have been written-Nom-Sg/written-Pl three
böcher.
books
b. Det har blivit tre böcher *skrivet/
there have been three books written-Nom-Sg/
skrivna.
written-Pl
c. Tre böcher har blev *skrivet/skrivna.
three books have been written-Nom-Sg/written-Pl
(Richards (2012: 205))

Thus, we can derive the following assumption from (81): If an expletive is generated in the upper *v*P layer, inflection appears in the lower *v*P layer, namely on the participle, whereas if an expletive exists in the lower *v*P layer, inflection does not appear in the lower *v*P layer. Thus, based on (81), we can derive the optionality of the appearance of inflection. Keeping this in mind, let us see actual derivations.

Firstly, the derivation for the examples where neither movement nor inflection is observed is shown below.

19 Since it makes no difference to my argument, I will not discuss the status of *har*, which corresponds to *have* in English: it is probably an Aspect head or another V head and is finally moved to the T head.

(83) [...Expl...*Prt_{-infl}/$Prt_{-\varphi}$...XP...] (=(69a), (70a), and (71a))

(84) a.

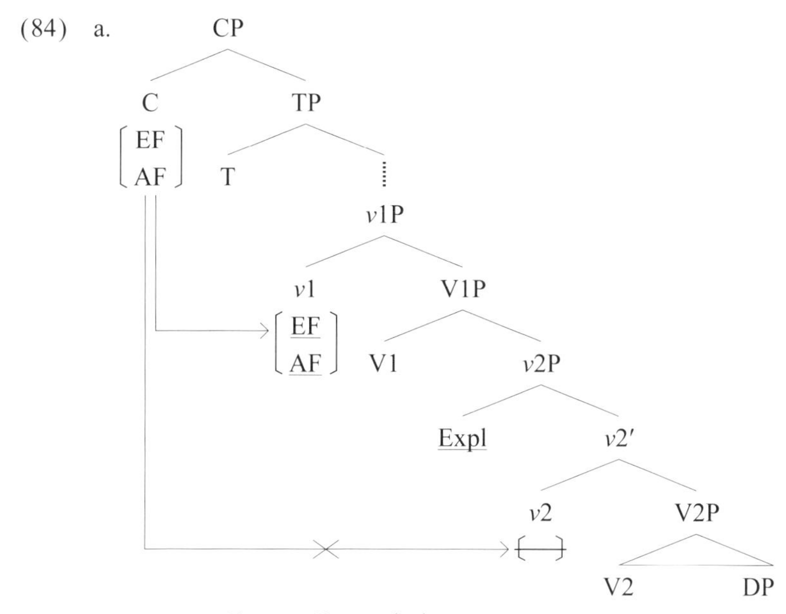

b.

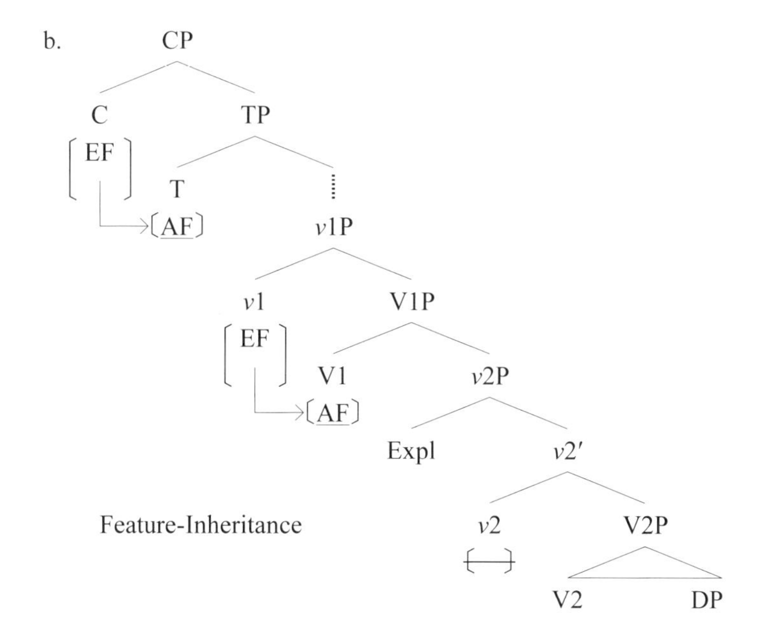

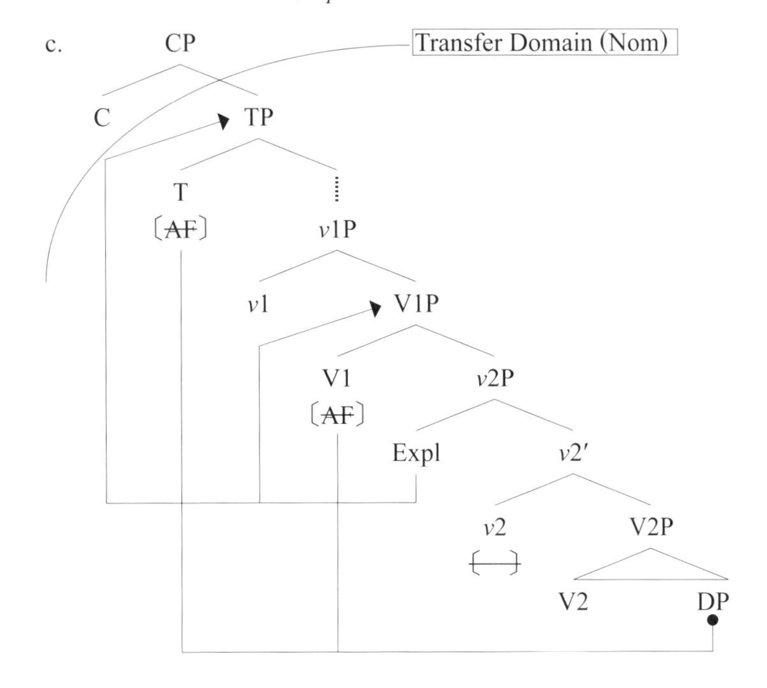

In this case, the expletive is base-generated in the lower (lowest) *v*P layer, namely, in the Spec of *v*2P. As is shown in (84a), Feature-Transcription is not applied to *v*2, following assumption (81). At this moment, let us pursue the possibility of simultaneous-derivation (we will revisit individual-derivation, later). Therefore, as is shown in (84b), Feature-Inheritance occurs from C to T and from *v*1 to V1, except from *v*2 to V2. Following that, the uninterpretable Agree Features on T and V1 start an Agree operation simultaneously.[20] They find the DP as their target.[21] Thus, the features are checked by the corresponding feature on the DP. In this book, I assume that when an agreement relation is established, some element has to be moved to the Spec of the head possessing the feature (cf. Miyagawa (2010) for relevant discus-

20 Although V1 as well possesses an AF here, there seems to be no phonetic manifestation pattern on V1 in the relevant languages and thus I assume that null-inflection is gained here.

21 Although being omitted here and in what follows, strictly speaking, the AF on T and V1 holds a partial Agree relation with the expletive before it holds a full Agree relation with the DP. I assume that the φ-features on the expletive are defective (although interpretable) and thus the AF cannot be checked completely when it holds an Agree relation with the expletive. Therefore, the AF has to undergo a bypass Agree operation suggested by Chomsky (2001) and hold an Agree relation with the DP. Concerning the bypass Agree operation, see footnote 29.

sion).[22] In this case, therefore, I claim that the expletive rather than the DP is moved to the relevant Specs, namely, to Spec-TP and Spec-V1P since the expletive occupies a higher position than the DP (also see footnote 21). In sum, the DP is not moved and inflection does not appear on V2, namely on the participle. Therefore, the situation in (79a), repeated as (83) is correctly derived.

Next, let us move to another case where both movement and inflection are found.

(85) [...Expl...XP...$V_{\text{-infl}}$/*V...*t*...] (=(69b) and (70b))

(86) a.

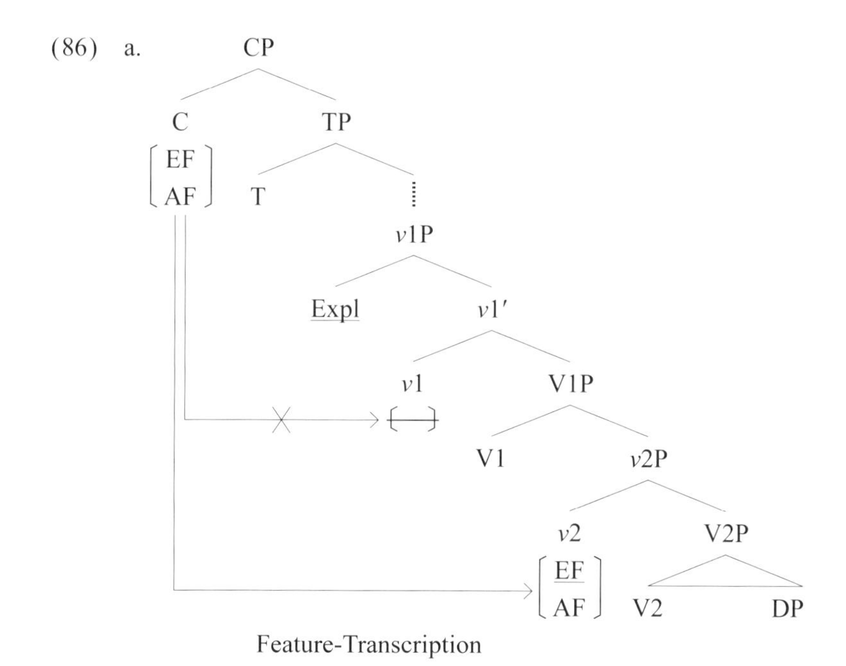

Feature-Transcription

22 I cannot present the reasoning of this assumption of movement here. However, Chomsky's (2013) Labeling Algorithm seems to shed the light on this problem: namely the expletive has to make a label with T in terms of their φ-features. Concerning the Labeling Algorithm, see chapter 6.

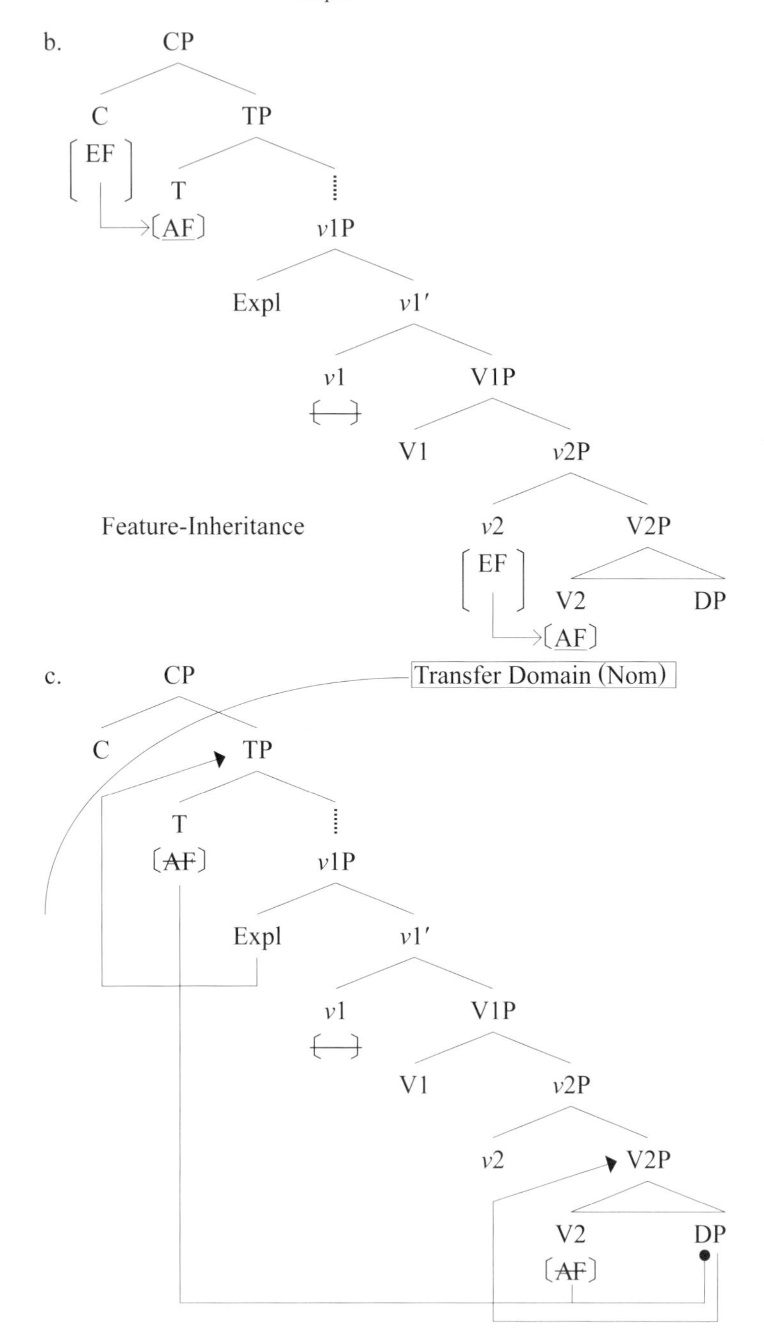
b.
CP
C
TP
EF
T
AF
v1P
Expl
v1′
v1
V1P
V1
v2P
Feature-Inheritance
v2
V2P
EF
V2
DP
AF
c.
CP
Transfer Domain (Nom)
C
TP
T
AF
v1P
Expl
v1′
v1
V1P
V1
v2P
v2
V2P
V2
DP
AF

In this derivation, Feature-Transcription does not occur onto *v*1, based on (81), since the expletive occupies the Spec of *v*1P. However, Feature-Transcription does occur onto *v*2 in this case, since no expletive is included in *v*2P. This is shown in (86a). Then, as can be observed in (86b), Feature-Inheritance is applied from C to T and *v*2 to V2. Therefore, the uninterpretable features on T and V2 start an Agree operation and find the DP. Since the uninterpretable Agree Feature exists on V2 and it is checked, inflection appears. Moreover, the expletive is moved to Spec-TP since it is closer to T than the DP is. When it comes to V2, however, it attracts the DP since the expletive is not within the c-command domain of V2. Thus, the movement of the DP is also observed. To conclude, through this derivation, both movement and inflection are derived as in (79b), repeated as (85).

The last case is examples without expletives.

(87) [...XP...$Prt_{\text{-infl}}$/*$Prt_{\text{-}\varphi}$...*t*...] (=(69c), (70c), and (71b))

(88) a.

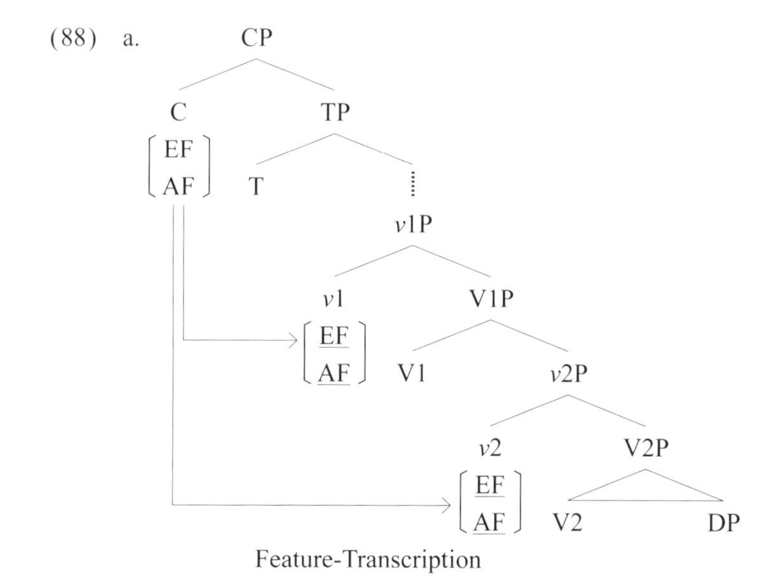

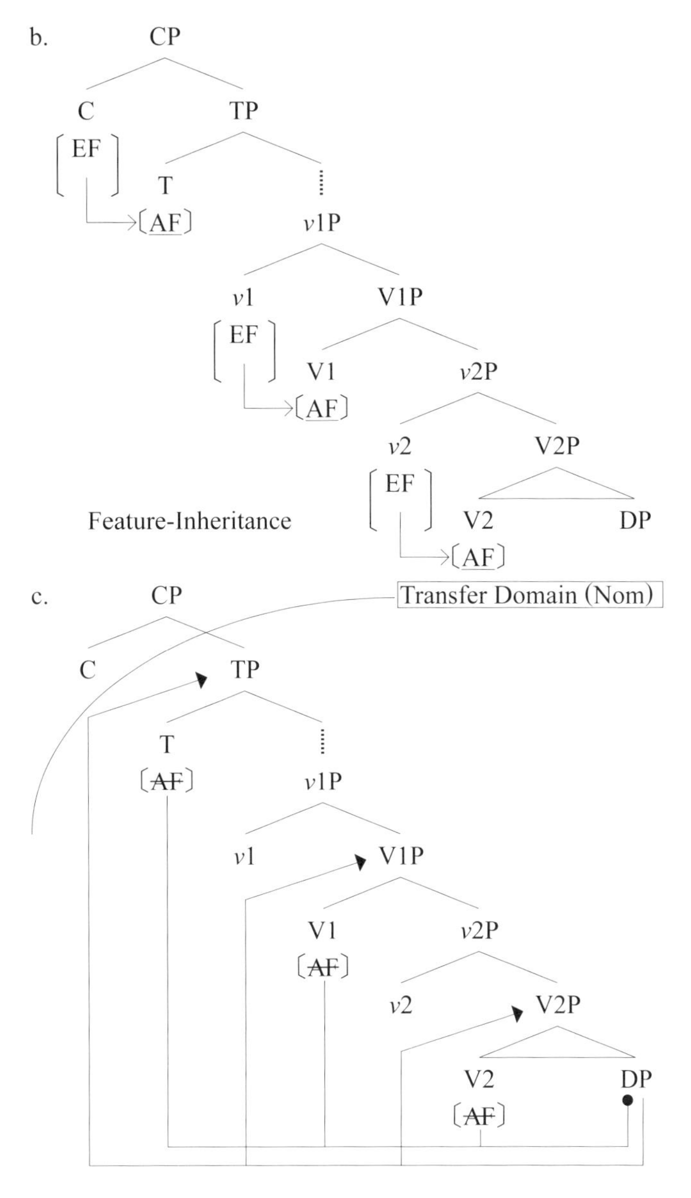

In this derivation, since no expletive is included, Feature-Transcription occurs to every possible head, that is, to *v*1 and *v*2. Feature-Inheritance follows the transcription from C to T, *v*1 to V1, and *v*2 to V2. The uninterpretable Agree Features on T, V1, and V2 start an Agree operation and find the DP, holding an Agree relation. Finally, the DP is moved to the relevant Specs, namely Spec-TP, Spec-V1P, and Spec-V2P. Through this derivation, again, both movement and inflection are observed and the situation in (79c), repeated as (87), is correctly derived.

Before closing this subsection, we need to consider the possibilities of individual-derivation in the derivations thus far, given that I proposed that two possibilities of derivations, namely, simultaneous-derivation and individual-derivation are always available in 3.5.1. However, I claim that the possibility of individual-derivation is excluded due to the PIC in all cases above. Let us have a brief look at the main point of the discussion.

(89) a.

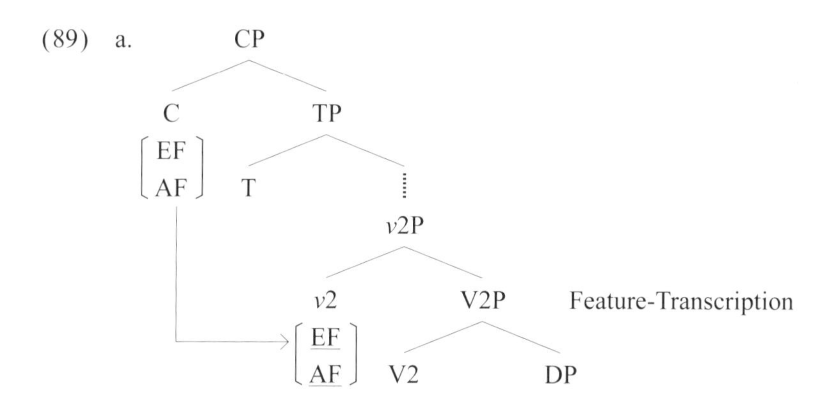

b.

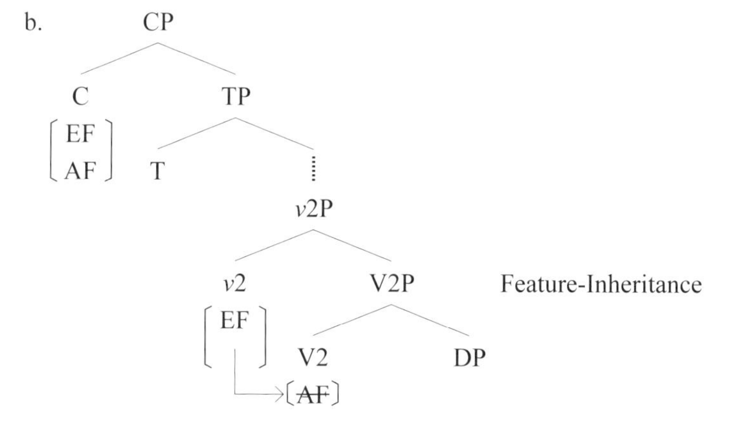

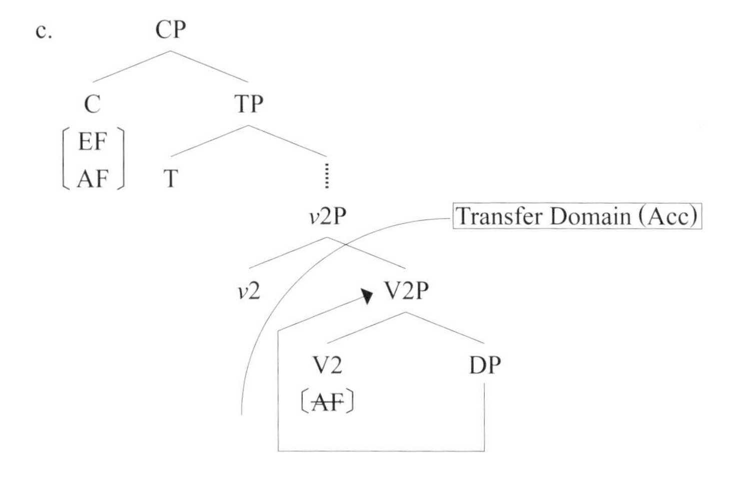

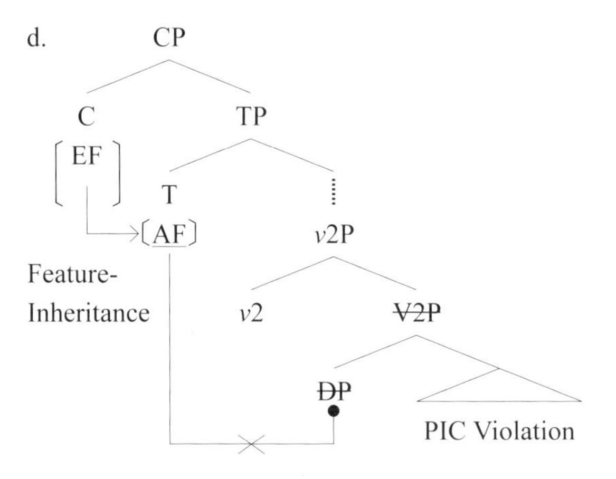

To simplify the discussion, let us observe only the case where the head of *v*2P, namely, the lower verbal layer, starts its syntactic operations in individual-derivation, because the exactly same discussion can be applied to *v*1P as well. As is shown in (89), in individual-derivation, the *v*2 head starts its operations after Feature-Transcription, before the C head. As in (89b), Feature-Inheritance occurs from *v*2 to V2 and the uninterpretable Agree Feature on V2 attracts the DP to its Spec as in (89c). When the movement occurs, the complement of *v*2P, namely, V2P is transferred. Hence, later on the derivation, the Agree Feature inherited by T cannot access the DP within VP due to the PIC as in (89d). Thus, the derivation is independently ruled out. Note that however many *v*P layers are included, derivations in passives do not converge in individual-derivation because of the reason just noted. Therefore, I will omit a discussion on the possibility of individual-derivation in passives in what follows.

4.1.3.2 A Solution to Richards' (2012) Problems

As was shown in the last subsection, the Feature-Transcription approach can also correctly explain the inflection-movement connection. Moreover, I claim that this approach can deal with Richards' (2012) problems.

The first problem I pointed out in 4.1.2.2 is how Richards (2012) can exclude a possibility where the DP is moved to Spec-TP but inflection does not appear. Recall that in Richards' (2012) approach, when inflection is not observed, a "completely" defective *v* head is included in the derivation. Since Richards (2012) assumes that the "completely" defective *v* head does not trigger transfer, it is wrongly expected that the DP within a "completely" defective *v*P can be extracted from within its domain if an expletive does not exist. Recall that Richards (2012), therefore, has to stipulate that an expletive necessarily exists in the Spec of a "completely" defective *v*P.

Under the Feature-Transcription framework, this problem does not arise. This is because we expect that when an expletive does not exist in the Spec of *v*P, inflection always appears in its domain. In other words, we can explain the series of problems concerning the inflection-movement connection from the opposite direction from Richards (2012) and thus the first problem in Richards' (2012) analysis does not occur in the Feature-Transcription framework in the first place. This is schematized in (90) (*F-T* stands for *Feature-Transcription*).

(90)	a.	Richards (2012)	no inflection	⇒	expletive is necessary
	b.	F-T framework	expletive	⇒	no inflection
			no expletive	⇒	inflection

Therefore, under our framework, there is no logical possibility to produce a situation where an expletive does not exist and inflection is not observed as well. In this way, the Feature-Transcription can deal with Richards' (2012) first problem.

Secondly, I have pointed out another problem concerning the Icelandic examples in (78), repeated below.

(91) a. Það hafa verið *skrifað/skrifaðar Þrjár bækur
Expl have been written-Sg/written-Pl three books
um Þetta
about this

b.* Það hafa verið Þrjár bækur skrifað/skrifaðar
Expl have been three books written-Sg/written-Pl
um Þetta
about this

(Richards (2012: 218))

As was already discussed in 4.1.2.2, Richards' (2012) analysis cannot deal with the examples in (91). Recall that this is because he assumes that when inflection is observed, IFM necessarily moves a DP out of the domain. Otherwise, the uninterpretable case feature on the DP is left unchecked, causing the derivation to crash. Thus, his approach raises a serious problem concerning the Icelandic examples in (91).

Under the Feature-Transcription framework, we can derive this fact easily. Notice that assumption (81), repeated as (92) below has been assumed so as to capture the inflection-movement connection.

(92) If a DP exists in the Spec of a weak-phase, the weak-phase head cannot be involved in Feature-Transcription. (=(81))

Note that in the assumption in (92), a term *a DP* is used. Therefore, if an expletive is analyzed as a DP in a language, (92) holds in that language. Nevertheless, if an expletive is not considered as a DP in another language, we expect that (92) does not hold in the language. Interestingly, Holmberg (2002) points out that how an expletive is treated is different depending on the language. More specifically, he claims that in some languages an expletive is analyzed as a DP, whereas in others it is treated as a locative pronoun. For expository purposes, let us call the two kinds of expletives nominal expletives and locative expletives, respectively. As one may expect, Icelandic expletives are locative expletives, corresponding to *there* in English.[23]

In addition, let us tentatively assume a licensing condition in (93) for such locative expletives.

(93) Licensing Condition on Locative Expletives[24]
A locative expletive has to be merged with the lowest *v*P (namely a participle phrase).

(93) is derived because locative expressions generally have to be merged with verbal phrases. Moreover, in this case, the locative expletive has to hold a relation with its associate DP somehow. I suggest that this relation is established by merging a locative expletive with the verbal phrase in which the DP originates. Namely, a locative expletive and its associate DP have to be generated within the same *v*P layer.

Now, a derivation for the Icelandic example in (91a), which is again schematically repeated as (94), is shown below.

(94) [...Expl...$\text{Prt}_{\text{-infl}}$/*$\text{Prt}_{-\varphi}$...XP...] (=(91a))

23 Such a locative expletive probably projects a null prepositional phrase and thus (92) does not hold since it is not a DP.

24 Of course, we need to assume some kind of licensing conditions for nominal expletives as well. Although I put aside the detailed discussion on that matter here, the licensing condition for expletives in the Scandinavian languages discussed thus far will be something like "a nominal expletive and its associate DP must be transferred within the same transfer domain." Interestingly, I evoke a loose version of the Distinctness Condition in Richards (2010) later (see 4.4). If we assume that this version of the Distinctness Condition holds in the Scandinavian languages, we can expect that if two DPs are included within one transfer domain, they violate the Distinctness Condition unless they are co-referential expletive-associate and need not to be distinguished. This reasoning may provide support for the licensing condition for nominal expletives. Interestingly, Japanese, in which I assume that this version of the Distinctness Condition does not hold, does not possess expletives. Thus, there may be a relation between the existence of the Distinctness Condition and of (nominal) expletives, although I will leave this possibility for future research.

(95) a.

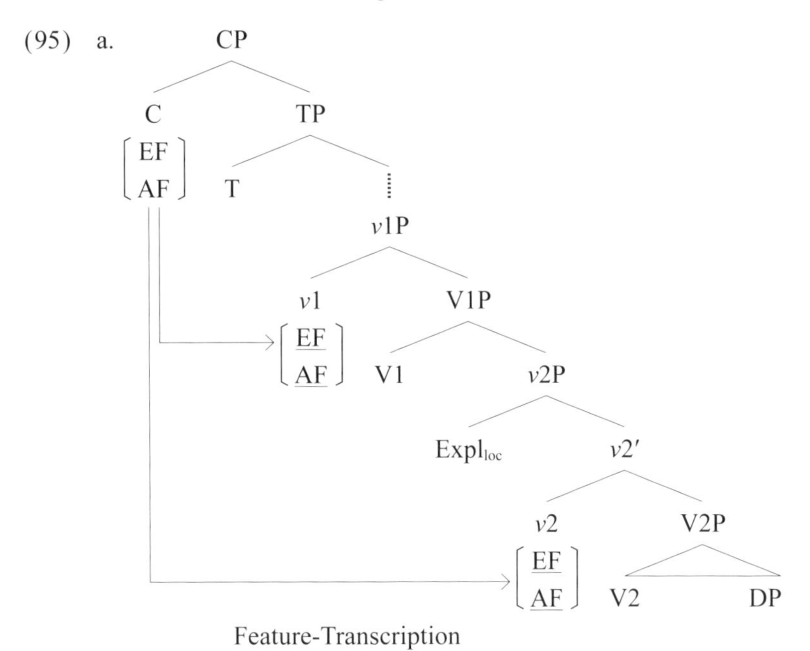

Feature-Transcription

b.

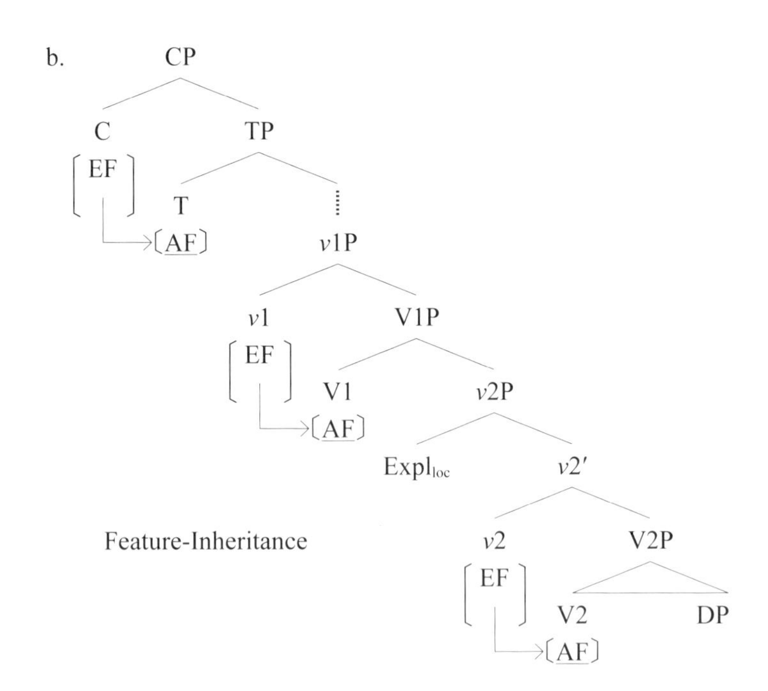

Feature-Inheritance

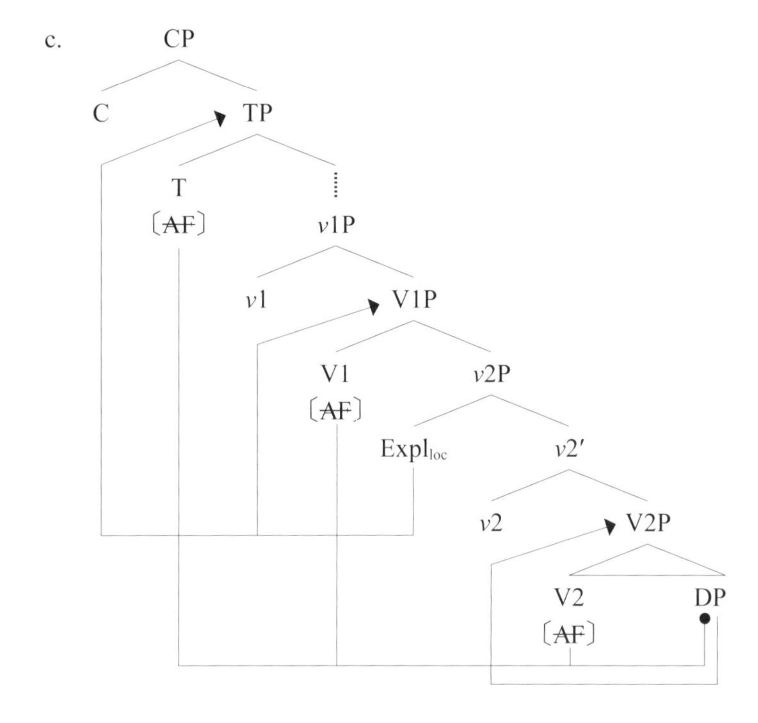

As is shown in (95a), based on (93), the expletive here has to be base-generated in the Spec of *v*2P, where its associate DP exists. Moreover, since this is a locative expletive, (92) does not hold and Feature-Transcription to *v*2 is not prevented. Thus, Feature-Inheritance occurs from C to T, *v*1 to V1, and *v*2 to V2, as can be seen in (95b). Finally, the uninterpretable Agree Features are checked by the DP. When this occurs, although T and V1 attract the expletive since it is nearer than the DP, V2 attracts the DP to its Spec since V2 does not c-command the expletive.[25] Here, following Zwart (1994), I assume that the participle, namely V2 is moved to the *v*2 position or higher. Thus, even though the DP is moved, it results in a lower position than V2.

25 Although I assume that the expletive is a kind of locative expressions, I claim that it possesses (defective) φ-features and thus can be moved to Spec-TP. In this way, the expletive is different from other normal locative adjuncts and can be in Spec-TP, although other locative adjuncts can also be in Spec-TP in locative inversions, which I will not address in this book.

(96)

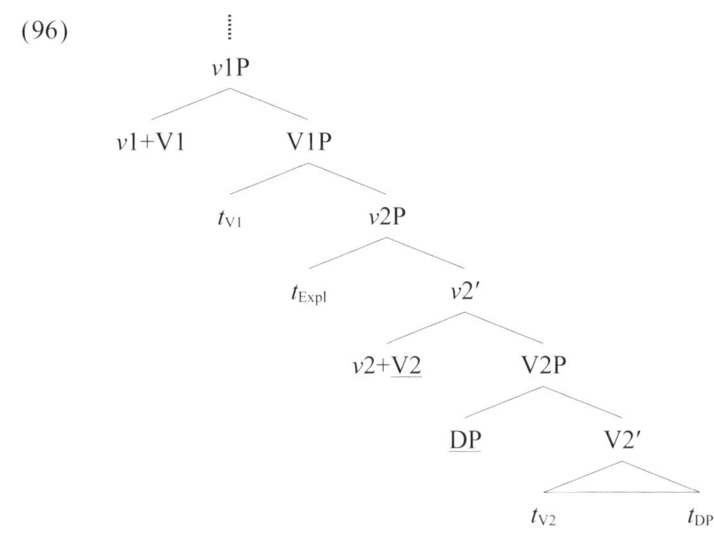

In sum, the example in (91a) without inflection is ruled out because Feature-Transcription is not prevented. In addition, (91b), where the DP is moved higher than the participle, is also excluded since the DP is moved no higher than to Spec-V2P and the V2 head is always moved above the DP. Moreover, notice that based on (93), the expletive has to be base-generated in the lower *v*P layer. Therefore, the situation in (91b) is not derived in the first place.

In this subsection, we have observed that the problems Richards' (2012) analysis suffers from are solved under the Feature-Transcription framework. In the next subsection I will explain Thematization/Extraction examples, which Richards (2012) also attempts to account for. Again, his approach raises a problem in explaining these examples and I claim that the problem can be solved within the Feature-Transcription framework.

4.2 Thematization/Extraction

4.2.1 Thematization/Extraction: Chomsky's (2001) Invention

In this subsection, we investigate Chomsky's (2001) proposal of Thematization/Extraction.

(97) a. There have been <three books> written <*three books> about that.

b. There were <three men> arrested <*three men> last night.
(Richards (2012: 221))

As can be seen in (97), in English, DPs cannot be located on the right of participles.[26] Chomsky (2001) attempts to capture this by assuming a phonetic operation called Thematization/Extraction (Th/Ex). According to Chomsky (2001) Th/Ex is an obligatory phonetic operation. Because of an idiosyncratic reason in English, a DP cannot remain in situ, namely, on the right of a participle. Therefore, Chomsky (2001) claims that Th/Ex must be applied to such a DP and it is obligatorily moved rightward or leftward to circumvent the undesirable situation.[27]

However, the nature of Th/Ex is quite unclear. In addition, although Chomsky (2001) claims that Th/Ex is a phonetic operation without semantic effects, there are researchers who argue against this position, claiming that it has semantic effects (e.g. see Svenonius (2001) and Holmberg (2002)).[28] In the following, I call examples like (97) the Th/Ex construction for simplicity.

---

26 Interestingly, these examples behave differently from a sentence including a past participle modifying a DP as in (ia). As can be seen in (ia), this sentence should be unnatural in that there is no possibility where a roasted pork may be alive. However, (ib) makes sense. This indicates that the sentence in (ib) is not a case of the existential *there* construction including a past participle modifying a DP but it belongs to a variety of passives which includes an expletive.

(i) a. #While you watch, there will be a roasted live pig.
b. While you watch, there will be a live pig roasted.
(Milsark (1994: 84))

27 The examples in (97) are cases of leftward Th/Ex according to Chomsky (2001). We can gain the rightward Th/Ex construction if the DP is posited after the adjunct at the end of the sentence.

28 For instance, Holmberg (2002) argues that a DP which undergoes Th/Ex "should preferably be quantified and especially should not be a bare plural (Holmberg (2002: 111))." This is exemplified by the instances below. Therefore, he claims that Th/Ex has a semantic effect in that a DP undergoing Th/Ex has to satisfy a requirement related to the meaning.

(i) a. Books were written.
b.??There were books written.
(Holmberg (2002: 111))

4.2.2 Richards' (2012) Approach and his Problem

Richards (2012) points out this problem and tries to explain it based on his weak-phase framework. Again, putting aside the problem of Improper Movement in Richards (2007), let us quickly view his main point. As we observed in 4.1.2, the two kinds of *v* heads are proposed under his framework: a "partially" defective *v* head and a "completely" defective *v* head. He claims that the Th/Ex construction is captured as an example including two *v*P layers, where the upper *v* head is "completely" defective, whereas the lower *v* head is "partially" defective. The derivation for the Th/Ex construction in his approach is shown below.

(98) a.

b.

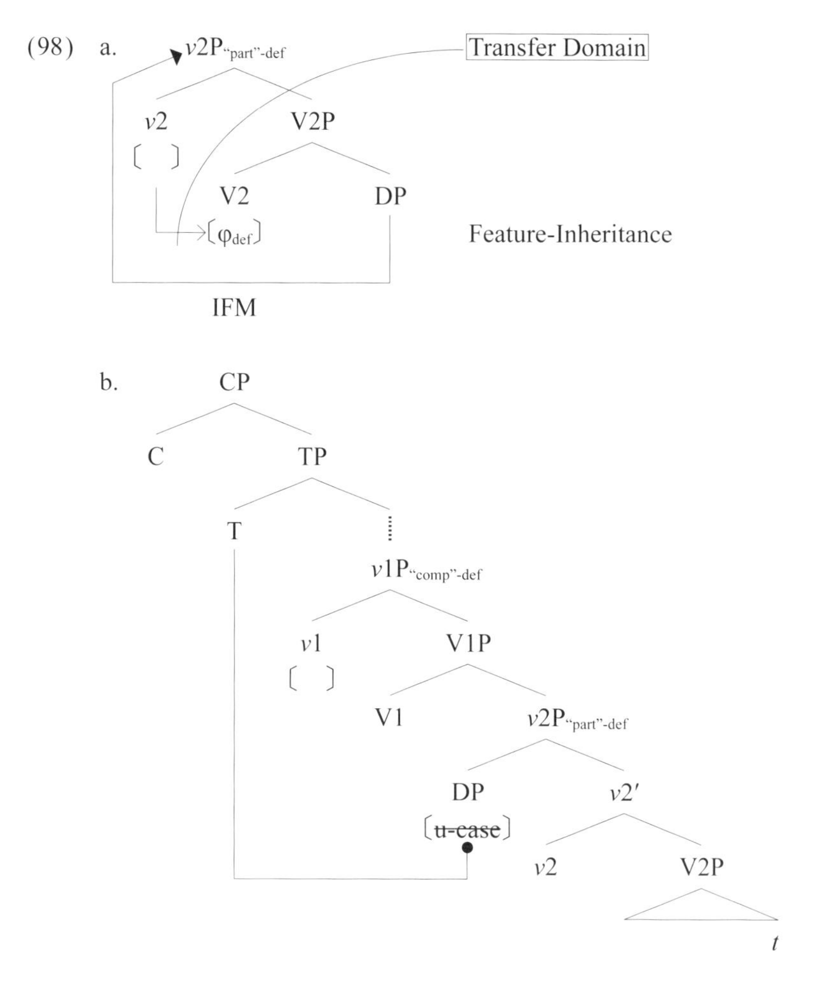

In his approach, as is shown in (98a), *v*2P serves as a normal phase since *v*2 is a "partially" defective head. Thus, Feature-Inheritance occurs from *v*2 to V2 as in a normal phase. However, since he assumes that the inherited feature is defective, the u-case feature on the DP is not checked. In order to prevent the unchecked u-case feature from causing the derivation to crash, IFM compels the DP to move to the Spec of *v*2P. The derivation continues by forming *v*1P, but *v*1 does not trigger syntactic operations since it is "completely" defective. When T and C are merged as in (98b), Feature-Inheritance occurs from C to T (although this is omitted for simplicity in (98b)), and the u-case feature on the DP in the Spec of *v*2P is checked by T; hence the derivation converges. As a consequence, the DP cannot remain on the right of the participle, since IFM forces the DP to move to the Spec of *v*2P. Otherwise, the derivation is doomed due to the unchecked u-case feature on the DP.

However, his approach to the Th/Ex construction also raises a problem. He claims that *v* in English is always "completely" defective in another part of his paper. This is because if English involves "partially" defective *v* heads, the sentences in (99) should be prohibited. Note that the agreement between T and the DP is prevented if "partially" defective *v* heads exist in the sentences since we expect that the domain including the DP is already transferred when the uninterpretable φ-features on T start an Agree operation. In other words, the *v* head in (99) should be a "completely" defective head so as to allow the DP to hold an Agree relation with T.

(99) a. [There seem to me [to appear to John [to be believed by Bill [...] [to be several dogs in the garden]]]]

b. [There seems to me [to appear to John [to be believed by Bill [...] [to be a dog in the garden]]]]

(Richards (2012: 216))

However, he claims that English includes "partially" defective heads only in the Th/Ex construction. Now, the question is why a "partially" defective head exists only in the Th/Ex construction in English. He argues that normal *v* heads in English are "completely" defective, but, on the other hand, *v* heads projecting above "lexical" passive participles, which have active counterparts (for instance *written* in (97), which has an active counterpart *write* taking an object), are "partially" defective. Nevertheless, the reasoning is unclear.

Moreover, clearly *believed* in (99) also possesses its active counterpart *believe* and it can assign case in the example of the ECM construction in (100).

(100) John believes her to be genius.

Thus, there is no denying that he has to assume an ad hoc stipulation in order to capture the Th/Ex construction and thus his explanation is not theoretically well-motivated.

4.2.3 An Alternative Account under Feature-Transcription

I claim that the Th/Ex construction is readily explained under the Feature-Transcription framework. What plays a crucial role here is the assumptions in (92) and (93), respectively repeated below.

(101) If a DP exists in the Spec of a weak-phase, the weak-phase head cannot be involved in Feature-Transcription. (=(92))

(102) Licensing Condition on Locative Expletives (=(93))
A locative expletive has to be merged with the lowest *v*P (namely a participle phrase).

I claim that English is also a language to which (102) is applied like Icelandic, since an English expletive *there* is a locative phrase. Thus, following these assumptions, the derivation below occurs for the Th/Ex construction.[29]

29 If the derivation in *v*2P in (104) occurs in an individual-derivation manner, it seems that no problems occur because the AF on V2 can be checked by the φ-features on the DP and the AFs on T and V1 can be dealt with by those on the expletive. If so, we wrongly expect that an example where the DP is assigned the accusative case is derived. However, we can avoid this problem by adopting a bypass Agree operation, which Chomsky (2001) proposes to derive the case assignment mechanism on participle heads. Namely, I claim that φ-features on the expletive are defective (though interpretable) and thus the AFs on T and V1 cannot be completely checked by them even if the Agree relations are held. Thus, the Agree operations must continue to find the DP so as to check the AFs on T and V1 completely. This assumption is supported by the fact that T does not show agreement with the expletive but with the DP in English (see (99)). Therefore, the case of individual-derivation is ruled out because such a bypass Agree operation is prevented in individual-derivation because the AFs cannot access the DP within *v*2P due to the PIC, causing the derivation to crash.

(103) There have been <three books> written <*three books> about that. (=(97a))

(104) a.

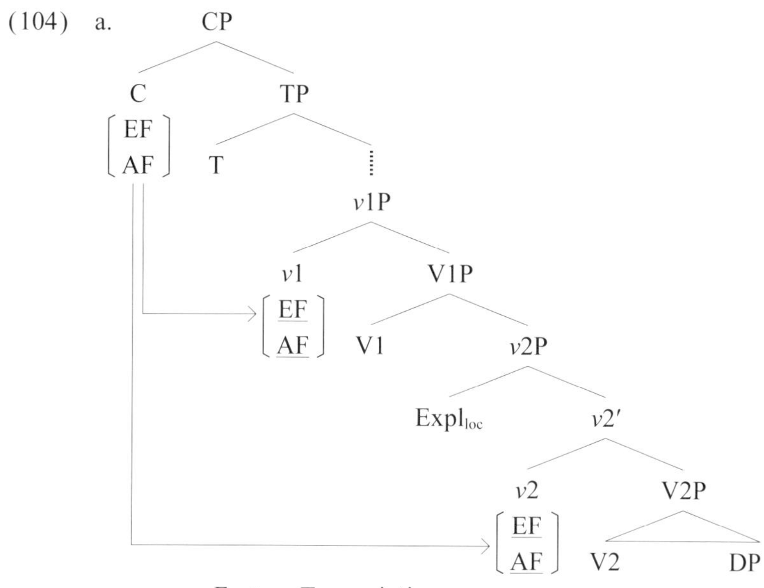

Feature-Transcription

b.

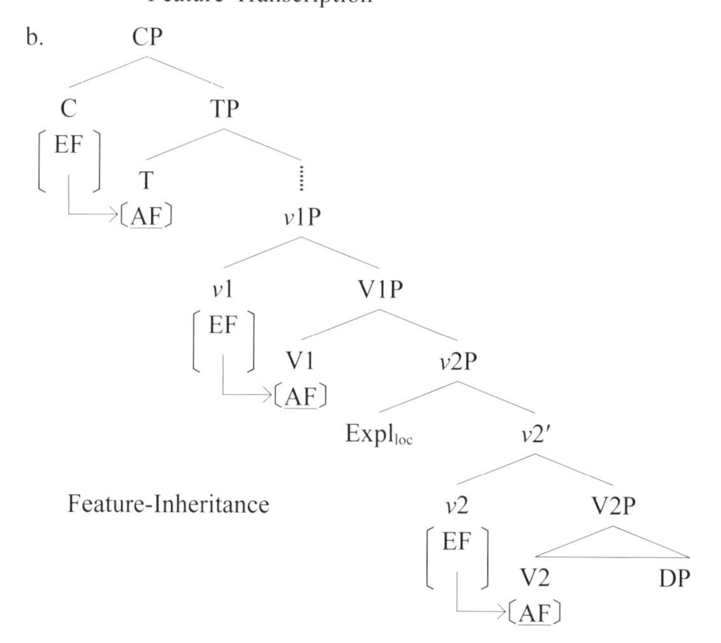

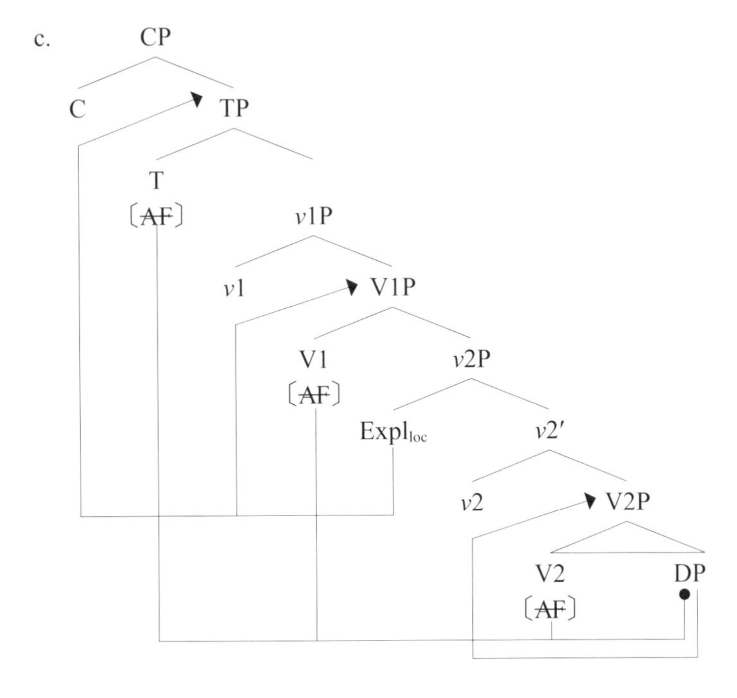

The derivation is basically the same as that in Icelandic in (95). In English as well, Feature-Transcription on *v*2 is not circumvented due to (101). Again, Feature-Inheritance occurs from C to T, from *v*1 to V1, and from *v*2 to V2. In analogy with the Icelandic derivation in (95), feature checking of each uninterpretable feature results in a situation where the expletive is moved to Spec-TP and Spec-V1 at the same time, whereas the DP is moved to Spec-V2. Here, following Pollock (1989) and Caponigro and Schütze (2003), I claim that V in English passives is not moved to *v*, unlike in Icelandic.[30] Therefore,

---

30 Caponigro and Schütze's (2003) discussion is based on the following data concerning adjunct placements. Following Bowers (1993) and Blight (1999), they assume that the adjuncts in (i) are always adjoined to VP. Thus, the positions of the verb (or the verbal active/passive participles) in (ia, b) imply that the verbal head exists below *v* in the passive sentence in (ia) but it does not in the active example in (ib). Thus they claim that in passive sentences V does not move to *v* unlike in active sentences.

(i) a. The house was poorly built.
 b. *They (have) poorly built the house.

(Caponigro and Schütze (2003: 297))

as is shown in (105), V2 always projects below the moved DP.

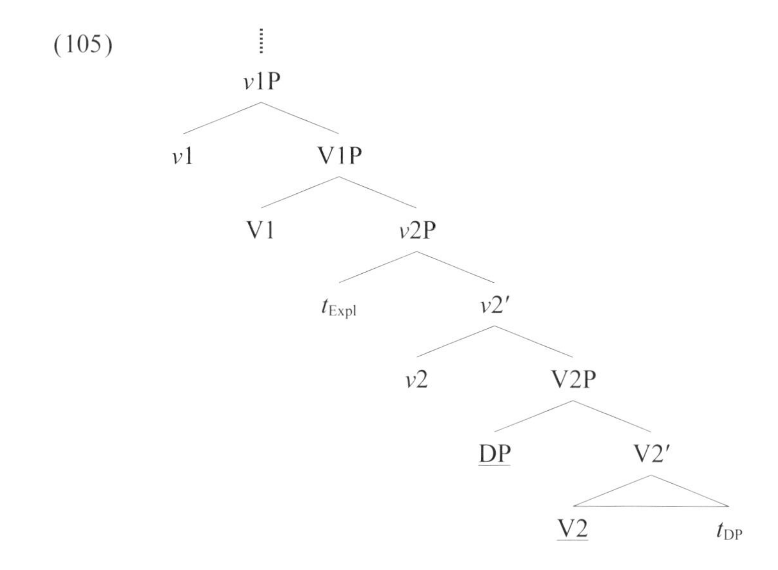

Thus, in English, the DP cannot remain on the right of the participle because it is necessarily moved above V2 since Feature-Transcription is applied to *v*2, and V2 remains in situ unlike in Icelandic.

To wrap up, in this section, I have argued that the Th/Ex construction, which has not gained a full-fledged explanation in previous research, can be accounted for under the Feature-Transcription framework. In the next section, we will move to phenomena of optional case manifestations in Japanese.

4.3 The Nominative/Accusative Case Conversion in Japanese

Thus far, we have observed explanations where simultaneous-derivation under the Feature-Transcription framework plays a crucial role. In this section, we pursue explanatory possibilities of the optionality of the two kinds of derivations in Feature-Transcription framework, namely simultaneous/individual-derivation, as discussed in 3.5.1. Recall that we assume the transfer-based case assignment mechanism in (66), repeated in (106) below. Then, it should be noted that if the C head transfers a DP inside a weak-phase *v*P in simultaneous-derivation, the DP is expected to receive the nominative case as in (107a), whereas, if individual-derivation occurs, the DP within *v*P is transferred by the *v* head and assigned the accusative case as in (107b). Here, we can derive an optionality concerning case manifestations.

(106) A phase head determines a DP's case within its domain, when it triggers Transfer. (=(66))

(107) a. $[_{CP}$ C̲ $[_{TP}...[_{vP}$ *v* $[_{VP}...DP_{Nom}...]]]]$ simultaneous-derivation
b. $[_{CP}$ C $[_{TP}...[_{vP}$ *v̲* $[_{VP}...DP_{Acc}...]]]]$ individual-derivation

In what follows, I claim that the Japanese nominative/accusative case conversion and its scope-related phenomena can be captured based on the optionality in (107).

Before moving on to the analysis, a small note is necessary concerning presuppositions in this book. Firstly, I assume that Japanese includes φ-feature agreement although it is not overtly expressed in most cases.[31] Secondly, I claim that Japanese nominative and accusative case is structural case, whereas other types of case, such as *-ni*/*-de*, are inherent case in that a DP with such a case is included within some projections (probably *p**P as discussed in chapter 6). Keeping in mind these assumptions, let us move to data in Japanese.

4.3.1 Previous Analyses

It has been pointed out that in Japanese, an object can be assigned the nominative case when a certain modal head exists.

(108) a. Taro-ga migime-o̲ tsumur-e-ru (koto).
Taro-Nom migime-Acc close-can-Prs (the fact)

31 Some researchers claim that Japanese honorific expressions include agreement. For instance, Mikami (1970) points out that *o- suru*/*ni naru* honorific expression shown below is similar to subject-verb agreement in some languages. Furthermore, Toribio (1990), Kishimoto (1996), Hasegawa (2005), and Boeckx and Niinuma (2004) attempt to treat such honorific expressions based on agreement. In this book, therefore, I assume that Japanese has agreement following these researchers.

(i) a. Shatyo-ga Taro-o o-wakarini-naru.
b. #Taro-ga Shatyo-o o-wakarini-naru.

b. Taro-ga migime-ga tsumur-e-ru (koto).
Taro-Nom migime-Nom close-can-Prs (the fact)
'(the fact that) Taro can close his right eye.'

The object in (108a) receives the accusative case, whereas the assigned case on the object in (108b) is nominative. Interestingly, these case manifestation patterns are completely optional. Moreover, there is no semantic difference between (108a, b) as far as I can see and thus I conclude that this phenomenon must be explained syntactically.

Although there is no apparent semantic difference, some researchers point out that when the expression *-dake* ("only") is introduced, there occurs a difference in scope interpretation.

(109) a. Taro-ga migime-dake-o tsumur-e-ru.
Taro-Nom right-eye-only-Acc close-can-Prs
'(the fact that) Taro can close only his right eye.'
b. Taro-ga migime-dake-ga tsumur-e-ru.
Taro-Nom right-eye-only-Nom close-can-Prs
'(the fact that) Taro only can close his right eye.'
(Takahashi (2011: 759))

As is shown in (109a), *-dake* ("only") in the accusative-object sentence has a narrow scope reading, where Taro has an ability to wink. On the other hand, *-dake* ("only") in (109b) has a wide scope reading, where *Taro* cannot close his left eye for some reason.[32]

Traditionally, this fact is explained based on a movement operation related to nominative case assignment (see, for instance, Tada (1992), Koizumi (1994), Ura (1996)). Regardless of the place to which the nominative marked object is moved (Spec-TP, Spec-AgrS, or so forth), the main point of these analyses is that the object DP has to be moved to a higher position to receive the nominative case and there it gains wide scope reading.

32 According to Koizumi (1994), the accusative object can take the wide scope interpretation if it is stressed. However, I will put aside the stress-related interpretation here and in what follows.

(110) a. Taro-ga migime-dake-o tsumur-e-ru. (=(109a))

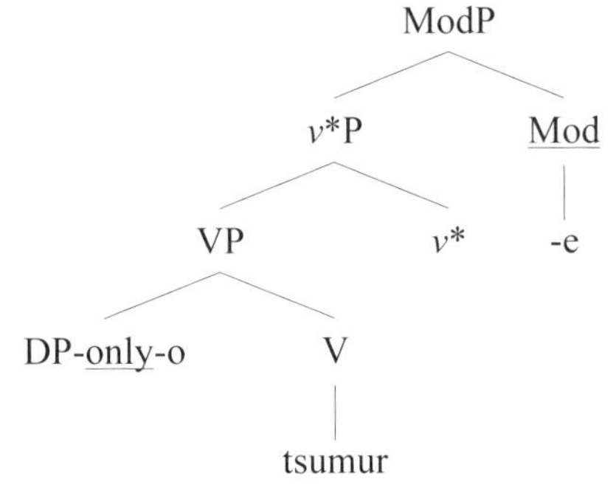

b. Taro-ga migime-dake-ga tsumur-e-ru. (=(109b))

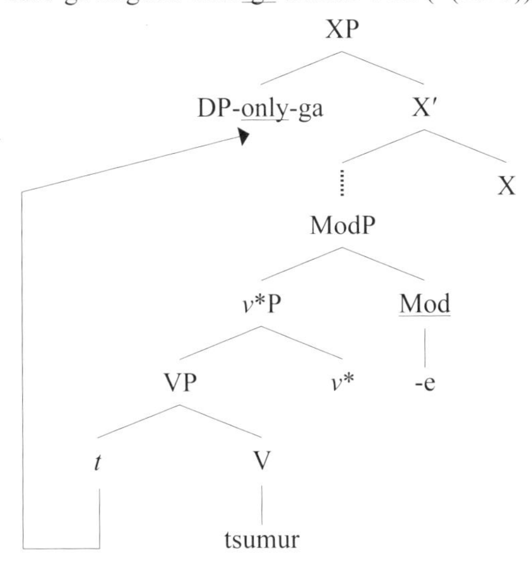

Assuming that scope relations are explained based on c-command relations, the object DP in (109b) is moved to a position which c-commands the position *-dake* ("only") occupies, as is shown in (110b).

Though such an explanation is quite elegant, the analysis faces a serious problem when Takahashi (2011) points out intriguing but complicated examples, which are seen in the next subsection.

4.3.2 Further Problems

Takahashi (2011) points out the following examples.

(111) a. Taro-ga sakana-o kosho-dake-de tabe-rare-ru
Taro-Nom fish-Acc pepper-only-with eat-can-Prs
(koto). (*only>can, can>only)
the fact
'(the fact that) Taro can eat fish only with pepper.'

b. Taro-ga sakana-ga kosho-dake-de tabe-rare-ru
Taro-Nom fish-Nom pepper-only-with eat-can-Prs
(koto). (only>can, ?can>only)
the fact
'(the fact that) Taro only can eat fish with pepper.'
(Takahashi (2011: 761))

Interestingly, again, when the object receives the accusative case, *-dake* ("only") in (111a) takes a narrow scope reading, where "Taro can eat fish with only pepper (Takahashi (2011: 761))." On the other hand, *-dake* ("only") in (111b) can take a wider scope interpretation, where "it is only pepper that Taro can eat fish with (Takahashi (2011: 761))." Now, notice that *-dake* ("only") in (111b) is attached to the adjunct phrase, not to the DP receiving case. Therefore, movement for the nominative case assignment can never affect the c-command relation between *-dake* ("only") and *-rare* ("can") here. Thus, the explanation in the last subsection is not tenable and we need an alternative account for the phenomenon without relying on the case assignment process directly.

4.3.3 Takahashi (2011)

4.3.3.1 A Phase-Based Approach

Takahashi (2011) proposes a phase-based alternative approach to this problem. Firstly, he suggests the following two assumptions.

(112) Takahashi's (2011) assumptions
a. Phase-ness corresponds to case assignment ability.
b. QR *dake* 'only' is bound to domains of case-valuation.
((112b) is cited from Takahashi (2011: 763))

As is shown in (112a), in his framework, phase-ness is related to case-assignment ability. Therefore, it is derived that when *v* can assign the accusative case to a DP, then it is analyzed as a phase *v** head and on the other hand when *v* cannot assign case, it is analyzed as a non-phase *v* head. In addition, he claims that *-dake* ("only") can undergo QR only within a case-valuing domain in (112b).

Then, he assumes (113) concerning Japanese modal head.

(113) Japanese modal heads can optionally absorb a case-valuation ability on *v*P.

Based on these assumptions, the phenomenon is explained as follows:

(114) a. Taro-ga sakana-o kosho-dake-de tabe-rare-ru. (=(111a))
(*only>can, can>only)

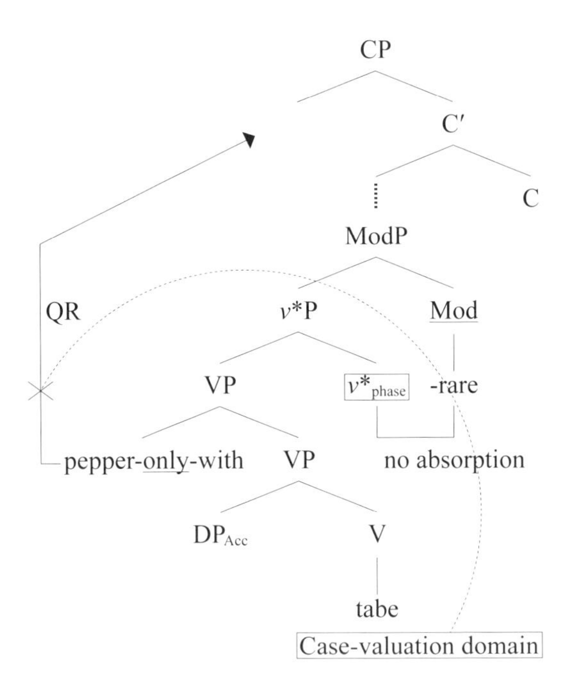

b. Taro-ga sakana-ga kosho-dake-de tabe-rare-ru. (=(111b))
(only>can, ?can>only)

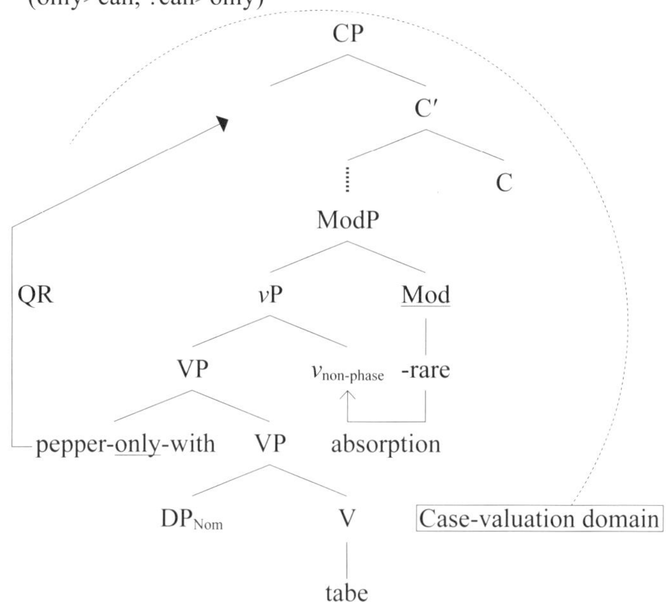

As is shown in (114a), when the modal head does not absorb the case-valuation ability on *v*P based on (113), *v*P serves as a phase *v**P and the object *sakana* receives the accusative case, since in his framework phase-ness and case-assignment ability correspond, following (112a). In this case, moreover, since the case-valuation occurs within the *v**P phase, the QR operation is applied only within the *v**P phase based on (112b). Given that operations concerning scope interpretation are considered to be A-bar movement and A-bar movement targets the Spec of a phase in Chomsky's (2008) Feature-Inheritance framework, this indicates that QR is applied to Spec-*v*P in this case (although Takahashi (2011) does not clearly note this). Therefore, *-dake* ("only") does not take a wider scope reading than the modal head *-rare* ("can") since the modal head c-commands the adjunct including *-dake* ("only"). On the other hand, as in (112b), when the modal head absorbs the case-valuation ability on *v*P based on (113), *v*P does not constitute a phase and the object *sakana* does not receive the accusative case following (112a). Therefore, the assumption in (112b) allows *-dake* ("only") to undergo a QR operation beyond *v*P, up to CP phase level. In this case, *-dake* ("only") can take a wide scope reading since it c-commands *-rare* ("can") due to the QR operation.

4.3.3.2 Problems in Takahashi (2011)

As we saw in the last section, Takahashi's (2011) approach largely relies on the assumption in (113). However, it seems that this assumption lacks sufficient motivation. For one thing, as we saw in 3.5.1, one possibility is selected in terms of economy when two choices exist in the MP. Thus, the optionality in (113) must be derived from some principled mechanisms. Moreover, a serious problem is that in (113) we need to rewind the derivation in order for the modal head, which exists outside *v*P, to change *v*P into a non-phase by absorbing its case-valuation ability. Let us see the details of this problem. Under Chomsky's (2008) Feature-Inheritance framework, a phase head starts its syntactic operations when it is merged into the derivation. Then, when the modal head is merged with *v*P, the syntactic operations within *v*P have already been finished whether or not the modal head absorbs the case-valuation ability of *v*P.

(115)

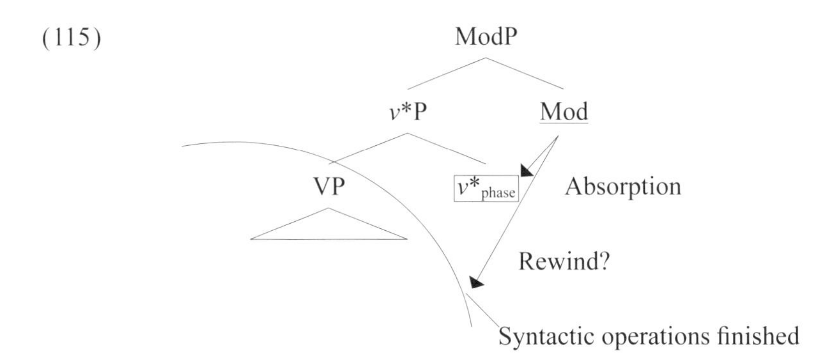

Of course, such a rewinding operation is not economical and therefore dispreferred in the MP. Moreover, even if we assume that such a rewinding operation is applicable because of some unknown reasons, the process must pose quite a heavy burden on the computation and thus the possibility of absorption should always be avoided in terms of economy. Thus, the derivation in (114b) is not accepted under any circumstances.

One may claim that the modal head does not exist outside *v*P, but rather it is merged directly to the *v* head. In that case, we can circumvent the rewinding problem above. However, note that Takahashi (2011) assumes that QR is applied within a domain of case-valuation. Notice that it is derived that the QR within *v*P is applied up to the Spec of *v*P, given that QR is a scope-related operation and such an operation is regarded as a case of A-bar movement in Chomsky's (2008) Feature-Inheritance framework. Hence, if modal head is directly merged to the *v* head, the QRed *only* always c-commands the modal head even in the case of (111a) and we wrongly expect that the wide scope reading is always possible in both (111a, b).

(116)

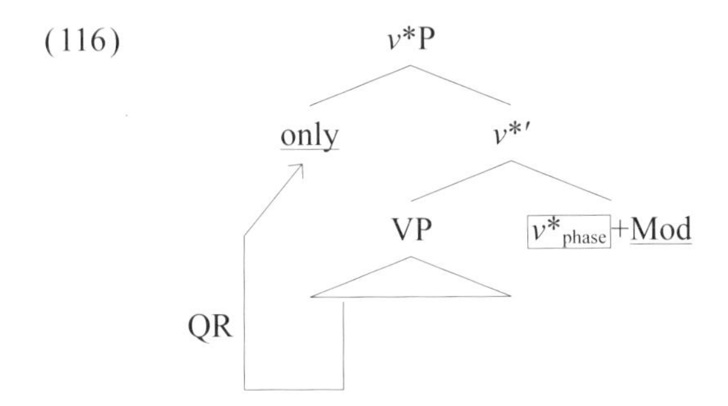

Thus, if we make the special assumption that the modal head is merged with the *v* head directly, still we cannot derive the proper c-command relation. In sum, although Takahashi's (2011) insight is quite interesting and elegant, his framework retains theoretical inadequacies.

4.3.4 An Alternative Account under Feature-Transcription

I claim that Takahashi's (2011) theoretical problem is readily solved under the Feature-Transcription framework. Note that I have derived optionality based on the two possibilities in derivation under Feature-Transcription in 3.5.1: simultaneous-derivation and individual-derivation. Then, I claim that Takahashi's (2011) assumption in (113) can be reanalyzed as in (117) under the Feature-Transcription framework.

(117) Japanese modal heads select a weak-phase *v*P as their complement.

In addition, I employ Takahashi's (2011) assumption in (112b) that QR is bound to domains of case-valuation, as is repeated in (118).

(118) QR *dake* 'only' is bound to domains of case-valuation.[33] (=(112b))

Again, recall that we have proposed the following assumption as a case assignment mechanism in this book.

(119) A phase head determines a DP's case within its domain, when it triggers Transfer.

Under the assumption in (119), (118) implies that QR is applied to the Spec of a (strong/weak-)phase whose head triggers transfer. Based on these assumptions, the examples in (111) repeated below are explained as follows:

(120) Taro-ga sakana-o kosho-dake-de tabe-rare-ru. (=(111a))
(*only>can, can>only)
a.

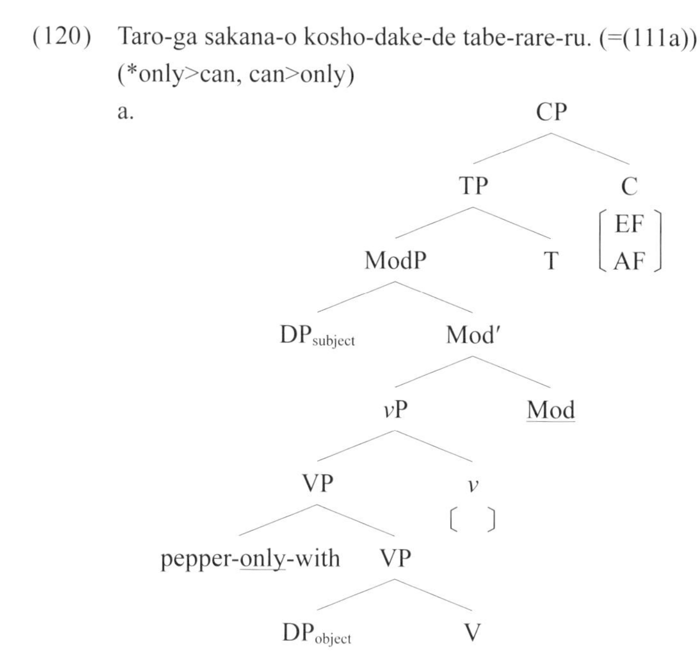

33 It is unclear whether this assumption is consistent with Fox's (2000) observation, where QR is optionally applicable in a long-distance relation if it affects scope-relations. I will, however, put aside the detailed discussion on scope relations since this is beyond the main scope in this book, and I simply adopt Takahashi's (2011) assumption in (118) in the discussion here.

b.

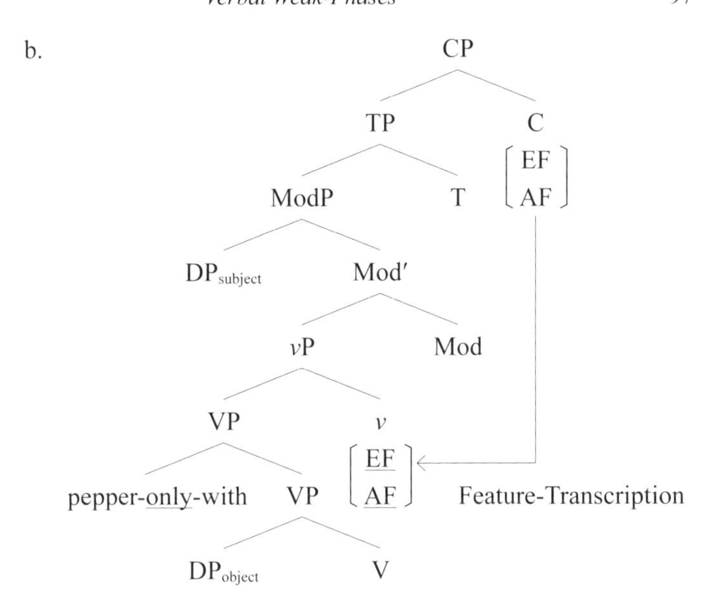
CP
TP
C
EF
AF
ModP
T
DP subject
Mod′
vP
Mod
VP
v
EF
AF
pepper-only-with
VP
Feature-Transcription
DP object
V

c.

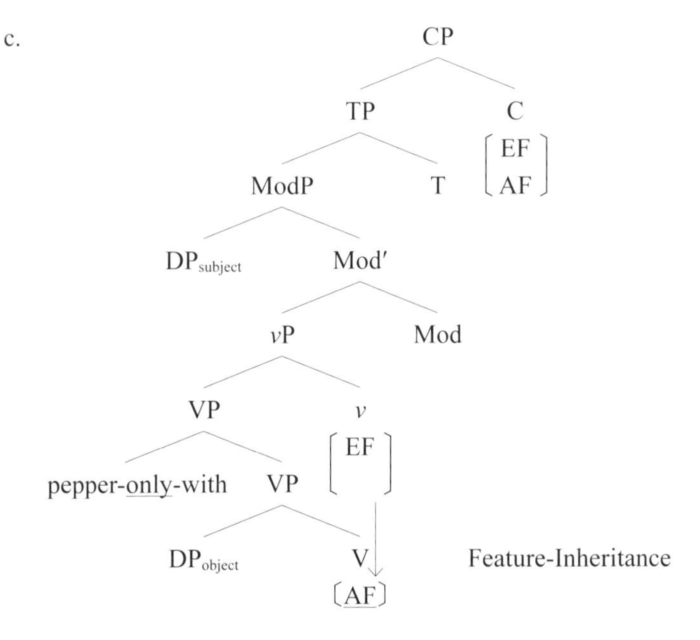
CP
TP
C
EF
AF
ModP
T
DP subject
Mod′
vP
Mod
VP
v
EF
pepper-only-with
VP
DP object
V
Feature-Inheritance
AF

d.

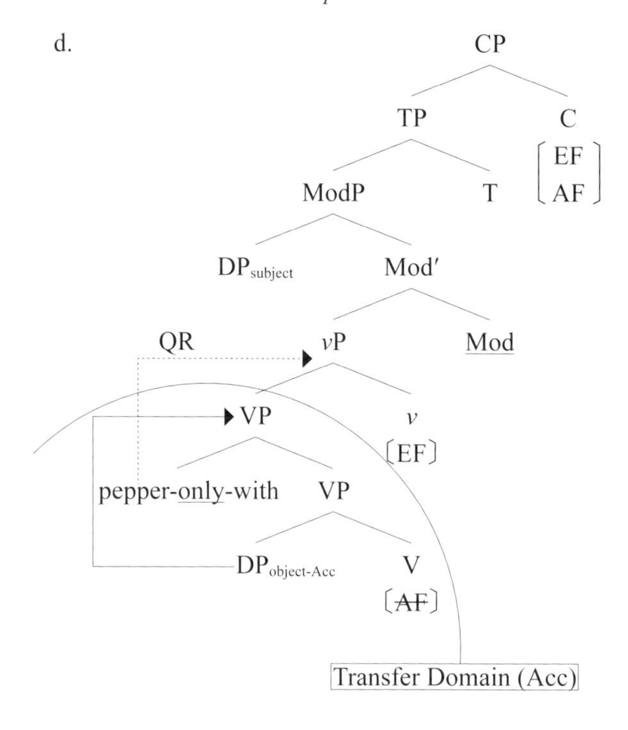

e.

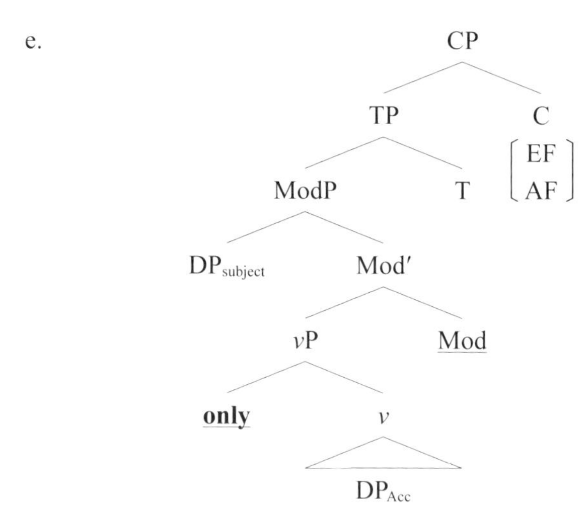

As is shown in (120a), the modal head selects *v*P in its complement based on (117). Moreover, since *v* is a weak-phase head, it does not introduce the subject DP in its Spec. I assume that it is base-generated in Spec-ModP, instead.[34] Since the *v* head is a weak-phase head without a DP in its Spec (cf. (81) in 4.1.3.1), Feature-Transcription is triggered from the C head to the *v* head. Then, the derivation here continues in an individual-derivation manner. At the C phase level, the syntactic operations in *v*P occur before those in CP. Feature-Inheritance is applied from *v* to V as in (120c). The AF on V holds an Agree relation with the object DP, and the DP is moved to Spec-VP. At the same time, the EF on *v* attracts *only* to Spec-*v*P as QR, as can be seen in (120d). As a result, the unpronounced copy of *only* exists in Spec-*v*P and this does not c-command the modal head as in (120e). Although I omit the derivation after it in CP since it makes no difference in the scope relation, the narrow scope reading is explained based on the c-command relation in (120e). Note that *only* cannot undergo QR further up to Spec-CP due to the assumption in (118) because if it does, it is posited outside of the domain of case-valuation, namely outside of *v*P. Finally, the DP within *v*P is assigned the accusative case since *v* transfers it.

Notice that the derivation may also occur in a simultaneous-derivation manner, since I assume the two derivation possibilities are always available as long as a weak-phase is included in the derivation. In this case, I claim that the wide scope reading is structurally supported.

34 This is applicable if we assume PRO, namely, an implicit subject exists in Spec-*v*P. However, if we take the Control as Movement approach (see, e.g. Hornstein (1999), Boeckx and Hornstein (2003), and Boeckx et al. (2010)), we can suggest that the subject is base-generated in Spec-*v*P but it is moved to Spec-ModP by an Edge Feature on the Mod head as a requirement of θ-roles before Feature-Transcription is applied (on the discussion on θ-roles and their relation to Edge Features, see 6.5). What is important here is that the subject is moved before Feature-Transcription occurs so that the *v* head can receive uninterpretable features. Otherwise, based on the discussion concerning the Scandinavian languages in 4.1, a weak-phase head would not be involved in Feature-Transcription because of the existence of a DP in its Spec.

(121) Taro-ga sakana-ga kosho-dake-de tabe-rare-ru. (=(111a))
(only>can, ?can>only)

a.

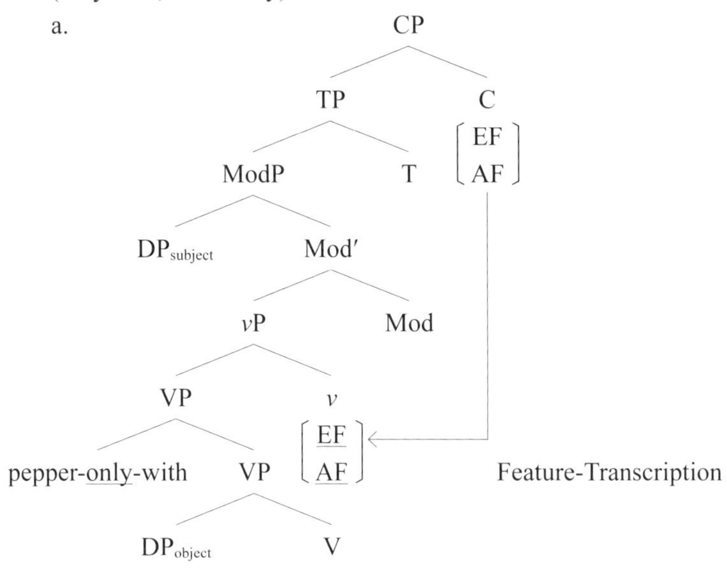

b.

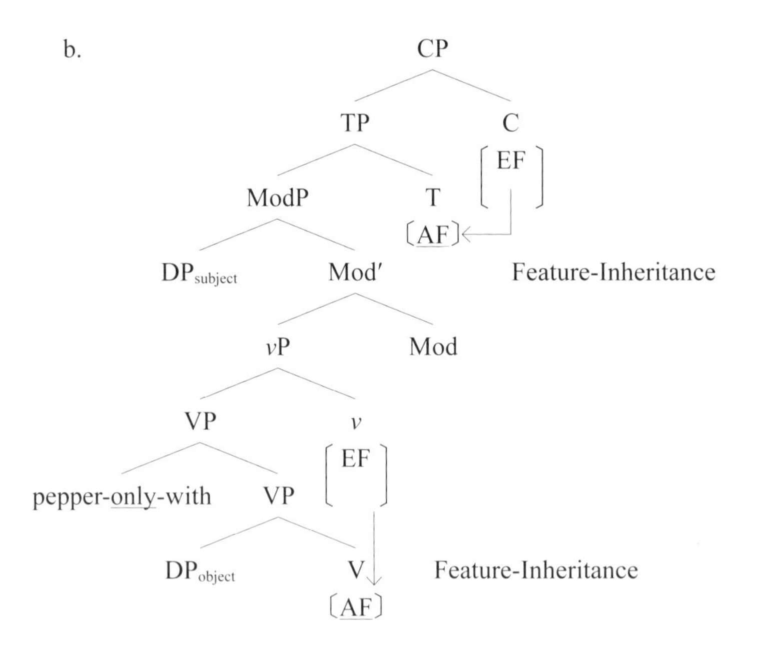

c.

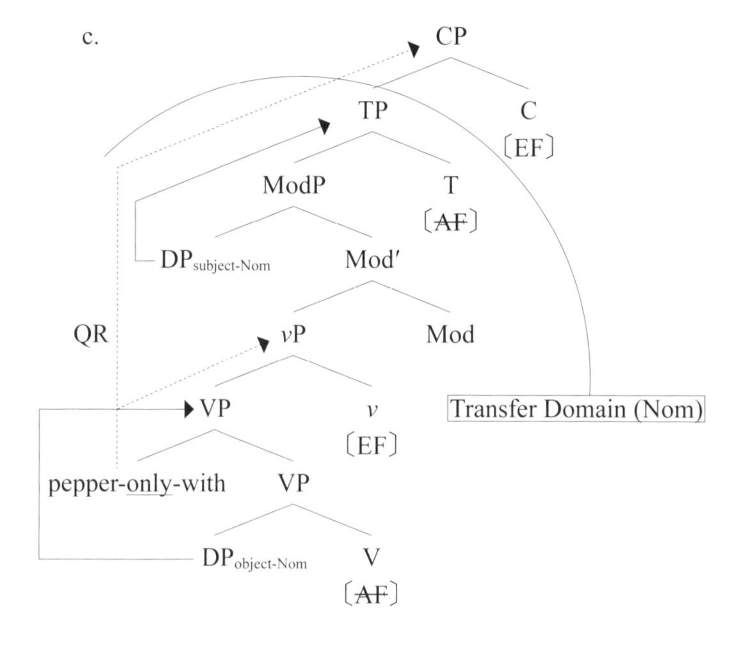

d.

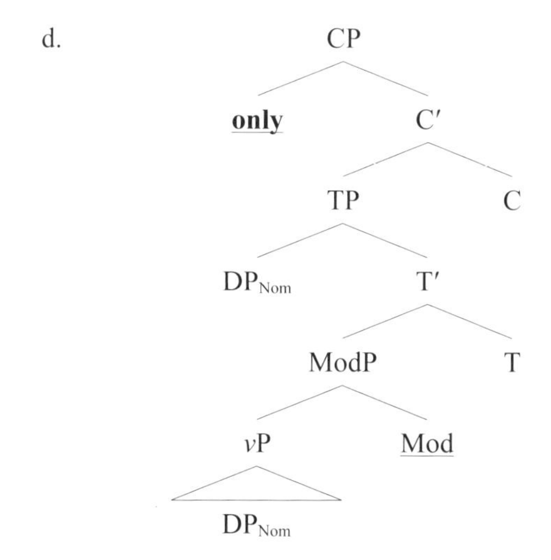

As can be seen in (121a), Feature-Transcription is triggered in a similar way as in (120b). However, in this case, the C head and the *v* head start their syntactic operations simultaneously. Feature-Inheritance occurs from C to T and *v* to V. Then, the AF on T holds an Agree relation with the subject DP and that on V, with the object DP. The DPs are moved to the respective Spec positions through this process. At the same time, *only* undergoes the QR operation based on the EF on C and *v*, simultaneously. Therefore, *only* in Spec-CP c-commands the modal head and thus the possibility of the wide scope reading is structurally captured. Notice that (118) is not violated here since the QR of *only* occurs within the case-valuation domain, namely, within CP (although it is beyond the "transfer domain" of CP, it is still within CP). Finally, both the subject DP and the object DP are transferred by C and thus they are assigned the nominative case.

In sum, under the Feature-Transcription framework, the nominative/accusative case conversion in Japanese is explained based on the two possibilities of derivations.

4.4 The Double Object Construction in English

4.4.1 An Overview of Some Analyses of the Double Object Construction

In this section, we will explore explanatory possibilities of Feature-Transcription by considering phenomena related to the Double Object Construction (the DOC) in English. The DOC has attracted the attention of quite a lot of researchers and contributed to the theoretical development of generative grammar. Before giving explanations to various problems, I present two brief summaries in research on the DOC, which is related to the discussions in this section. In the next two subsections, we will witness discussions on VP-shells, which led us to the assumption of *v*P, and discussions on differences (and similarities) between the DOC and the Prepositional Dative Construction (the Prepositional DC).

4.4.1.1 VP-shell and *v*P

It is fair to say that nowadays the existence of *v*P is taken for granted when we analyze verbal phrases. The introduction of *v*P, however, has much to do with the DOC. Since the main problem in this book is strongly connected to the existence of *v*P, let us take a look at a brief overview of Larson's (1988) VP-shell analysis.

It has been pointed out that English has two types of ditransitive constructions with almost the same semantic interpretation: the DOC and the Prepositional DC as presented below.

(122) a. John gave Mary a book. (the DOC)
b. John gave a book to Mary. (the Prepositional DC)

The fact that one language has the two apparently redundant constructions is quite intriguing. Interestingly, Amano (1998) points out that German has only the construction corresponding to (122a), whereas French has only the case of (122b).

(123) a. Das Mädchen shenkte dem Jungen ein Buch. (German)
the girl gave the boy a book
'The girl gave the boy a book.' (Amano (1998: 359))
b. Je donné un livre à Paul. (French)
I give a book to Paul
'I give a book to Paul.' (Amano (1998: 5))

Moreover, the DOC includes quite a lot of complicated facts, as have traditionally been pointed out. One of the most prominent discussions in the DOC is concerned with a c-command relation between Indirect Object and Direct Object pointed out by Barss and Lasnik (1986).

(124) a. I showed Mary herself (in the mirror).
b. *I showed herself Mary (in the mirror).
c. I gave every $worker_i$ his_i paycheck.
d. *I gave its_i owner every $paycheck_i$.
e. I showed no one anything.
f. *I showed anyone nothing.
(Barss and Lasnik (1986: 347–350))

As is shown in (124), Barss and Lasnik (1986) claim that Indirect Object asymmetrically c-commands Direct Object.[35] This fact is quite problematic because ternary branching structure as in (125a) or complicated binary branching structure in (125b) used to be traditionally assumed for the DOC (*IO* and

35 Strictly speaking, Barss and Lasnik (1986) originally claim that Indirect Object simply *c-commands* Direct Object. However, Larson (1988) argues that Indirect Object has to *asymmetrically c-command* Direct Object in order to capture the examples in (124).

DO stand for *Indirect Object* and *Direct Object*).

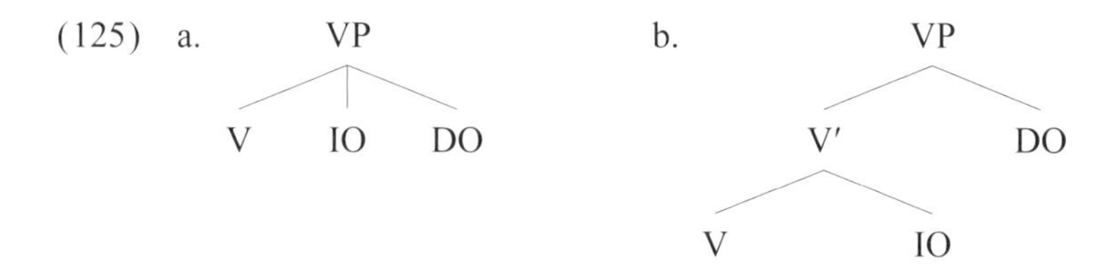

However, it is obvious that in both structures in (125), Indirect Object never asymmetrically c-commands Direct Object. In (125a), the gained situation is a mutual c-command relation between Indirect Object and Direct Object, not the asymmetrical c-command relation. In addition, the theoretical validity of ternary branching structures has been controversial. On the other hand, in (125b), the opposite asymmetrical c-command relation holds, making matters worse. Thus, the main topic of discussion related to the DOC in the 1980's used to be how to derive the proper c-command relation in the binary branching framework.

Research which sheds light on this problem is Larson (1988). He suggests a path-breaking assumption of VP-shell analysis that is now well-known. His claim is quite simple; there are two VP layers in the DOC.

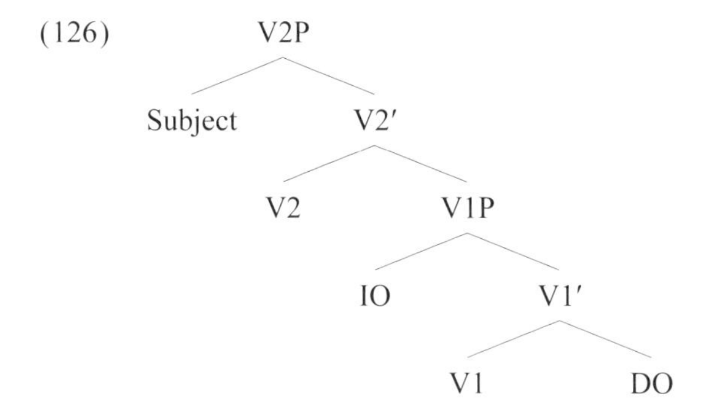

By assuming this, the proper c-command relation is gained. As can be seen in (126), Indirect Object can asymmetrically c-command Direct Object. Moreover, the verb is moved from the V1 position to the V2 position, deriving the proper word order. As one may already realize, the two layers of VP have been rephrased as *v*P-VP layers and thus Larson's (1988) core idea still survives until today. Therefore, it is fair to say that the DOC gave us a cue for the introduction of *v*P, without which the discussions in this book on weak-phases would not exist.

4.4.1.2 Are the Two Constructions Related or Not?

In this subsection, we will look at a brief history of discussions concerning similarities and differences between the DOC and the Prepositional DC. In early generative grammar, a lot of transformational operations were assumed. Due to the similarity in thematic relations in the two constructions, there used to be a lot of researchers who assume that the DOC and the Prepositional DC are basically the same construction and they are generated through a transformational operation of "dative shift." For instance, Larson (1988) is a representative among them and he provides an analysis based on a passive-like dative shift. However, many researchers have casted doubt on such an alternation. They have pointed out many differences between the two constructions and claimed that they are independent constructions, against approaches based on dative shift. Thus, roughly speaking, there are two big groups in analyzing these two constructions: *alternation approaches* and *non-alternation approaches*.[36]

It seems to me that non-alternation approaches are recently dominant given the following discoveries, which differentiate the two constructions. Of course, I cannot present all of the discussions concerning the differences between the two constructions because they include too much research. Picking up a couple of them, we can raise the fact that Indirect Object in the DOC must be animate whereas a DP within a *to* phrase in the Prepositional DC need not, and that there is a possessing interpretation in the DOC, which is not necessary in the Prepositional DC. Bruening (2010b) also raises asymmetries in scope relations and nominalizations between the DOC and the Prepositional DC.

Among the differences, furthermore, it is worth noting that a plenty of debates have been conducted concerning idiom formations in the DOC and the Prepositional DC. Because the discussions in idiom formations cause

36 Strictly speaking, alternation approaches are further subdivided into two groups, namely, altering the Prepositional DC into the DOC (for instance, Larson (1988), Baker (1997), Oba (2005)) or altering the DOC into the Prepositional DC (e.g. Takano (1998)). However, in this section, I will refer to them as alternation approaches since the difference is not significant here.

Bruening (2010a) to assume R-dative shift, which is partly employed in this book, let us take a brief look at the main point of the discussions here. Note that some kinds of idioms must be used only in the DOC or the Prepositional DC.

(127) a. The lighting here gives me a headache.
b. *The lighting here gives a headache to me.
c. The count gives me the creeps.
d. *The count gives the creeps to me.
(Bruening (2010a: 288))

Although Richards (2001) claims thats the two constructions are basically same by arguing that some of the idioms can be used in the both constructions, such an approach faces a problem concerning the examples in (127). If both of the constructions have basically the same semantic interpretations, the straightforward expectation is that all idioms should be used in both the constructions.[37] However it is obvious that many idioms can be used only in either of the constructions. For instance, in (127), *give* (*someone*) *a headache* can be used only in the DOC.

Interestingly, Bresnan et al. (e.g. see Bresnan et al. (2007) and Bresnan and Nikitina (2010)) argue against the discussion here. They claim that even such idioms as in (127) can be utilized in the Prepositional DC under some circumstances. They offer the following examples to support the alternation approach.

(128) a. … a stench or smell is diffused over the ship that would give a headache to the most athletic constitution.
(Bresnan and Nikitina (2010: 4))
b. This story is designed to give the creeps to people who hate spiders. (Bresnan et al. (2007: 72))

The examples in (128) seem to bring rays of hope to alternation approach in that even some idioms which have to be used in the DOC can appear in the

37 Although Richards (2001) also tries to capture the difference in (127), his approach still contains problems as he noted in his Appendix.

Prepositional DC under proper context.

However, Bruening (2010a), again, demolishes the claim. He argues that the examples in (128) are not cases of the Prepositional DC, but they are "disguised" as the Prepositional DC. This indicates that the instances in (128) are actually examples of the DOC, contrary to their appearances, and are not exceptions to (127) (we will move back to the detail of this claim in 4.4.2.2.2).

Therefore, judging from the differences between the two constructions, I conclude that the non-alternation analysis is superior to the alternation analysis. Moreover, in this book, I basically follow Bruening's (2010a) position in that the DOC can sometimes be "disguised" as the Prepositional DC. Now, in the next subsection, let us observe problems not fully explained thus far, to the best of my knowledge.

4.4.2 Asymmetries between Indirect Object and Direct Object

4.4.2.1 Problems

Now, let us move to the main problems of this section in the DOC. There are phenomena which have repeatedly been discussed in previous research but have not yet been given a convincing explanation: asymmetries between Indirect Object and Direct Object.

(129) a. Tom was given the book.
b. *The book was given Tom.

(130) a. *Who did you give *t* a book?
b. What did you give John *t*. (Wh question)
c. *This is the person who he gave *t* that book.
d. This is the book which he gave the person *t*. (Relativization)
e. *It is John that he gave *t* that book.
f. It is that book that he gave John *t*. (Cleft construction)
g. *John is impossible to give *t* that book.
h. That book is impossible to give John *t*. (Tough construction)
i. *John, he gave *t* that book.
j. That book, he gave John *t*. (Topicalization)
(Oba (2005: 61))

As can be seen in (129), Indirect Object can be moved to Spec-TP, whereas

Direct Object is incapable of being moved to the subject position in passives in the DOC. Therefore, when it comes to A-movement, there is a preference of Indirect Object over Direct Object. Apparently, this fact seems to be explained based on superiority since Indirect Object is posited in a higher position than Direct Object (or since the former asymmetrically c-commands the latter as we already saw in 4.4.1.1).

However, the situation becomes quite complicated with the other examples in (130). As Oba (2005) sums up, it has traditionally been argued that Indirect Object cannot undergo A-bar Movement. In (130), Direct Object can undergo A-bar movement such as a *wh*-phrase, while Indirect Object cannot be moved by *wh*-movement. That is to say, there is a preference of Direct Object to Indirect Object, contrary to the situation under A-movement. Here, we face asymmetries between Indirect Object and Direct Object in A/A-bar movement as is summed up in (131).[38]

(131)

	Indirect Object	Direct Object
A-movement	Ok	*
A-bar movement	*	Ok

4.4.2.2 Previous Analyses

Many researchers have attempted to account for these facts. In this subsection, we will take brief looks at Oba (2005) and Bruening (2010a) as repre-

38 As an anonymous reviewer points out, the asymmetry is idiosyncratic characteristics of the English DOC and we can find a wide variety of (un)acceptability of A/A-bar movement in other languages (see e.g. Citko (2011)). For instance, many languages allow both Direct/Indirect Object to undergo A-bar movement and in some languages, both objects can be A-moved (for instance, Norwegian and Icelandic) or only Direct Object can be the subject of a passive sentence (for example, German and Spanish). The exhaustive research on this topic requires a great amount of pages and this is the reason why I limit the discussion here to English. However, note that the idiosyncrasy of the English DOC discussed in this section is derived from an assumption that an English Appl head is involved in a weak-phase (AspP). This indicates that other languages may have Appl within a strong-phase (then, A-movement should be strictly limited), or they may have other phasal projections to ensure the dative case assignment (if so, the dative DP cannot undergo A-movement, while the other object may). Although it is possible to capture some of the varieties of the A/A-bar movement (un)acceptability in this way, I will not go into the detailed discussions, since the topic of this book is "weak-phases."

sentatives of the researchers. However, neither of the researchers is free from problems as will be made clear after the introductions.

4.4.2.2.1 Oba (2005)

Oba (2005) utilizes Thematization/Extraction (Th/Ex) as suggested by Chomsky (2001), and witnessed in 4.2 above, to account for the phenomena. Recall that Chomsky (2001) argues that Th/Ex is a phonetic operation. Therefore, once Th/Ex is applied to an element, the element cannot be syntactically moved further since phonetic operations including Th/Ex occur after the syntactic component. As can be seen in (132), Oba (2005) takes a dative-shift approach, where the DOC is derived from the Prepositional DC, and suggests that the relevant movement for Indirect Object is Th/Ex. More specifically, Indirect Object is moved via Th/Ex to the Spec-VP (expressed by the broken line) and the P head is incorporated into the V head through head movement. The V head is moved to the *v* head position and the proper linear order is gained. In this derivation, it is predicted that phonetically moved Indirect Object cannot be moved further at the syntax component and thus A-bar movement of Indirect Object is excluded.

(132)

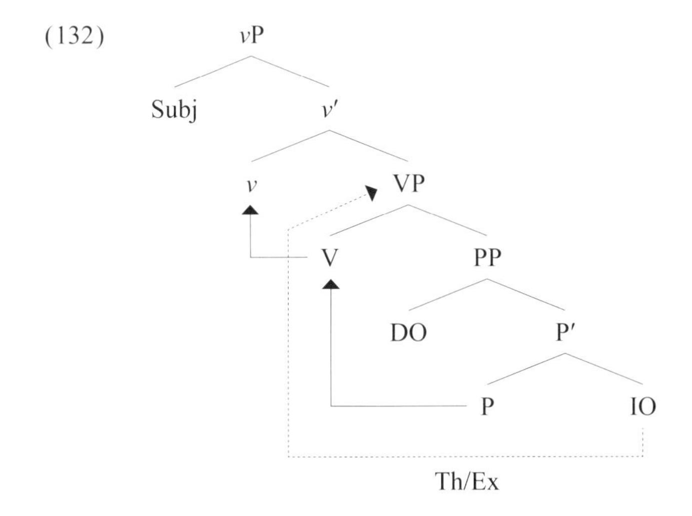

However, Oba's (2005) approach needs some assumptions to deal with the A-movement related asymmetry. On the one hand, when Indirect Object is moved to Spec-TP, it has to be moved directly there without Th/Ex. This is because if Indirect Object undergoes Th/Ex before the A-movement, the moved Indirect Object cannot be further moved, even in A-movement as in (133a). However, without Th/Ex, Direct Object is originally posited at a higher place than Indirect Object and superiority wrongly derives A-movement of Direct Object to Spec-TP as in (133b). Thus, Oba (2005) cannot account for the A-movement asymmetry without some assumptions.

(133) a.

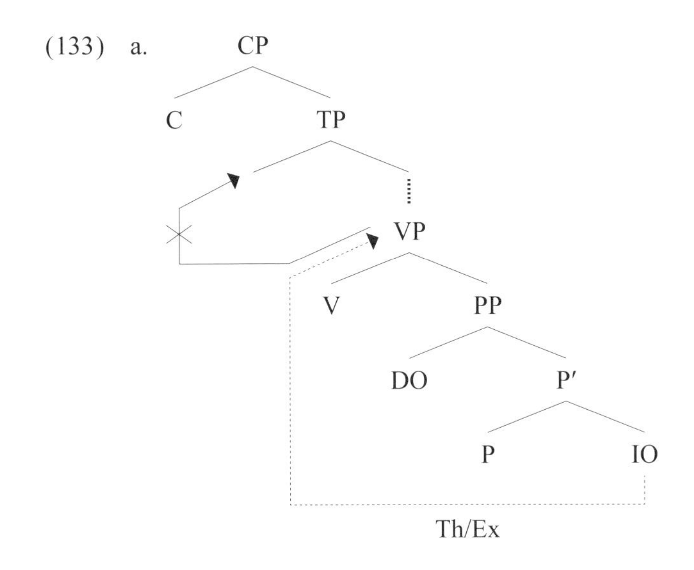

b.

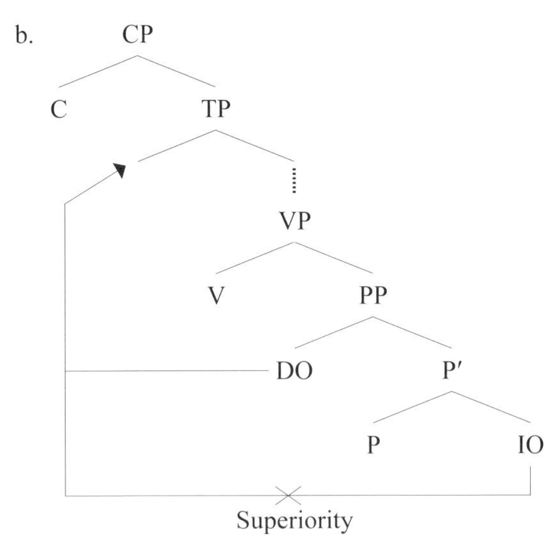

Moreover, if Th/Ex is truly a phonetic operation, it is expected that in an active sentence, the movement of Indirect Object does not have an effect in the C-I Interface, where c-command relations are arguably evaluated, even though Indirect Object is moved to the positon asymmetrically c-commanding Direct Object in (132). This implies that Oba's (2005) approach cannot account for the c-command relation in 4.4.1.1.

Taking into the consideration that the nature of Th/Ex is unclear as we observed in 4.2, it is concluded that although Oba's (2005) approach is quite radical and interesting, some problems remain.

4.4.2.2.2 Bruening (2010a)

The other research we will take a look at is Bruening (2010a), which we already touched on in 4.4.1.2. Bruening's (2010a) claim is that when A-bar movement is applied to Indirect Object, R-dative shift necessarily occurs before the application of A-bar movement. That is to say, Indirect Object, which exists in Spec-Appl(icative)P in his approach (see 4.4.3.2 concerning the Appl head), is moved rightward and "to" phonetically appears before Indirect Object as in (134b). Therefore, it is not that Indirect Object cannot undergo A-bar movement in the DOC, but that when Indirect Object is moved as part of A-bar movement, the sentence is "disguised (Bruening (2010a: 287))" as a Prepositional DC. Consequently, A-bar movement of Indirect Object in the DOC cannot be observed because in such a case the DOC is indistinguishable from the Prepositional DC.

(134) a.

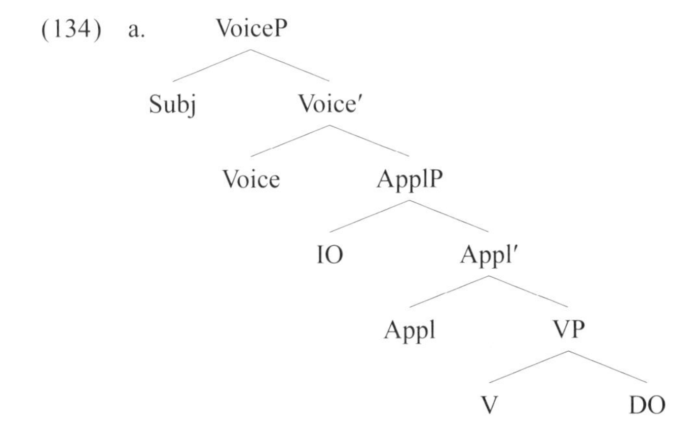

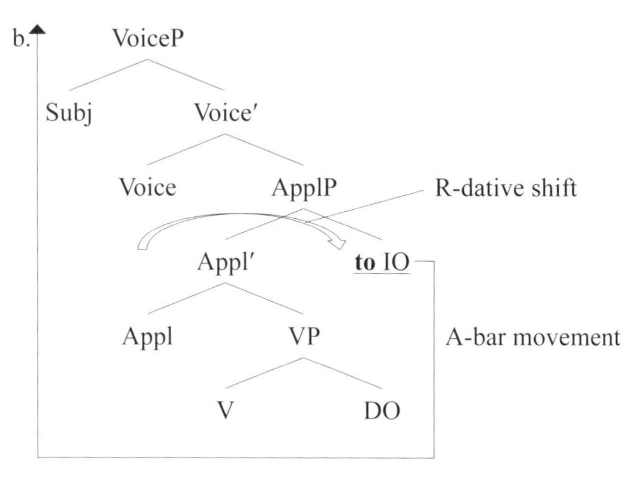

Moreover, his approach can explain the preference of Indirect Object to Direct Object in terms of A-movement. Note that Bruening (2010a) assumes that R-dative shift is applied only when A-bar movement is involved. Thus, when Indirect Object undergoes A-movement, R-dative shift does not occur. In addition, since Indirect Object occupies a higher position than Direct Object in his analysis as in (134a), superiority prevents Direct Object from moving beyond Indirect Object.

However, I claim that his assumption of R-dative shift is problematic; the detailed mechanism of R-dative shift is quite obscure. If he assumes that a preposition *to* is introduced during the derivation when R-dative shift is applied, then the assumption violates the Inclusiveness Condition in the MP, which bans an introduction of new elements once the derivation is started. He might escape this problem by assuming that the appearance of *to* is a result of realization of inflection, namely, an operation at the SM Interface, which is free from the Inclusiveness Condition. Nevertheless, still it is unclear why this occurs only when A-bar movement is triggered. At any rate, there is no denying that his R-dative shift is a mere stipulation without theoretical motivation. Although Bruening's (2010a) insight is worth noting, I claim that his analysis of R-dative shift holds theoretical inadequacies.

4.4.3 The Structure of the Double Object Construction

4.4.3.1 Null-P

In this subsection, I will present an alternative account to the asymmetries between Indirect Object and Direct Object. I take basically the same position as Bruening (2010a). Namely, I assume that it is not that Indirect Object in the DOC cannot undergo A-bar movement, but the sentence is necessarily *disguised* as the Prepositional DC and A-bar movement of Indirect Object in the DOC is unobservable.

However, instead of assuming R-dative shift, I propose that Indirect Object in the DOC is included in PP. In this book, I assume three kinds of PP, namely, bare PP, weak-phase *p*P, and strong-phase *p**P (see chapter 6 for the details). What projects above Indirect Object is the first one, the bare PP, which does not act as a strong/weak-phase at all. I claim that this P head is normally unpronounced by being attached to a verb.

One motivation for the assumption of a bare PP is that with the introduction of PP, two variations of lexical selection by a verbal root in the DOC and the Prepositional DC can be unified. Let us take an example of *give* here. Note that many kinds of ditransitive verbs can be used in both the DOC and the Prepositional DC. Then, if we assume that a lexical head determines its selection of arguments, we need to assume two kinds of selection of each ditransitive verb as follows:

(135) Two possibilities of selection by ditransitive verbs
a. DP1 (Subject) DP2 (IO) DP3 (DO) (the DOC)
b. DP1 (Subject) DP2 (Object) PP (the Prepositional DC)

(135a) represents a verb's selection for the DOC, whereas (135b) expresses that for the Prepositional DC. Nevertheless, once we suggest that Indirect Object is included within PP, the two selection patterns in (135) can be unified into one selection in (136).

(136) Selection by ditransitive verbs (a unified version)[39]
DP1 (Subject) PP (IO in the DOC) DP2 (DO in the DOC)

Therefore, the introduction of PP in the DOC provides a more economical possibility in a verb's selection, as we can deduce the two possibilities in

39 I assume that a prepositional phrase in the Prepositional DC is base-generated above the other object and the object is moved higher in the later derivation. Concerning the structure for the Prepositional DC, see chapter 6.

(135) into the one in (136). Based on this theoretical advantage, I suggest that Indirect Object in the DOC is included within PP in this book.[40]

4.4.3.2 An Applicative Head and an Aspect Head

Given the fact that a verb in the DOC introduces one more argument (namely, Indirect Object) than in usual transitive sentences, it is reasonable to assume that such a verb projects richer layers than normal transitive verbs. Actually, Marantz (1993) proposes that an Applicative (Appl) head, which was found in Bantu languages by Baker (1988), exists in the DOC in English as well. Given that this assumption has recently been supported by some researchers (see e.g. Pylkkänen (2008), Miyagawa (2010), and Bruening (2010a, b)), I assume that an Appl head exists within verbal layers in the DOC following Marantz (1993).

Moreover, I clam that in the DOC, an Aspect (Asp) head plays an important role. Beck and Johnson (2004) argue that the DOC includes a *progressive* possessive interpretation. Their claim is based on the fact that a possessive interpretation in the DOC, namely an implication that Indirect Object possesses Direct Object, can be denied. Citing Beck and Johnson's (2004) example, we usually expect that "Thilo sewed Satoshi a flag (Beck and Johnson (2004: 115))" implies that "Satoshi received a flag." But this can be denied in that "things could have gone wrong after the sewing … and … Satoshi never actually received the flag (Beck and Johnson (2004: 115))." If the DOC necessarily includes a possessive interpretation as was shortly touched on in 4.4.1.2, this fact cannot be expected. However, Beck and Johnson (2004) claim that the situation is similar to a sentence with progressive aspect. "We would normally expect that if Mary was opening the door at some past time, then the event continued until the door was open, and so Mary in fact opened the door. However, this is not necessarily the case: Mary could have been interrupted and never finished opening the door (Beck and Johnson (2004: 116))." Based on this fact, Beck and Johnson (2004) claim that the DOC includes a progressive possessive interpretation and thus it is deniable. Hence, following their claim, I assume that an Asp head exists in

40 Moreover, some researchers also assume the null P and its incorporation into the verb based on their own reasoning (see, e.g. Pesetsky (1995) and Oba (2005)). Thus, I emphasize that the assumptions of the null P and its incorporation in this subsection are not mere stipulations but independently motivated.

verbal layers and it plays an important role in the DOC.[41]

4.4.3.3 A Structure for the Double Object Construction

Based on the discussions shown so far, I propose a structure for the DOC, adopting null P, an Appl head, and an Asp head. I claim that a verb in the DOC projects the *v**-Appl-Asp-V layers. In addition, I propose that *v** serves as a strong-phase head as in usual transitive sentences and Asp acts as a weak-phase head. Let us see the detail of the derivation for the DOC in (137).

(137) a.

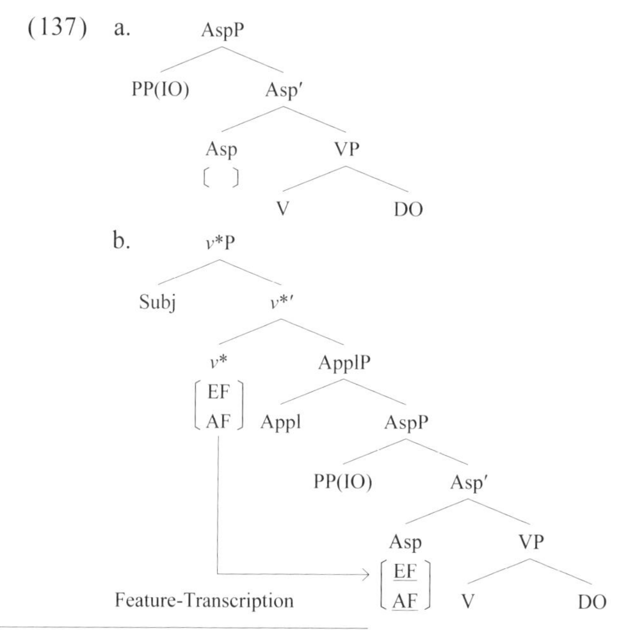

41 Although I have not assumed an Asp head in other transitive sentences thus far, Travis (2010) claims that such an inner aspect exists even in normal transitive sentences. However, if I adopt this assumption, it may complicate the definition of verbal phases in Chomsky's (2008) Feature-Inheritance framework: if an Asp head exists in all verbal layers, it is unclear whether the Asp head serves as a phase head or not, and whether Feature-Inheritance occurs on it or not if it is not a phase head.

However, it may be possible to assume that such an Asp head is involved within a phase head *v** in normal transitive sentences, but it splits into *v** and Asp heads when necessary such as in the DOC. This assumption is reminiscent of Rizzi's (1997) fine structures for the left periphery. Actually, Maeda (2013) claims that such fine structures for CP can be found in a verbal phase layer as well. Although the discussion here may have something to do with such a verbal phase left periphery, I leave the possibility for future research, since it is beyond the scope of the discussion here.

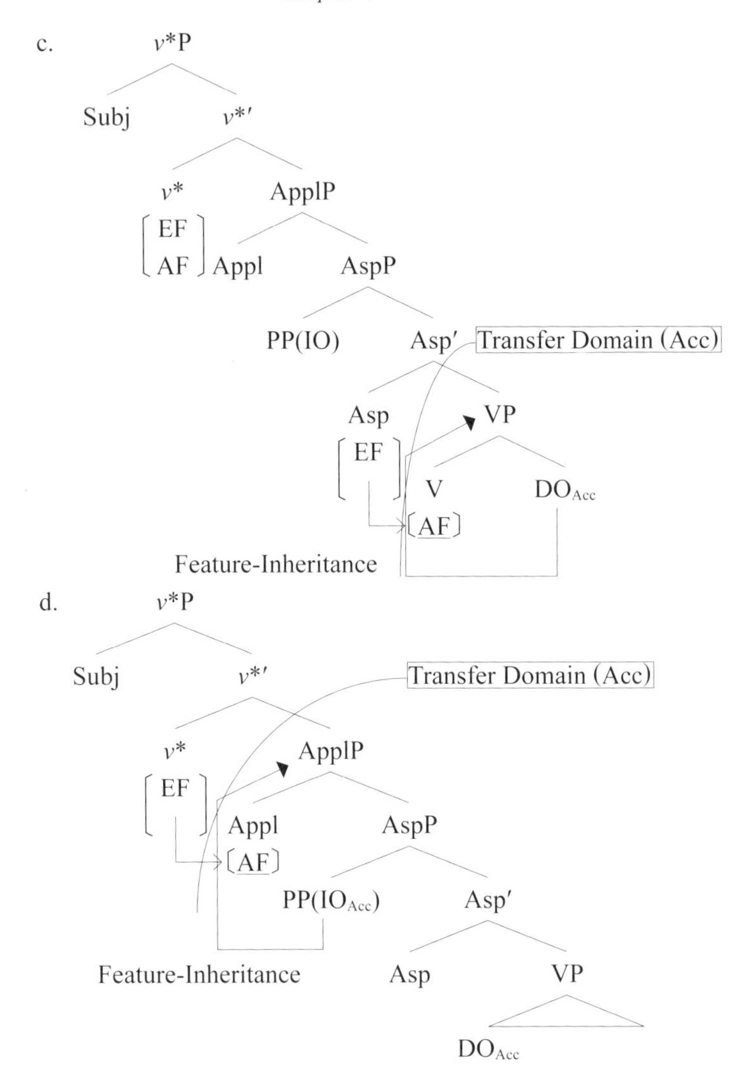

As can be seen in (137a), the weak-phase AspP is constructed by merging V, Direct Object, and an Asp head. When a PP including Indirect Object is merged, the weak-phase AspP is completed. However, since this is a weak-phase without uninterpretable features under the Feature-Transcription framework, syntactic operations are not triggered at this moment. As in (137b), the derivation continues by the merger operations of an Appl head and a *v** head in sequence. The subject DP is introduced in the Spec of *v**P, and v*P is completed. Since v* is a strong-phase head, Feature-Transcription from v* to Asp is triggered and their syntactic operations are started.

Although we always assume the two possibilities shown in 3.5.1 in derivations including weak-phases, in this case I claim that the possibility of simultaneous-derivation is excluded. Putting aside the reason, to which we will return later, let us consider the further derivation in the individual-derivation pattern. As in (137c), firstly, the syntactic operations in AspP are triggered. Asp transmits its AF to V and the AF on V agrees with Direct Object. Since Direct Object is transferred by the weak-phase head Asp and this is a part of verbal layers, Direct Object is assigned the accusative case based on the assumption in 3.5.2. After the syntactic operations in AspP, v*P starts its syntactic operations. Feature-Inheritance occurs from v* to Appl and the transmitted AF holds an Agree relation with Indirect Object. As a consequence, Indirect Object is moved out of PP to Spec-ApplP. Therefore, the proper c-command relation between Indirect Object and Direct Object as was shown in 4.4.1.1 is ensured.[42] Moreover, Indirect Object is transferred by v* and therefore its value determined as the accusative case.[43, 44] Although omitted here, the derivation continues by merging T and C. When CP is completed, the syntactic operations in CP are triggered and the derivation converges.

In addition, I suggest that the V head undergoes successive-cyclic head movement via Asp and Appl, up to v*, and the proper word order is derived.[45]

---

42 Here, we need some mechanisms to ensure the licensing condition on c-command-related matters beyond transfer domains. See Nishimura (2013) for the licensing mechanism beyond phases named "take over."

43 It is controversial whether the case on Indirect Object is accusative or dative as in German. In this book, I claim that it is assigned the accusative case since no obvious empirical evidence against this assumption is observable in English; even when Indirect Object is a pronoun, its case pattern is the same as accusative as can be seen in *I gave him a book*.

44 Note that in this case the P head cannot assign any case to Indirect Object since it does not constitute a strong/weak-phase. This is because I assume the transfer-based case assignment mechanism and the non-phase P head cannot trigger transfer.

45 Of course, the head movement occurs at each level. Namely, when AspP starts its syntactic operations, V is moved to Asp, and when v*P starts, up to v*. I will put aside the discussion on the status of head movement here, that is, whether it is an operation in the SM Interface or the narrow syntax.

Also, as an anonymous reviewer points out, the process of head movement of P here is unusual. However, the incorporation of P into a verb is independently motivated (see footnote 40) and therefore the process should somehow be accepted, whatever kind of operations may be involved.

When this head movement occurs, I assume that the null P head in PP is attached to the V head. Since the P head is phonetically incorporated into a verb, it is not pronounced as "to."

(138)

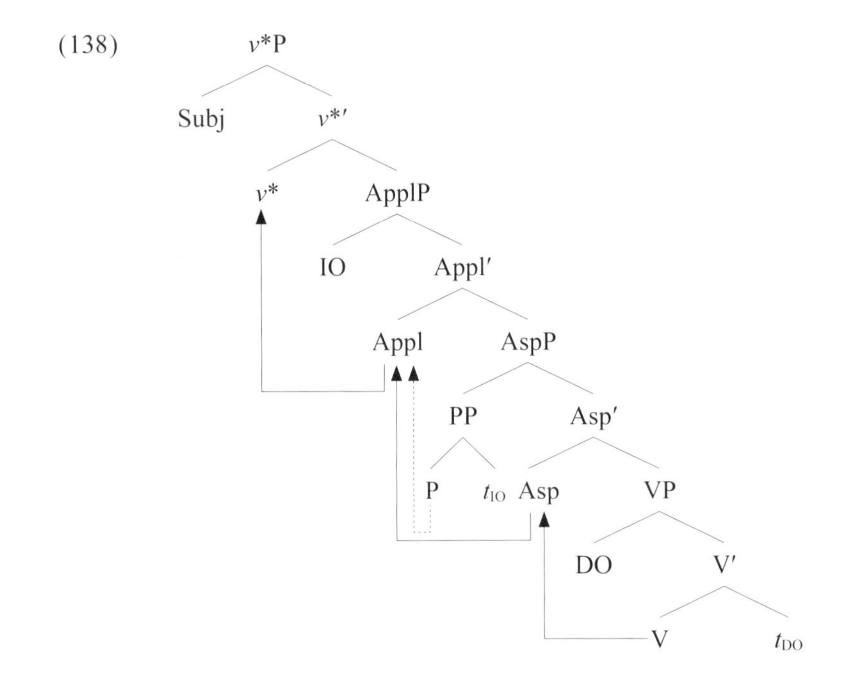

Now, note that if the derivation of *v**P including the weak-phase AspP occurs in simultaneous-derivation fashion, the two DPs, namely Direct/Indirect Object, are included within the single transfer domain. I claim that this situation violates Richards' (2010) Distinctness Condition shown below.

(139) The Distinctness Condition
If a linearization statement <α, α> is generated, the derivation crashes. (Richards (2010: 5))

Richards (2010) argues that the condition is derived from the assumption that when two elements are included in one domain, their linear order cannot be determined under the assumptions in the MP. To be more specific, because we cannot utilize indexes in the MP due to the Inclusiveness Condition, the computation cannot realize that the two elements are independent items and it wrongly expects that contradictory information is sent. For instance, when two DPs are included in one domain, the information that "a DP precedes V" and "a DP follows V" is sent to the Interface and this causes a crash since the computation does not know that the involved DPs are two different DPs.

However, Richards' (2010) reasoning seems to me to be problematic. Under the assumption of Bare Phrase Structure in MP, it is expected that the computation does not see the category of an item but its actual label (namely, a head, or a bundle of features). Thus, if lexical items *John* and *Mary* are included in one domain, the computation treats them not as DP and DP but *John* and *Mary* as they are. Therefore the computation can distinguish them even without indexes. If so, the problem of linear order is not predicted. Moreover, it is clear that some kinds of same-categorical items can exist in a phase. For instance, multiple adjectives can be placed in one DP like *a big red rubber balloon*, or multiple passive participles can exist in one phase such as *The man is considered to be expected to be genius*. Thus, the original version of the Distinctness Condition holds theoretical and empirical inadequacies.

Thus, this book recaptures the Distinctness Condition as in (140).

(140) A loose version of the Distinctness Condition
Two DPs cannot exist within the same transfer domain.

(140) is derived because if two DPs exist in one transfer domain, case assignment process will be complex under the transfer-based case assignment mechanism assumed in this book. Moreover, the revised version in (140) has two theoretical consequences. Firstly, (140) is only applied to DPs which are related to case assignment. Secondly, in some languages which allow such a complex case assignment, (140) may not hold.[46] Leaving a further

46 Actually, I assume that Japanese at least allows two DPs to exist in one transfer domain as we saw in 4.3 with double nominative. Moreover, as an anonymous reviewer points out, Japanese allows multiple nominative DPs in one sentence as follows:

(i) Bunmeikoku-ga dansei-ga heikinzyumyoo-ga mizikai
civilized countries-Nom male-Nom average-life-span-Nom short-is
'The average life-span of males of civilized countries is short.'

(Kuno (1973: 34))

detailed discussion for the future research, I assume a loose version of the Distinctness Condition in (140) in this book.

Note that although Richards (2010) defines (139) based on a phase domain, the loose version of (140) in this book holds based on a transfer domain. Therefore, the derivation of the DOC cannot occur in the simultaneous-derivation pattern because, if it does, the indirect object and the direct object are transferred within one transfer domain and this violates (140).

Now that the derivation in the DOC and the condition in (140) are proposed, we are ready to explore an explanation for the problems in the DOC. Let us move to the actual data in the next section.

4.4.4 A Solution to the Problems

In this subsection, let us revisit the problems summed up in (131), which is repeated below, and offer an explanation under the Feature-Transcription framework.

(141)

	Indirect Object	Direct Object
A-movement	Ok	*
A-bar movement	*	Ok

In order to explain the asymmetries in (141), let us investigate each case in the DOC in sequence. Firstly, we will look at the asymmetry in A-movement.

4.4.4.1 The Impossibility of A-Movement of Direct Object

I claim that the impossibility of A-movement of Direct Object is explained based on the Distinctness Condition in (140). Consider a case of passive movement of Indirect Object and Direct Object.

I suggest that Japanese has overt case particles and can afford to permit complex case assignment processes because of them. Hence, I claim that the multiple case assignment is accepted in Japanese.

(142)

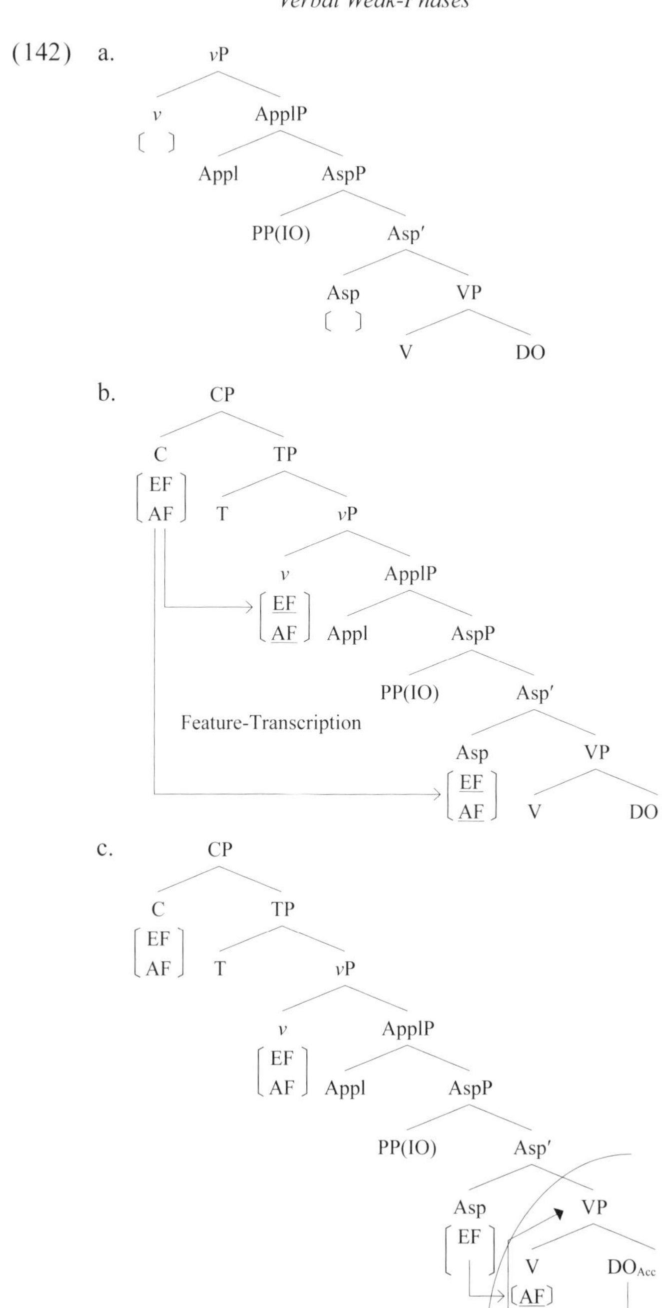
a.
vP
v
ApplP
Appl
AspP
PP(IO)
Asp′
Asp
VP
V
DO
b.
CP
C
TP
EF
AF
T
vP
v
ApplP
EF
AF
Appl
AspP
PP(IO)
Asp′
Feature-Transcription
Asp
VP
EF
AF
V
DO
c.
CP
C
TP
EF
AF
T
vP
v
ApplP
EF
AF
Appl
AspP
PP(IO)
Asp′
Asp
VP
EF
V
DOAcc
AF
Feature-Inheritance
Transfer Domain (Acc)

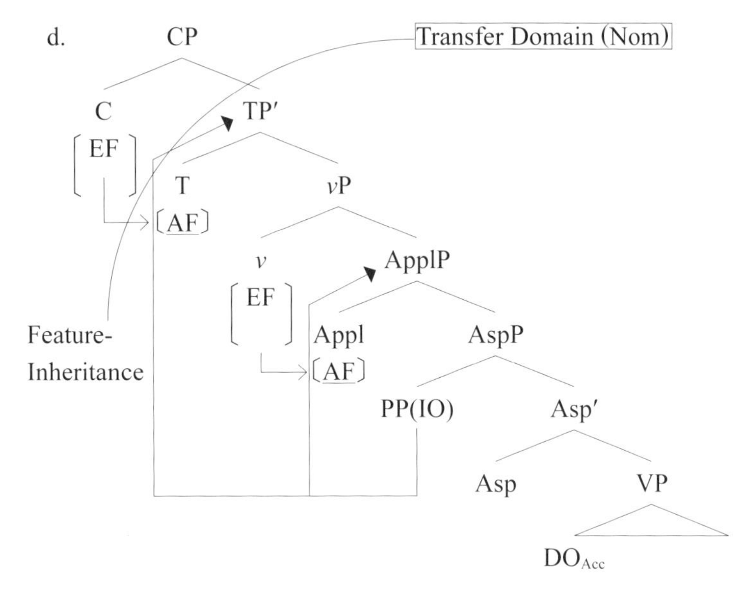

As can be seen in (142a), when the DOC is passivized, I assume that the strong-phase head *v** becomes a weak-phase head *v*, as is in other normal transitive passives. Therefore, it lacks an external subject DP in its Spec. As is shown in (142b), the derivation in AspP occurs in individual-derivation because otherwise the Distinctness Condition in (140) is violated due to Indirect Object and Direct Object existing in one transfer domain. The Asp head transmits its AF to the V head and the AF is checked by Direct Object. Since Direct Object is transferred by the weak-phase head Asp, it is assigned the accusative case under the transfer-based case mechanism. The case assignment process to Direct Object in passive the DOC has been puzzling in that only Direct Object, not Indirect Object, can be assigned case by the verb even in passive sentence. However, this is readily explained under the transfer-based case assignment mechanism and the Feature-Transcription framework.

After the operations, the syntactic operations in CP and *v*P occur in simultaneous-derivation.[47] C and *v* pass their AFs to T and Appl, respectively.

47 Since we assume that individual/simultaneous-derivation is always selectable, when two weak-phases *v*P and AspP are included, we have more possibilities than when only one weak-phase is involved. Namely, CP=*v*P=AspP (all simultaneous as in (143)), CP=*v*P<AspP (simultaneous-individual as in (142)), CP<*v*P=AspP (individual-simultaneous), and CP<*v*P<AspP

The AFs hold an Agree relation with Indirect Object simultaneously and Indirect Object is moved out of PP to each Spec simultaneously.

Now, let us move to passivization of Direct Object. Note that if AspP starts its operations in an individual-derivation manner as in (142), Direct Object cannot be moved to Spec-TP due to the PIC. Thus, passivization of Direct object requires that CP, *v*P, and AspP all start their operations at the same time in simultaneous-derivation. However, in this case, the two objects are necessarily included in the transfer domain of C, which violates the Distinctness Condition in (140), as is shown in (143) (the details of feature-checking are omitted here for simplicity).

(143)

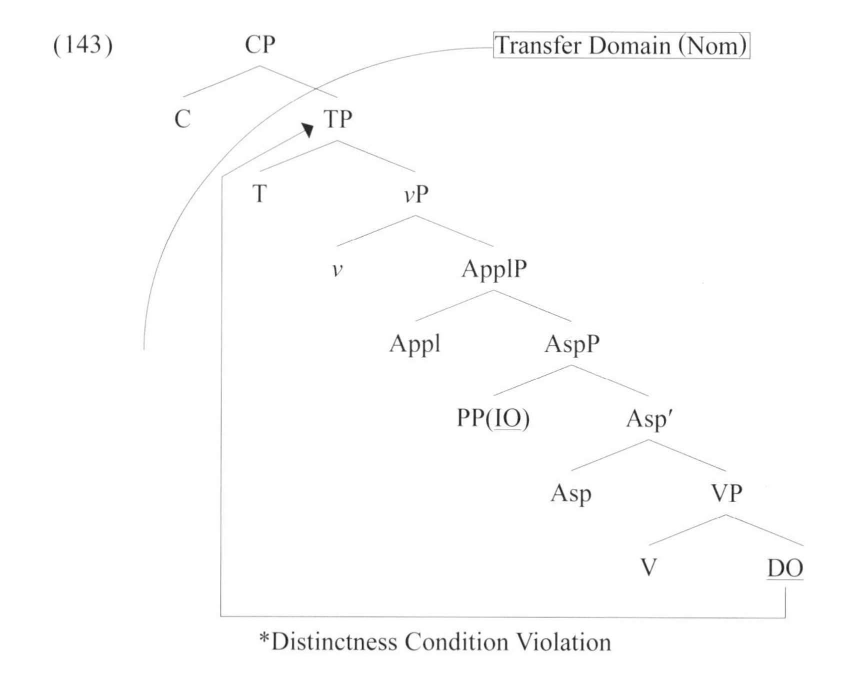

Thus, passivization of Direct Object cannot converge and the asymmetry in A-movement is captured.

(all individual) may be possible. However, the PIC and Distinctness Condition exclude the other possibilities and only CP=*v*P<AspP survives as shown here. I will omit the details of the other possibilities because they are not significant here.

4.4.4.2 The Impossibility of A-Bar Movement of Indirect Object

4.4.4.2.1 On A-Bar Movement of PP

Now, let us move to the impossibility of A-bar movement of Indirect Object. So as to explain the impossibility, we need to consider what happens to PP when it is involved in A-bar movement. Once we assume that Indirect Object in the DOC is included in PP, should Indirect Object be moved, stranding P, or should PP as a whole be moved in A-bar movement? In this subsection, I claim that PP as a whole has to be moved due to the concept of economy. The reasoning is shown below.

Recall that, in Chomsky's (2008) framework, A-bar movement is triggered by an Edge Feature a phase head possesses. Then, it should be noted that checking of an Edge Feature does not involve an Agree operation. This is derived from the assumption that an Edge Feature is satisfied even by an external merge, which is not related to Agree. Namely, the Edge Feature itself can attract anything, as long as the moved item induces proper effect after the movement (that is, in this case, as long as an element with a *wh*-feature is located in the phase edge; also see the discussion in 6.5.4). Given the fact that English allows prepositional phrases including a *wh*-phrase to occupy the sentence initial position as a *wh*-operator, a *wh*-feature on Indirect Object should be percolated into PP. Thus, it is concluded that, concerning A-bar movement of Indirect Object, the Edge Feature can optionally attract either Indirect Object only or PP as a whole, both of which possess a *wh*-feature. Therefore, a question is which movement operation is chosen in terms of economy in the MP.

Then, note that when only Indirect Object is moved, stranding P, the movement step is longer than when PP as a whole is moved. This is because Indirect Object has to pass PP to move out of PP.[48] Thus, the movement operation of PP as a whole is more economical than stranding of P when it comes to the length of the movement. Based on this reasoning, I conclude that PP as a whole should be moved regarding A-bar movement, unless

---

48 For example, if we calculate the length of movement in terms of containment of movement path following Hornstein (2009), the movement path of Indirect Object always includes PP, but when PP as a whole is moved, it does not, as in (i).

(i) a. Path of P stranding: {TP, *v**P, ApplP, <u>PP</u>} longer
  b. Path of P pied-piping: {TP, *v**P, ApplP}

inevitable factors exist (see chapter 6 for an analysis of preposition-stranding in English).

Notice that Indirect Object is moved, stranding P, when it comes to A-movement, as is shown in (137) and (142). This is because A-movement includes an Agree operation by the Agree Feature unlike A-bar movement. Now, let us move to an explanation keeping the discussion on A-bar movement in mind.

4.4.4.2.2 An Explanation

Based on the discussion in 4.4.4.2.1, we can conclude that regarding A-bar movement, PP including Indirect Object has to be moved to the sentence initial position. Then, I claim that the P head in the moved PP is not attached to V and it has to be pronounced as "to." Let us see the reasoning for this.

Recall that I assume the P head is usually attached to V via head movement as in (144a). However, if PP including Indirect Object undergoes A-bar movement, this movement of PP as a whole violates Takano's (2000) constraint, which states "[r]emnant movement of α is impossible if the head of α has moved out of α (Takano (2000: 151))." He calls this "illicit remnant movement." Hence, PP as a whole cannot be moved if its head P is moved outside of PP via head movement, since the movement of PP results in a case of illicit remnant movement.

Nevertheless, notice that extraction of Indirect Object from PP is dispreferred in terms of economy, as was discussed in the last subsection. Therefore, a possible solution to this problem of illicit remnant movement is to assume that if PP including Indirect Object is moved, the derivation cannot involve the head movement of P and P has to remain within PP.[49] In this way, it is derived that P cannot be incorporated into V and it has to be phonetically expressed as "to" as the last resort, when IO undergoes A-bar movement. Therefore, we can derive Bruening's (2010a) stipulation of R-dative shift from a principled mechanism.

49 Note that this is not a case of "look ahead" because all operations occur at the *v**P phase level and they are evaluated at that level. Under the normal situation, incorporation of P into V is preferred because of some characteristics of P. Thus, the derivation including head movement of P is preferred in the normal sentence, whereas, if PP as a whole is moved, the derivation involving the head movement of P does not converge because the derivation results in including illicit remnant movement. Thus only the derivation without the head movement survives.

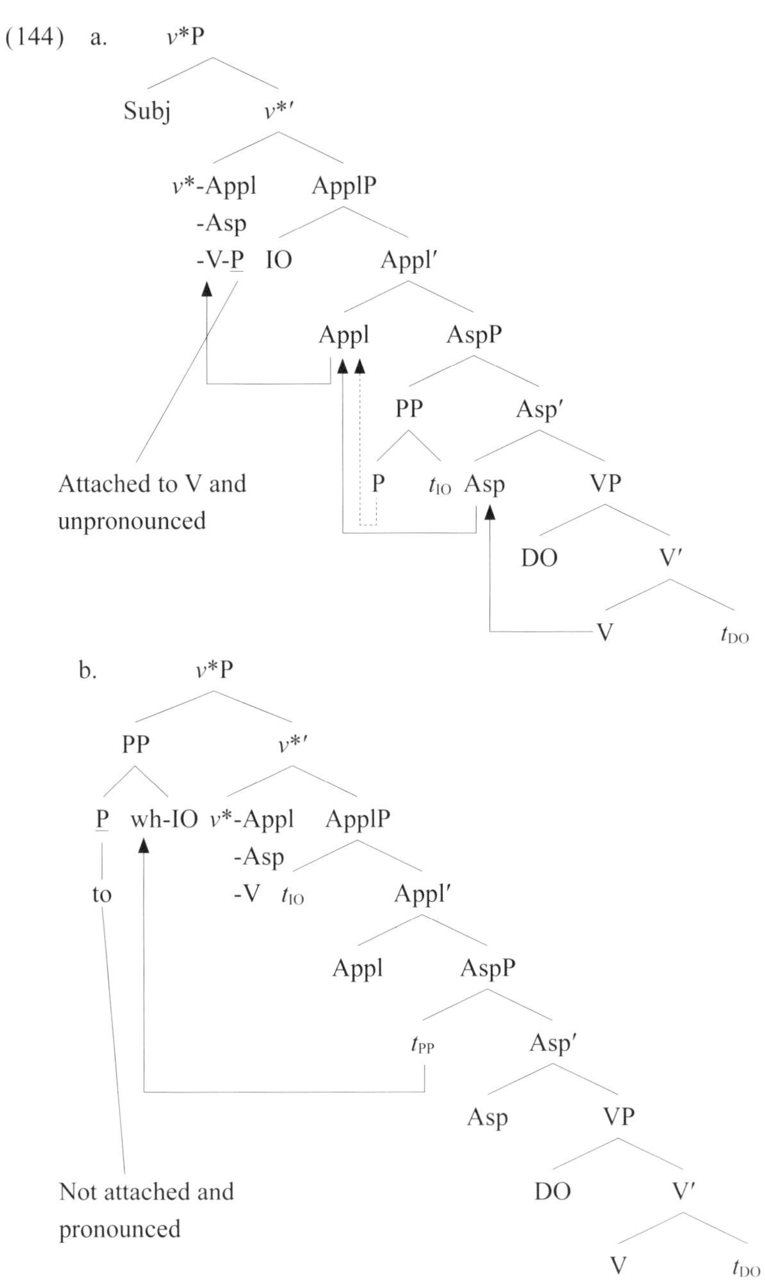

Therefore, the impossibility of A-bar movement of Indirect Object in the

DOC is explained as follows: (a) in A-bar movement, PP as a whole has to be moved due to economy, (b) therefore, the P head cannot be attached to V and thus is pronounced as "to," and (c) the resulting sentence is equivalent to the Prepositional DC. Although omitted here, notice that Direct Object can be moved via successive-cyclic A-bar movement, since there is no factor to prevent it. In this way, the asymmetry in A-bar movement is also captured.

4.4.4.3 Exceptions

Importantly, there are exceptions to the asymmetries we have discussed thus far. Namely, some speakers accept passivization of Direct Object in the DOC and other speakers allow A-bar movement of Indirect Object. Before closing this section, let us consider how these exceptions can be accounted for in this book.

Firstly, concerning passivization of Direct Object, it should be noted that this is ruled out based on the Distinctness Condition in (140), repeated as (145).

(145) The Distinctness Condition (a loose version in (140))
Two DPs cannot exist within the same transfer domain.

Then, we expect that if this condition is not violated somehow, Direct Object can be passivized. It should be noted that passivization of Direct Object is widely accepted if Indirect Object is a pronoun, even for speakers who do not normally allow passivization of Direct Object. Moreover, interestingly, the sentence is not grammatical if the pronominal Indirect Object is emphasized as Larson (1988) points out.

(146) a. A letter was given 'im by Mary.
b.* A letter was given HIM by Mary.
(Larson (1988: 364))

Larson (1988) claims that such pronominal Indirect Objects are cliticized to the verb and thus cannot be emphasized. Following this assumption, we can predict that when Indirect Object is attached to the verb as a clitic as in (147), it is no longer treated as a DP and the Distinctness Condition in (145) is not violated since only Direct Object exists in a transfer domain. Therefore passivization of Direct Object is accepted.

(147) [$_{CP}$ C [$_{TP}$...DO...given-him...]]

If we extend this assumption and suggest that if a speaker allows even non-pronominal Indirect Object to be cliticized, we can expect that passivization of Direct Object should be accepted by such a speaker (for other types of varieties in other languages, see footnote 38).

On the other hand, when it comes to A-bar movement, we can expect two possibilities; the normally-unpronounced P head loses its pronunciation form as "to," or even such a P head does not exist at all. Interestingly, the difference is expected to affect the acceptability of passivization of Direct Object. Note that passivization of Direct Object should be excluded if Indirect Object is not included in PP, because in that case superiority bans movement of Direct Object beyond Indirect Object as can be seen in (148), even if Indirect Object is attached to the verb to circumvent the Distinctness Condition.

(148)

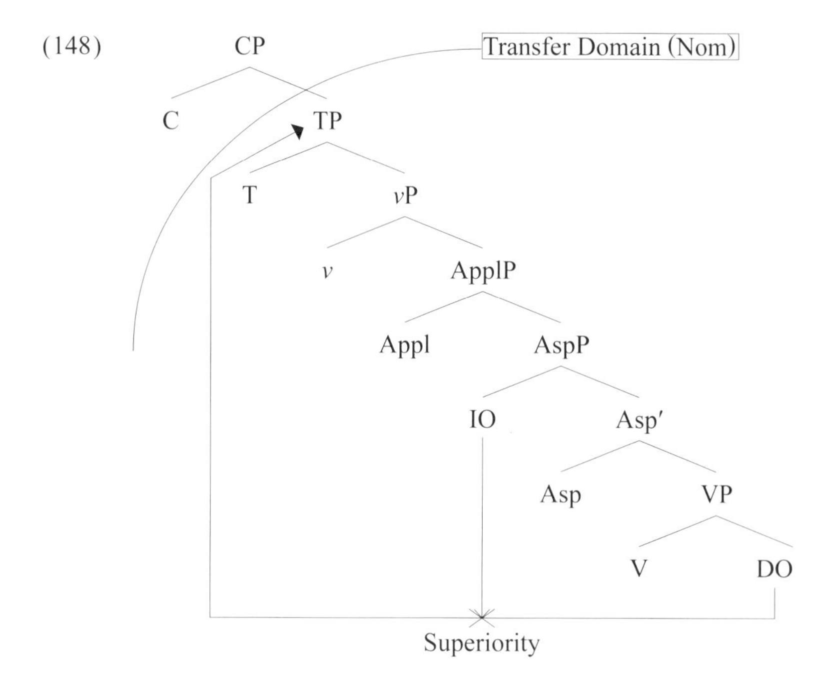

Therefore, if a speaker who accepts A-bar movement of bare Indirect Object does not allow passivization of Direct Object, we can expect that such a speaker loses a P projection entirely. Such a speaker probably somehow develops a special selection for the DOC against the unified selection by ditransitive verbs I proposed in (136) in 4.4.3.1. On the other hand, if a speaker allows both A-bar movement of Indirect Object and passivization of Direct Object, we expect that the DOC for the speaker should include the null P head, but its pronunciation pattern should disappear. Thus, passivization of Direct Object is accepted for such a speaker due to the cliticization strategy of Indirect Object noted above.

To wrap up, based on the discussion above, I have shown that the Feature-Transcription framework captures not only the impossibilities of passivization of Direct Object and A-bar movement of Indirect Object, but also accounts for major exceptions.

4.5 Summary

In this chapter, we have solved the problems related to verbal weak-phases. Firstly we have observed the inflection-movement connection in passives cross-linguistically. Then we have moved to Japanese nominative object examples and their scope-related puzzles. Finally, we have witnessed explanatory possibilities for the problems with the DOC in English. However, as we will see in the next chapter, I argue that even clausal projection can act as a weak-phase.

5

Clausal Weak-Phases

In this chapter, I will investigate clausal weak-phases, namely weak-phase CPs. Kanno (2008) claims that some kinds of CP form defective phase boundaries. If we assume that such defective boundaries are weak-phases, we can extend the analysis of Feature-Transcription to phenomena related to clauses. Although there are relatively fewer examples related to weak-phase CPs, in this chapter, we will witness examples of floating quantifiers in the ECM construction in an Irish dialect of English in 5.1 and the Japanese Raising-to-Object Construction, which I assume is a Japanese counterpart of the ECM construction in English, in 5.2. In 5.3, the last section in this chapter, we will briefly look at examples of complementizer agreement in West Flemish and explore an explanatory possibility.

5.1 The ECM Construction in an Irish Dialect of English

5.1.1 Does the ECM Construction Include TP or CP?

The structure of what is called the ECM construction exemplified in (149a) has often been discussed.

(149) a. I believe him to be genius.
b. I believe that he is genius.

The interpretation of (149a) is almost the same as that in (149b), where a sentence is embedded in the normal way. However, interestingly, the case manifestation patterns are different between (149a, b). In (149b), the subject of the embedded clause receives the nominative case, whereas in the relevant example in (149a), the case assigned to the subject of the infinitive clause is accusative. Since the accusative case is normally assigned by verbs, it is agreed that the accusative case in (149a) is valued by the verb *believe*. This fact has been explained by assuming that ECM verbs such as *believe* take TP complement and that the T head is defective and cannot assign case to the ECM subject. Therefore, the verb has to determine the case manifestation pattern on the ECM subject in Spec-TP in an unusual way, which is why the ECM construction is named "Exceptional Case Marking."

In the GB era, where many relations were captured based on the concept of "government," researchers assumed that V can assign case to the ECM subject exceptionally beyond TP (although in those days it was called "IP"). In the early MP, this was reframed within an assumption based on Agr projections and now it is explained based on Agree operations. Under the Agree strategy, a DP can be assigned case if it is c-commanded by a proper case assigner. Therefore, the ECM construction does not include "Exceptional Case Marking" any longer, although the term itself survives until now.

Nowadays, the mainstream analysis on the ECM construction is based on the assumption that the ECM complement is TP, as was already noted. Although the assumption of TP complement is widely accepted in the MP, McCloskey (2000) offers problematic examples in an Irish dialect of English. Let us observe his main claim and propose an account for the problem he points out in the ECM construction based on the Feature-Transcription framework.

5.1.2 McCloskey (2000)

McCloskey (2000) points out interesting facts in an Irish dialect of English.[50] As exemplified in (150), floating quantifiers in the Irish dialect behave unlike those in Standard English; floating quantifiers can be stranded in intermediate positions of A-bar movement in the Irish dialect.

(150) a. What all did he say (that) he wanted *t*?
b. What did he say all (that) he wanted *t*?
(McCloskey (2000: 61))

Interestingly, floating quantifiers in the Irish dialect seem to be stranded

50 According to McCloskey (2000: 57) the dialect is "a variety spoken in an area west and east of the river Foyle in the northwest of Ireland."

not in any A-bar traces, but only in Spec-CP. As McCloskey (2000) argues in footnotes, Spec-*v*(*)P is not qualified as a host for them. The Spec of prepositional phrases is not the position for floating quantifiers, either, as can be seen in (151).

(151) a.* Who did you talk all to?
b.* What were you laughing all at?
(McCloskey (2000: 65))

Thus, the phenomena can be summed up as in (152).

(152) Floating quantifiers in an Irish dialect of English can be stranded in Spec-CP.

Now, keeping this observation in mind, let us see (153) below.

(153) a. Who did you want your mother all to meet *t* at the party?[51]
b. Who did you expect your mother all to meet *t* at the party?
(McCloskey (2000: 70))

As (153) exemplifies, although floating quantifiers in this dialect can be stranded only in Spec-CP, they are allowed to be posited at the left of *to* in the ECM construction.

Under the normal assumption, this *to* is analyzed as a T head. Thus, this example raises a problem. If the ECM complement is TP, the distribution in

51 In usual analyses, *want* is considered to select a null *for* CP complement rather than ECM complements. However, McCloskey (2000) claims that this is a case of ECM verbs, pointing out the following examples.

(i) a. Who did you arrange all for your mother to meet *t* at the party?
b. *Who did you arrange for your mother all to meet *t* at the party?
c. *Who did you want all your mother to meet *t* at the party?
d. *Who did you expect all your mother to meet *t* at the party?
(McCloskey (2000: 70))

In (i), the distribution of floating quantifiers in the *want* example is different from those in the *arrange* examples, which are generally assumed to select an overt for-CP complement. In this light, the *want* example behaves similarly to the *expect* example (at least, in this dialect). Therefore, in this book, I assume that *want* selects the ECM complement following McCloskey (2000).

(153) cannot be expected based on (152), since floating quantifiers in the dialect are not stranded in Spec-TP. Of course, it is possible to assume that these floating quantifiers can be stranded in both Spec-CP and Spec-TP. However, in that case, we wrongly predict such examples as in (154), where quantifiers are floated in Spec-TP in a finite clause, to be grammatical. Such examples are needless to say ungrammatical.

(154) a.* What did he say (that) he all wanted *t*?
b.* What did he all say (that) he wanted *t*?

Of course, it is possible to presume further that floating quantifiers in the dialect are stranded mainly in Spec-CP but only in the ECM construction they can be stranded in Spec-TP as well. Nevertheless, such an assumption lacks theoretical motivation. Thus, it is reasonable to assume that the ECM complement is CP (at least in this Irish dialect of English) to explain (153).

However, in turn, if we assume that the ECM complement is a normal strong-phase CP, the assumption obviously raises problems; movement of the ECM subject out of CP should be banned due to a PIC violation as in (155a) or Improper Movement as in (155b). Therefore (153) cannot be derived.

(155) a.* [$_{v\text{*P-Ph}}$...your mother...[$_{\text{CP-Ph}}$ C [$_{\text{TP}}$...*t*...]]] PIC violation
b.* [$_{v\text{*P-Ph}}$...your mother...[$_{\text{CP-Ph}}$ C [$_{\text{TP}}$...*t*...]]] Improper Movement

In the next subsection, I claim that the problem is readily solved under the Feature-Transcription framework if we assume this CP is a weak-phase.

5.1.3 A Solution

In this subsection, I argue that the examples in (153) are readily derived by assuming that the ECM complement is a weak-phase CP. In this book, I claim that stranding of *all* is optional following McCloskey (2000), and if there is an intermediate trace in Spec-CP, it can be stranded there.[52] Let us

52 Of course, we have to derive this optionality based on some mechanism. Although I cannot

see the derivation of the ECM construction under the Feature-Transcription framework. In (157), CP_{weak} represents a *weak-phase CP*.

(156) Who did you expect your mother all to meet *t* at the party? (=(153b))

(157) a.

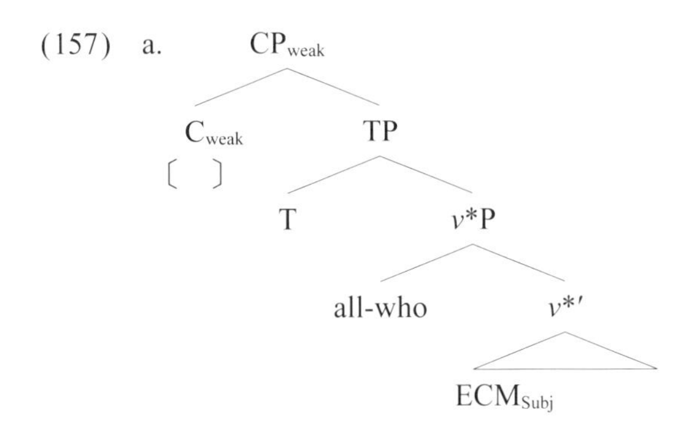

b.

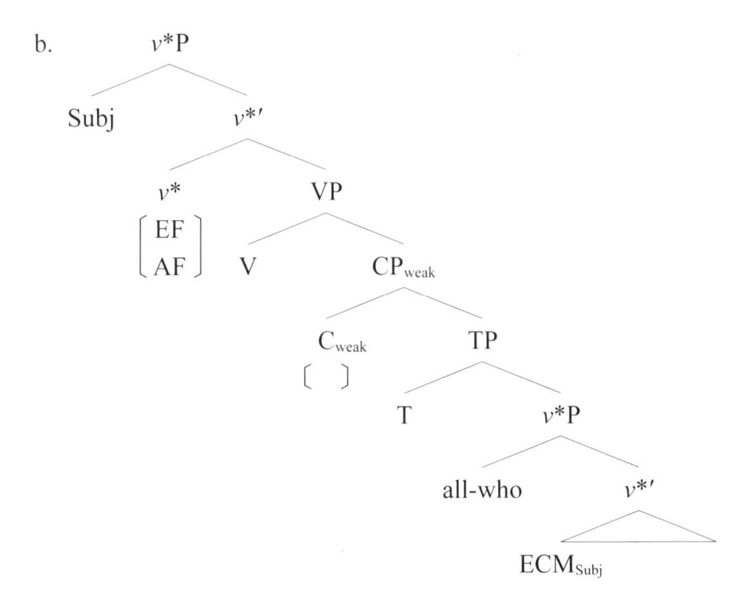

present a full-fledged explanation here, the labeling on *all* and *DP* may shed light on the optionality.

c.

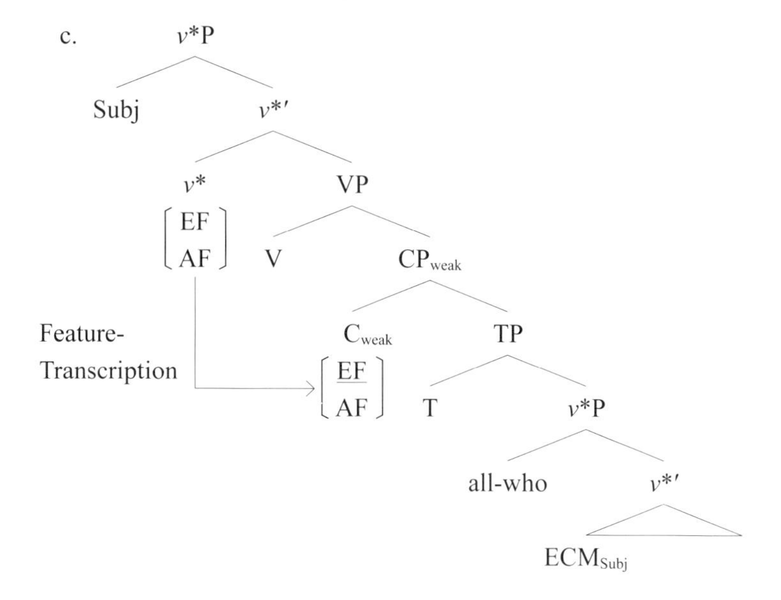
v*P
Subj
v*′
v*
VP
EF
AF
V
CPweak
Feature-
Transcription
Cweak
TP
EF
AF
T
v*P
all-who
v*′
ECMSubj

d.

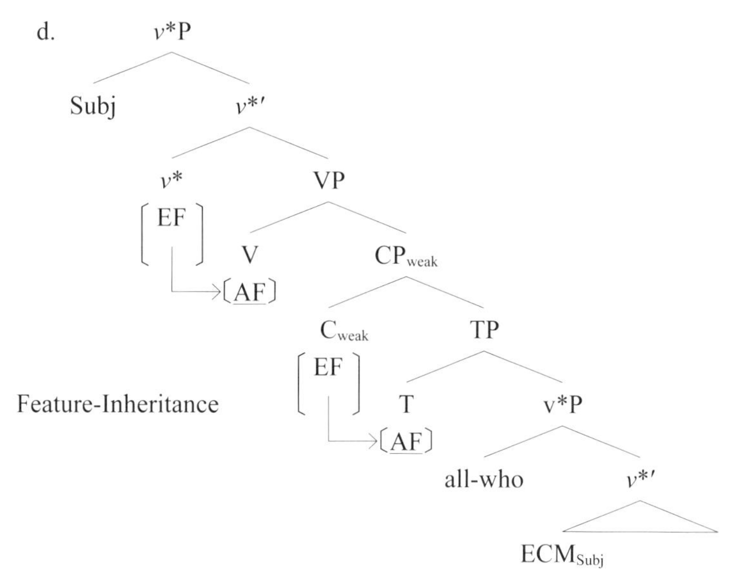
v*P
Subj
v*′
v*
VP
EF
V
CPweak
AF
Cweak
TP
EF
Feature-Inheritance
T
v*P
AF
all-who
v*′
ECMSubj

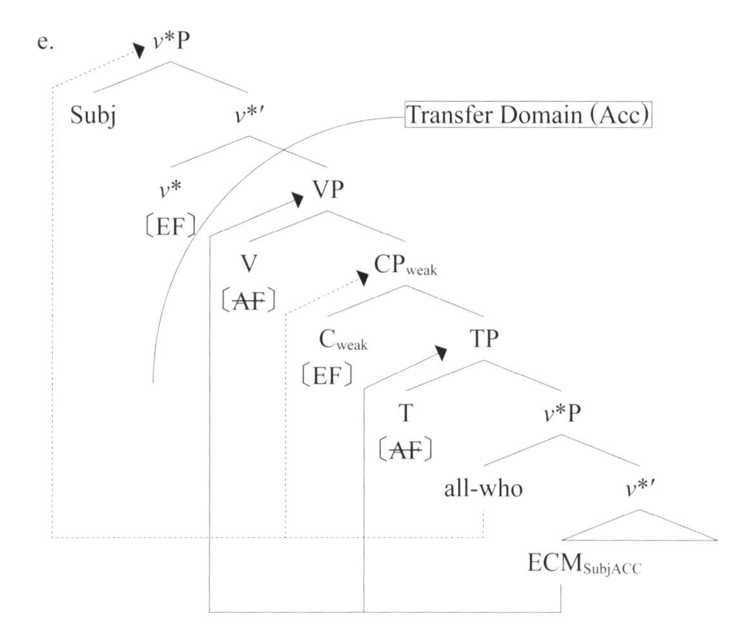

Although I have omitted it here, before CP is formed, syntactic operations in the lower v*P are triggered. As a consequence, the *wh*-element *all-who* is located in the outer Spec of v*P and the ECM subject is posited in the inner Spec of v*P, as is shown in (157a). Then, the ECM complement, namely, a weak-phase CP, is constructed by successive merger operations of T and C. When CP is formed, since it is a weak-phase in this case, syntactic operations in CP are not triggered at this moment as in (157a).

Sequentially, the v*P phase is constructed by merger of V and v* as in (157b). When the v*P is completed with the (matrix) subject in its Spec, the syntactic operations occur. Firstly, Feature-Transcription occurs from v* to C to activate the weak-phase C head in (157c). Following that, the syntactic operations in CP and v*P are triggered simultaneously. The AFs on v* and C are transmitted on V and T via Feature-Inheritance as in (157d). Then, the AFs start an Agree operation and find the ECM subject, holding an Agree relation with the ECM subject simultaneously. At the same moment, the EFs on v* and C attract *all-who* in the outer Spec of v*P to each Spec simultaneously. Therefore, an intermediate position for floating quantifiers is formed in Spec-CP. Finally, v* transfers its complement including CP. Since the ECM subject is transferred by v*, it is assigned the accusative case. Thus, the proper situation for (153) is derived.

Before closing this section, recall that we always have two possibilities in derivations. If the derivation continues in an individual-derivation manner, the weak-phase C head transfers its complement and thus the ECM subject receives the nominative case as can be seen in (158a) (in (158a), the derivation until Feature-Transcription is omitted since this is completely equivalent to that in (157)). However, in the later derivation, the AF on V remains unchecked as in (158b) and the derivation crashes.

(158) a.

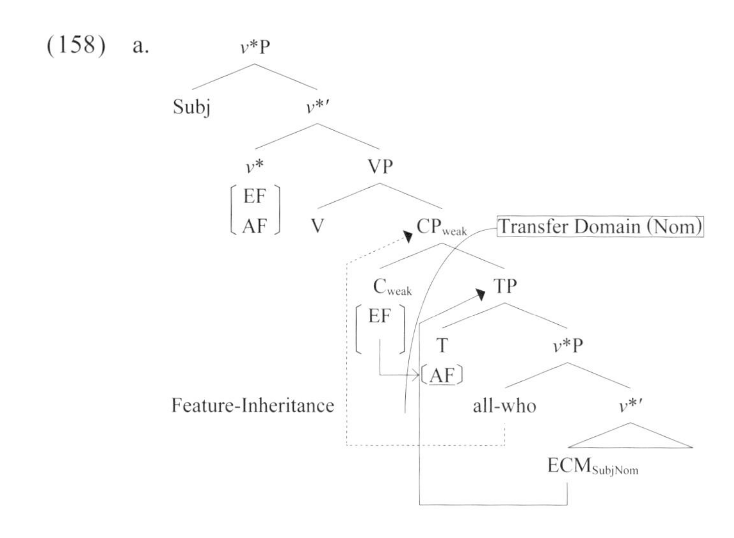

b.

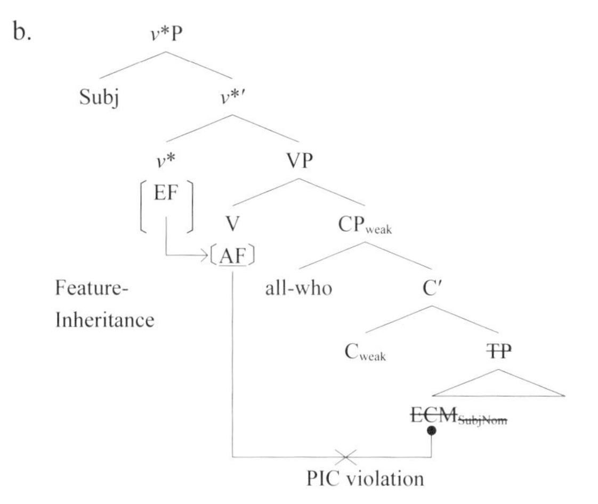

Nevertheless, it is expected that if a language has some strategies to circumvent this situation, the language produces two possibilities for case manifestations, namely, an nominative/accusative case conversion in the ECM construction. I claim that Japanese is a candidate for being such a language, which is the topic of the next section.

5.2 The Japanese Raising-to-Object Construction

5.2.1 Another Case Conversion in Japanese

Although we have witnessed one type of case conversion in Japanese in 4.3, Japanese has another interesting case conversion shown below. This is sometimes called the Raising-to-Object Construction.

(159) a. Taro-wa Yuki-o [baka da to] omot-teiru.
Taro-Top Yuki-Acc [stupid COP COMP] think-Prog
'Taro thinks that Yuki is stupid.'
b. Taro-wa [Yuki-ga baka da to] omot-teiru.
Taro-Top [Yuki-Nom stupid COP COMP] think-Prog
'Taro thinks that Yuki is stupid.'
(Takeuchi (2010: 101))

Example (159a) seems to be similar to the ECM construction in English shown in the last section. However, interestingly, Japanese has an alternative case manifestation as can be seen in (159b). As far as I can see in previous research, and to the best of my understanding, there is no significant semantic difference between these examples.

Now, in the following subsections, I claim that this case of case conversion can be explained based on basically the same structure for the ECM construction in English in the last subsection. Before moving on to the explanation, however, let us see previous analyses to know how the examples have been treated.

5.2.2 Previous Analyses

Concerning the Raising-to-Object Construction, there have been many debates. Some researchers assume that the DP with the accusative case in (159a) is base-generated and *pro* exists in the embedded clause (e.g. see Saito

(1985), Oka (1988), and Takano (2003)). On the contrary, many other researchers claim that the DP with the accusative case is moved from within the embedded clause into the matrix clause (see Sakai (1998), Tanaka (2002), Hiraiwa (2005), and Ura (2007)). Ura (2007) convincingly concludes that this "Raising-to-Object" approach is on the right track and I assume that the accusative DP in (159a) is base-generated within the embedded clause and is moved to the main clause following these approaches.[53]

However, concerning the optionality of the case manifestation patterns, not so many debates have been conducted as far as I know. In this subsection, as a candidate for analyses of the optionality in the MP, let us see Takeuchi (2010), who attempts to derive this optionality based on Chomsky's (2008) Feature-Inheritance framework.

When we consider the examples in (159), we have two possible positions to take; the C heads in the two examples are different independent items or they include the same C head behaving differently. If we assume that these C heads are different independent elements, say, a phase head C and a non-phase head C, we can derive these facts. However, since their phonological realizations are both "to," there is no denying that the assumption of the two complementizers is not theoretically well-motivated. Moreover, under such an approach, we cannot derive the optionality. As can be seen in (160), if another C head *ka* is involved, the optionality disappears. If we assume that both instances of *to* are different C heads, we cannot capture the behavioral difference between *to* and *ka* because if we do so, we have to claim that Japanese incidentally has two types of phase/non-phase *to*, but concerning *ka*, Japanese has only one type. This is not a principled explanation.

(160) a. Taro-wa [Yuki-ga baka (da) ka] siritagat-teiru.
Taro-Top [Yuki-Nom stupid (COP) Q] wonder-Prog
'Taro wonders whether or not Yuki is stupid.'

b.* Taro-wa [Yuki-o baka (da) ka] siritagat-teiru.
Taro-Top [Yuki-Acc stupid (COP) Q] wonder-Prog
'Taro wonders whether or not Yuki is stupid.'

(Takeuchi (2010: 103))

53 Ura's (2007) discussion on the validity of the "Raising-to-Object" approach is based on the facts of adverb placement and quantifier scope, although I will omit the details of the discussion here.

Thus, Takeuchi (2010) tries to account for this optionality by assuming the same single C head *to*. He assumes that an AF on C can optionally remain without being transmitted on T. Under this approach, the examples in (159a, b) are accounted for as follows:

(161) Taro-wa Yuki-o [baka da to] omot-teiru. (=(159a))

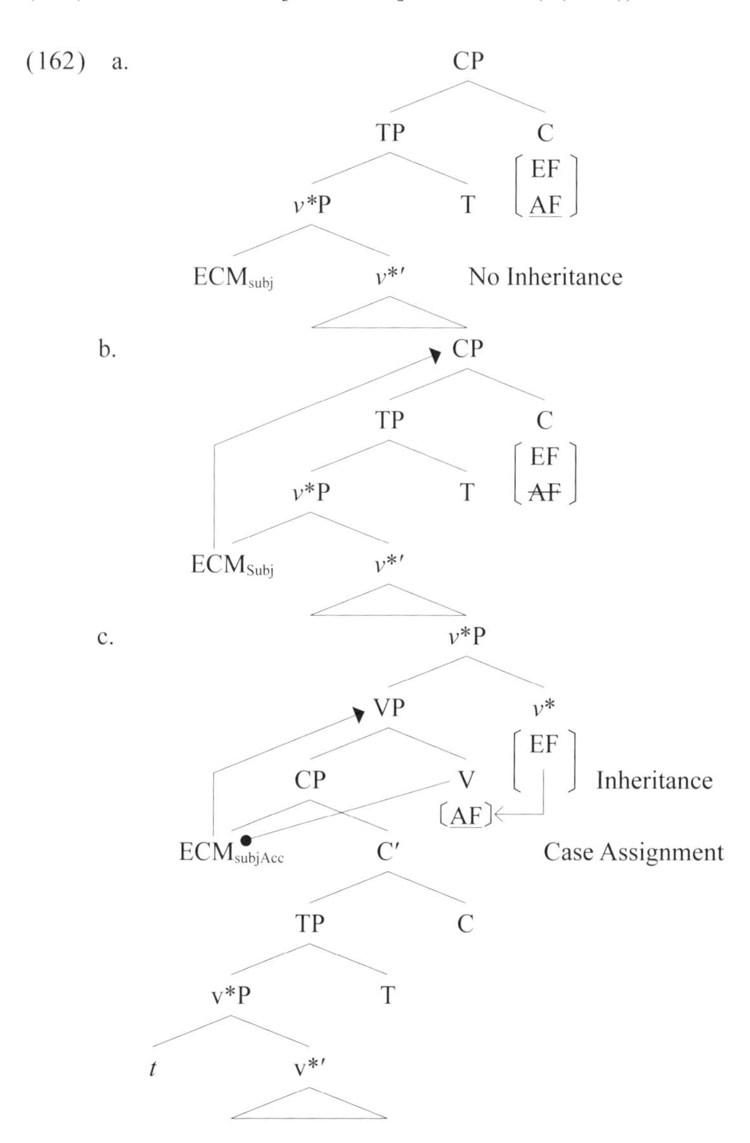

As is shown in (162a), if the AF on C remains there without the inheritance in the embedded clause, the ECM subject can be moved to Spec-CP. He assumes that the nominative case is assigned by T with an AF, and thus in this case T cannot assign the nominative case to ECM subject since there is no inheritance of the AF on T. At first glance, this movement to Spec-CP seems to be a case of A-bar movement. However, Takeuchi (2010) claims that the movement of the DP to Spec-CP is a case of A-movement, since AF checking is involved. Therefore, he argues that the movement to Spec-VP in the main clause via Spec-CP is not Improper Movement. Thus, the accusative example in (161) is derived.

On the other hand, if the AF is transmitted on T as in (164a), the AF on T is checked by the DP and in his framework the DP is assigned the nominative case since T has an AF in this case as in (164b).

(163) Taro-wa Yuki-ga [baka da to] omot-teiru. (=(159b))

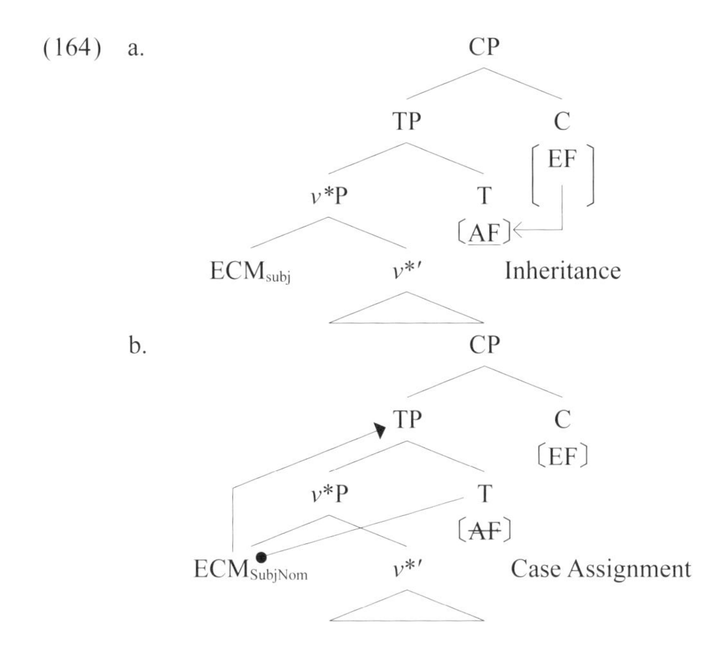

Through this optionality of inheritance, he captures the optionality of the nominative/accusative case conversion.

However, as we witnessed in 2.3 in this book, Feature-Inheritance is assumed to occur obligatorily. Otherwise, the simultaneity problem we saw in 2.3.2 remains unsolved (namely, the AF remains on C cannot be transferred when checked). Thus, Takeuchi's (2010) approach needs to make clear the mechanism of the optionality. Obviously, if we assume Feature-Inheritance is not triggered, the simultaneity problem arises and, moreover, even if we can abandon Richards' (2007) reasoning and derive an optional Feature-Inheritance mechanism, then, Feature-Inheritance is expected not to occur. This is because if the derivation converges without Feature-Inheritance, the operation need not be applied since it is redundant and should be avoided in the MP in terms of the last resort. Thus, Takeuchi's (2010) approach has a mechanical problem.

5.2.3 An Alternative under Feature-Transcription

In this book, the optionality can be captured based on the two possibilities of derivations, namely, simultaneous-derivation and individual-derivation. I assume that the Japanese Raising-to-Object Construction has exactly the same structure as the ECM construction in English shown in 5.1. Thus, as has been shown in the last section, the embedded clause is analyzed as a weak-phase CP. I claim that when simultaneous-derivation occurs, the accusative example in (161) results, whereas the nominative example in (163) is generated under individual-derivation.

Firstly, let us consider the case of simultaneous-derivation. As can be seen in (166), the structure is exactly the same as that in the ECM construction in English in the last section, with the only difference being the position of the respective heads (due to the head parameter).

(165) Taro-wa Yuki-o [baka da to] omot-teiru. (=(161))

(166) a.

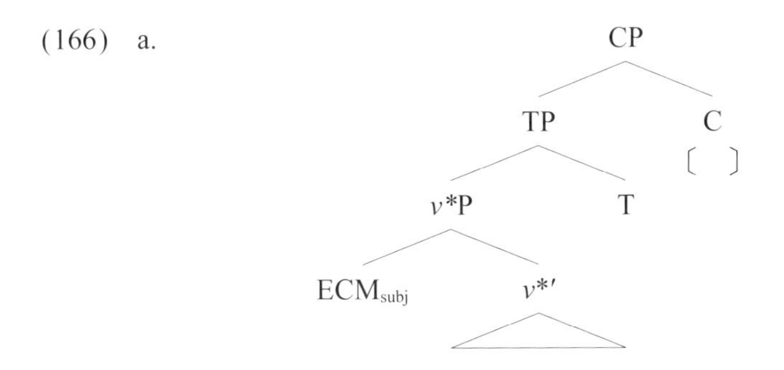

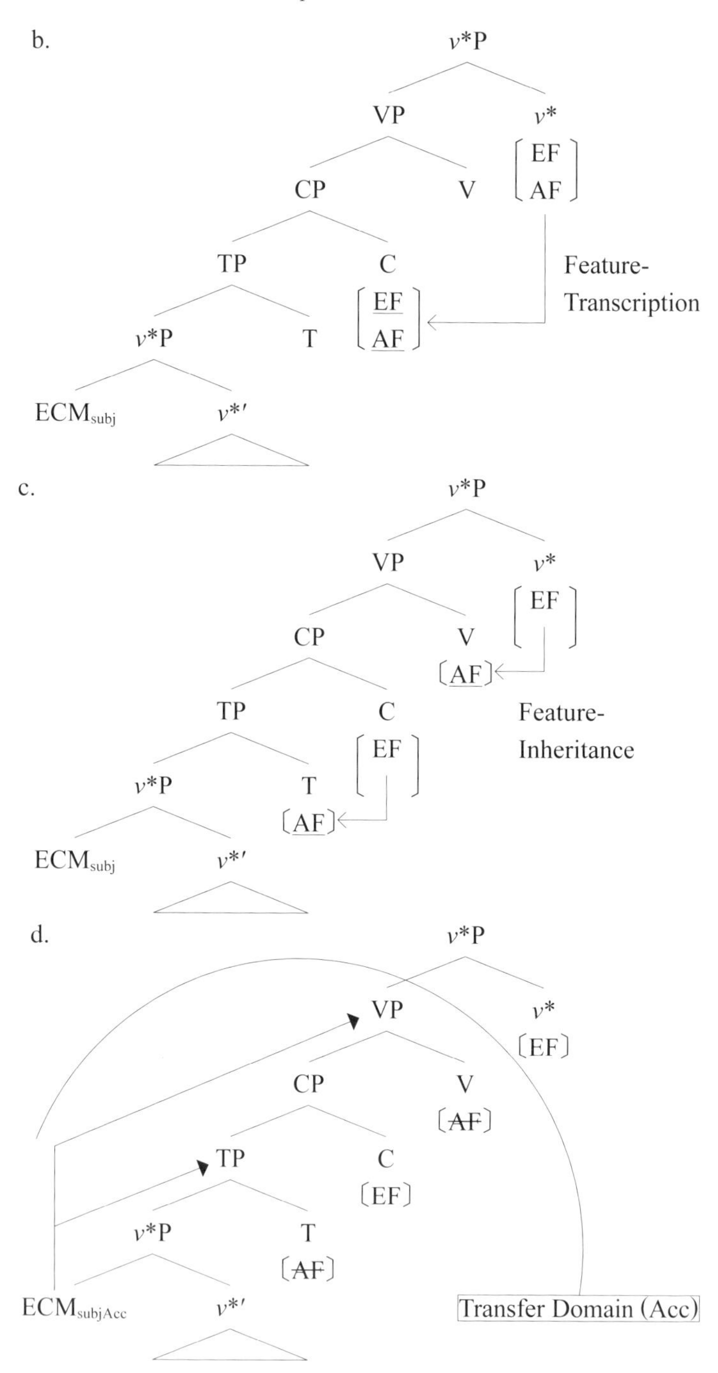
b.
v*P
VP
v*
EF
AF
CP
V
TP
C
Feature-
Transcription
EF
AF
v*P
T
ECMsubj
v*′
c.
v*P
VP
v*
EF
CP
V
AF
TP
C
Feature-
Inheritance
EF
v*P
T
AF
ECMsubj
v*′
d.
v*P
VP
v*
EF
CP
V
AF
TP
C
EF
v*P
T
AF
ECMsubjAcc
v*′
Transfer Domain (Acc)

When the weak-phase CP is constructed as in (166a), syntactic operations in CP are not triggered since this is a weak-phase. When *v**P is formed, Feature-Transcription occurs from *v** to C and the syntactic operations are triggered. In this case, the derivation continues in a simultaneous-derivation manner. The AFs on V and T start an Agree operation and they are checked by the ECM subject, simultaneously. Since the ECM subject is transferred by *v**, it is assigned the accusative case in this derivation.

When it comes to the nominative counterpart, individual-derivation derives this pattern.

(167) Taro-wa Yuki-ga [baka da to] omot-teiru. (=(163))

(168) a.

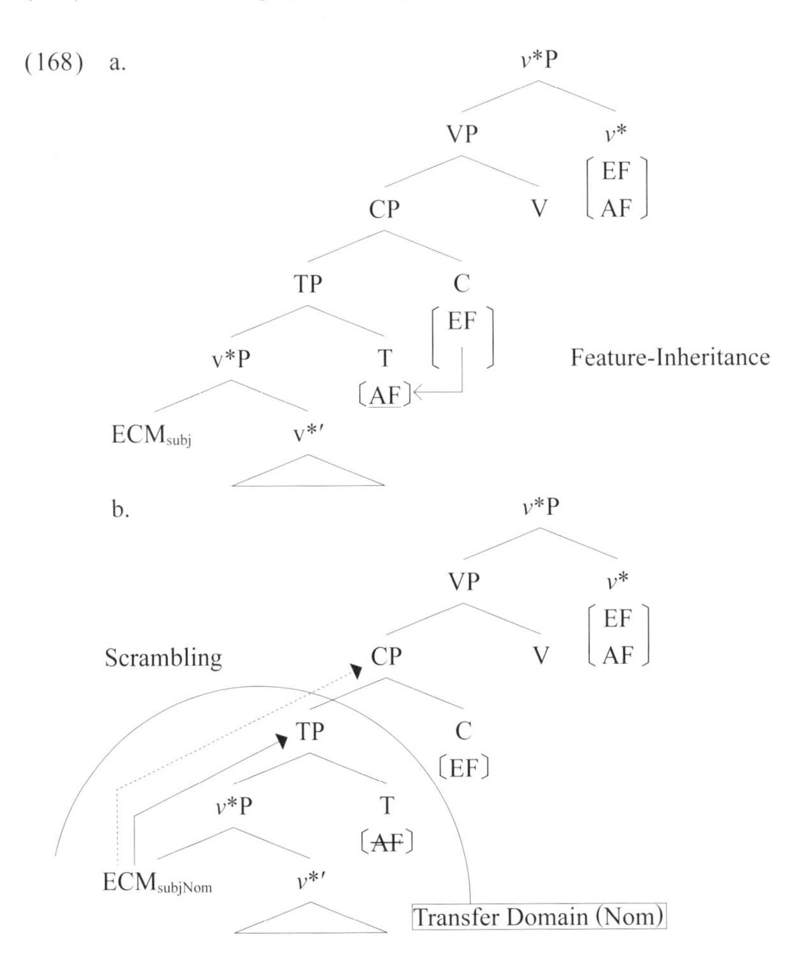

c.

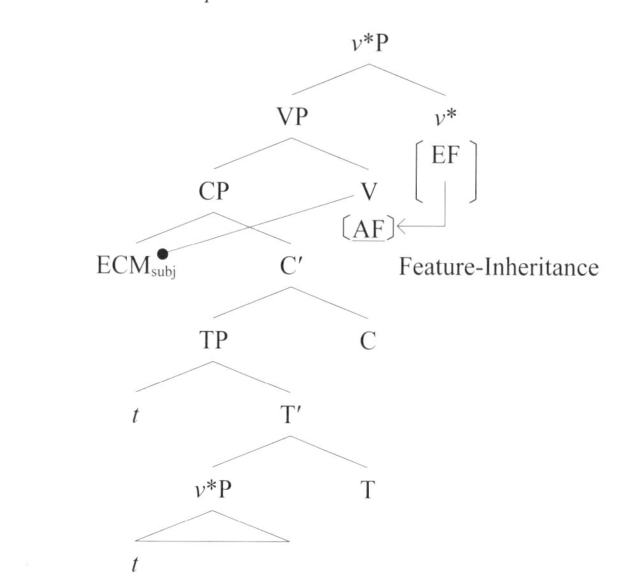

Here, the derivation before Feature-Transcription is omitted since it is the same as in (166a, b). Again, when CP is formed, syntactic operations are not triggered as before, and when v*P is constructed, Feature-Transcription occurs from v* to C. Then, the lower weak-phase CP firstly starts its syntactic operations in individual-derivation as in (168a). The AF on T is checked by the ECM subject and C transfers TP including the ECM subject. Therefore, the ECM subject is assigned the nominative case based on the transfer-based case assignment mechanism. Now, what is different from the case with the English ECM Construction in 5.1 is that Japanese is a language which allows scrambling. In this book, I claim that the ECM subject is attracted by an Edge Feature on C to Spec-CP as an instance of scrambling as in (168b).[54] Therefore, after the operations in CP finish, syntactic operations in v*P start and the AF on V can be checked by the scrambled ECM subject.[55] Thus, the

54 Of course, we have to consider a mechanism for scrambling. I suggest that a scrambled item has some discourse-related feature and based on it, an Edge Feature attracts the item (see 6.5.4 as well). However, I will omit further details of the mechanism and leave them for future studies. Moreover, the analysis here should be extended to other languages which allow scrambling. An important point is whether such languages also possess a weak-phase version of CP and allow case conversion. Again, this will be the future topic for research of weak-phases.

impossible derivation in the last section, namely, individual-derivation in the ECM construction, is rescued by the existence of scrambling in Japanese.

In sum, the Feature-Transcription framework can derive both case patterns of what is called the Raising-to-Object Construction in Japanese, based on the assumption that both cases include the same weak-phase C head and the inherent derivation possibilities of simultaneous/individual-derivation. It should be noted that we do not need to assume two redundant C heads, nor do we have to assume optional Feature-Inheritance. Moreover, I have shown that the possibility of scrambling in the relevant language plays an important role in this explanation to the acceptability of nominative ECM subjects.

5.3 Complementizer Agreement in West Flemish

5.3.1 A Puzzle of Complementizer Agreement

In the last section of this chapter, let us take a brief look at a case of complementizer agreement in West Flemish. Before beginning, it should be noted that complementizer agreement is a troublesome phenomenon in Chomsky's (2008) Feature-Inheritance framework. As was shown in 2.3, Feature-Inheritance has an important theoretical consequence of explaining the checking-transfer simultaneity pointed out by Epstein and Seely (2002) and Richards (2007). However, the discussions of the simultaneity problem lead to a puzzle concerning complementizer agreement. The discussion by Richards (2007) leads us to an expectation below (since the strong/weak distinction in phases is not important at this moment, I refer to them simply as *phase*).

(169) Checked uninterpretable features cannot remain on a phase head.

Now, notice that complementizer agreement is a case where agreement appears on a C head. Given that a C head is a phase head, complementizer agreement seems at first sight to be the exact case that the assumption in (169) prohibits.

---

55 I assume that the scrambled ECM subject does not move further to Spec-VP in the main clause and therefore this derivation does not involve Improper Movement. Concerning the validity of the assumption that the φ-features on the scrambled ECM subject can be utilized in the later derivation in Japanese, see Obata (2012).

Therefore, some researchers have searched for the way to solve this problem (e.g. see Ackema and Neeleman (2004), Chomsky (2007), and Miyagawa (2010)). Their main claim is that the agreement on C is not an actual agreement made by syntactic feature checking. Rather, complementizer agreement is a case of concordance at the phonological component. If this has nothing to do with syntactic operations, the simultaneity problem does not occur since the simultaneity problem is a syntactic problem. However, this phonological approach raises a problem in complementizer agreement in West Flemish as we will witness in the next subsection.

5.3.2 Haegeman and Koppen (2012)

The claim that complementizer agreement is derived from an operation in the SM Interface faces a problem pointed out by Haegeman and Koppen (2012). They find out a piece of evidence that complementizer agreement actually sees an inside structure of the relevant element.

Firstly, let us observe what Haegeman and Koppen (2012) call External Possessor in West Flemish.

(170) ...omda-n die venten toen juste underen computer
because-Pl those guys then just their computer
kapot was.
broken was
'...because those guys' computer broke just then.'
(Haegeman and Koppen (2012: 444))

In West Flemish, a possessor can be separated from its possessee when an adjunct exists within them as in (170). In (170), *underen* ("their") refers to *die venten* ("those guys") and the gained interpretation is that *die venten* possesses *computer*. Interestingly, this separation affects complementizer agreement.

(171) a. ...omda-n/*omdat André en Valère toen juste
because-Pl/because André and Valère then just
underen computer kapot was.
their computer broken was

b. ...omdat/*omda-n André en Valère underen computer
because/because-Pl André and Valère their computer
kapot was.
broken was
'...because André and Valère's computer broke (just then).'
(Haegeman and Koppen (2012: 449))

As can be seen in (171a), the C head agrees only with the possessor if a possessor is separated, whereas if it is not separated, the DP including the possessor and possessee as a whole agrees with C.

Now, if we explain this based on phonetic adjacency, a problem arises. Firstly, concerning (171a), we should expect that only *André* agrees with the C head since it is in adjacent situation as in (172a). Thus, (171a) seems to be problematic based on phonetic adjacency. However, we can circumvent the problem if we assume *André en Valère*, namely, conjoined NPs are treated as one item phonetically, and therefore it is adjacent to the C head as in (172b). However, even if we assume this, we are not capable of analyzing (171b). As is obvious, the agreement on C is based on the relation with the C head and the DP *underen computer* ("their computer") beyond *André en Valère* as (172c) indicates.

(172) a. ...C André and Valère their computer
b. ...C André and Valère their computer (=(171a))
c. ...C André and Valère their computer (=(171b))

This agreement can be captured only if we assume that *André en Valère* and *underen computer* form one constituent which *underen computer* heads. Given that constituency is a concept in syntax, (171b) is never explained unless we assume this agreement is ensured in syntax. Once we admit that complementizer agreement is a syntactic phenomenon, we have to take the simultaneity problem into consideration.

5.3.3 A Possible Solution

Now, I claim that the problem noted in the last subsection can be explained under the Feature-Transcription framework, evoking Rizzi's (1997) split CP structures. In this book, following Maeda (2013), I assume that a phase head

C is introduced into the derivation as a single element, but it splits into the well-known left periphery (or cartography) proposed by Rizzi (1997). Based on the Labeling Algorithm suggested by Chomsky (2013), which we will look at in chapter 6, Maeda (2013) argues that C possesses Focus/Topic/Force features as in (173a) and they have to constitute a label. Then, for instance, when an XP with a Topic feature is moved to Spec-CP, the Topic features on XP and C form a label of TopP in (173b). However, there remains a Force feature to form a label on C. Thus, the C head has to undergo head movement and forms another layer with the label determined as ForceP as in (173c).

(173)

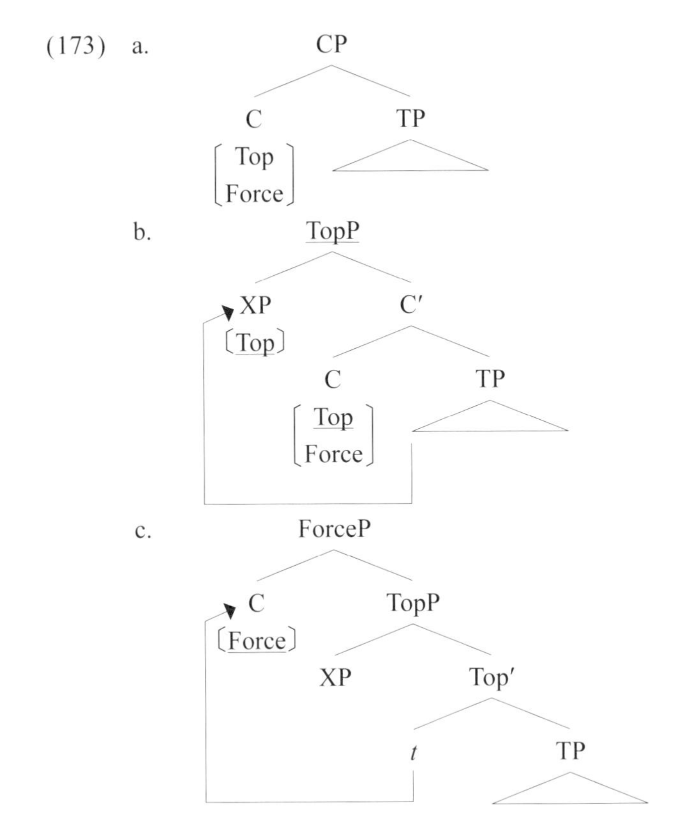

Therefore, under Maeda's (2013) approach, the left periphery is constructed derivationally through the Labeling Algorithm and head movement.

Now, notice that although a C head is a phase head, when the left periphery is formed, it already finishes its task as a phase head. In other words, the topmost split C head, which becomes the Force head, is treated as a phase head without uninterpretable features, because the uninterpretable features are already checked and transferred at the CP phase level. "A phase head without uninterpretable features" is exactly the same as the characteristics of a weak-phase head under the Feature-Transcription framework. Thus, it is reasonable to assume that a strong-phase head may act as a weak-phase head after it finishes its syntactic operations.

Now, let us see the derivation for (171a), where the possessor is separated. *EP* in (174) stands for *External Possessor*.

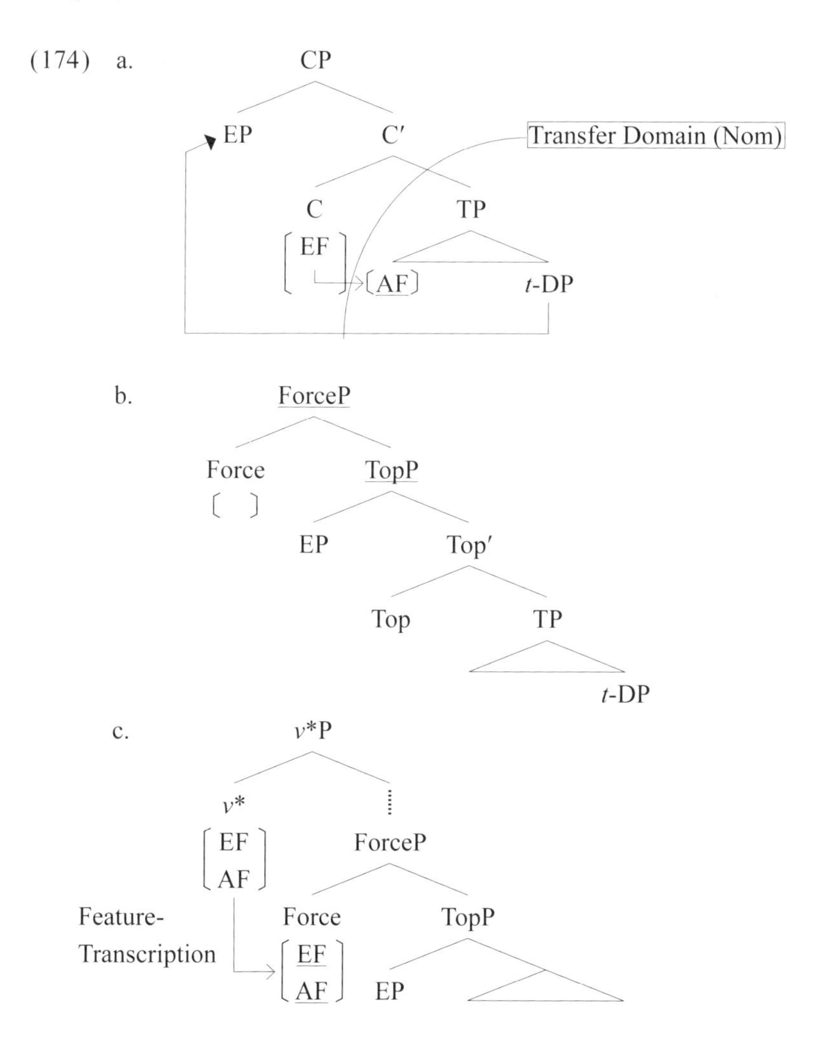

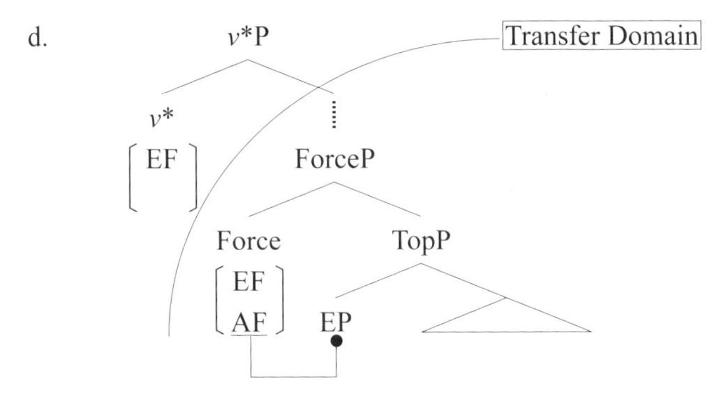

Firstly, as can be seen in (174a), syntactic operations in CP (namely, Feature-Inheritance, feature checking, and transfer) are finished and the External Possessor is moved to the Spec of CP stranding the possessee DP. Then, following Maeda (2013), the left periphery is constructed through the Labeling Algorithm as in (174b).[56] Here, I claim that complementizer in West Flemish exists on a Force head. Moreover, based on the discussion above, it serves as a weak-phase head in the next strong-phase level. Therefore, Feature-Transcription occurs from *v** to Force as can be seen in (174c).[57] Importantly, if Feature-Inheritance occurs from Force to Top in this case, the transmitted AF on Top cannot be checked since the Top head does not c-command the External Possessor and thus an Agree operation becomes impossible. Hence, I claim that the AF on Force starts its Agree operation without the inheritance. The AF on Force holds an Agree relation with the External Possessor as in (174d) and is transferred by *v**. Thus, the agreement is ensured by this derivation. Notice that although omitted here, *v** also triggers Feature-Inheritance and its AF is checked by a DP within its domain, simultaneously with checking of the AF on Force. In addition, I will not present the derivation for (171b), because the derivation is exactly the same except that the moved element to Spec-CP in (174a) is not only the External Possessor but the DP including it as a whole.

56 I tentatively assume that EP exists in Spec-TopP. However, a precise consideration on the site of EP is needed.

57 Here, I assume that ForceP is adjoined to VP. Therefore, *v** can c-command Force and Feature-Transcription is possible. However, even if it is adjoined above *v**P, no problem occurs because it is c-commanded by another strong-phase C head and Feature-Transcription is possible.

Importantly, although the AF on Force is checked through this derivation, the checking and transfer can occur simultaneously because the checking occurs at the *v**P phase level. Thus, Richards' (2007) theoretical proposal is preserved. Moreover, note that if this derivation occurs in individual-derivation manner, the derivation does not converge since the checked AF on Force remains un-transferred because the Force head transfers its complement TopP in this case.

One question remains in this approach; whether or not the process of Feature-Transcription on a C head which has already finished its syntactic operations always occurs cross-linguistically even if the relevant language does not allow complementizer agreement. For instance, can the process shown in (174) be found in English as well? At this moment, I will leave this possibility open, only showing that even complementizer agreement, which is truly problematic under Richards' (2007) assumption, can be explained by assuming Feature-Transcription.

5.4 Summary

In this chapter, we have observed explanatory possibilities of clausal weak-phases, namely, a weak-phase CP. By arguing that weak-phases are also found in CP, we have solved the problems in the distribution of floating quantifiers in the ECM construction in an Irish dialect of English, the Japanese nominative/accusative case conversion in the Raising-to-Object Construction, and complementizer agreement in West Flemish, all of which have not been accounted for properly in the previous research. In the next chapter, we will move to the last putative cases of weak-phases discussed in this book, namely, prepositional weak-phases.

6

Prepositional Weak-Phases

In the last chapter of this book, we will investigate prepositional weak-phases. The discussion in this chapter is mainly related to adjunct islands. I propose a possible explanation for adjunct islands based on the Labeling Algorithm suggested by Chomsky (2013) (although this book does not adopt Chomsky's (2015) latest framework based on Free Merger, as was discussed in footnote 1).

Firstly, I discuss a possibility of the existence of prepositional phases in 6.1. Following that, I claim that prepositional phases can be subdivided into strong-phase *p**Ps and weak-phase *p*Ps. Then, our discussion moves to adjunct islands in 6.2. After reviewing a previous analysis of Uriagereka (1999), I propose an analysis based on Chomsky's (2013) Labeling Algorithm. After introducing the Labeling Algorithm, I will consider how modification relations are ensured in syntax and propose a special variety of Edge Features, namely, Lexical Edge Features. Then, I claim that based on the Labeling Algorithm, Lexical Edge Features, and the Phase Theory, adjunct islands are captured. After the discussion, we move to actual explanations for optionality in prepositional-stranding/pied-piping in leftward movement in 6.3 and impossibility of prepositional-stranding in rightward movement in 6.4. Finally, I will examine the validity of the assumption of Lexical Edge Features in 6.5.

6.1 Prepositional Phases

6.1.1 A Strong-Phase *p**P

When we discuss what element counts as phases, prepositional phrases are sometimes raised as a candidate (for instance, see Matsubara (2000), Abels (2003), and Drummond et al. (2010)).[58] Matsubara (2000) claims that a prepositional phrase constitutes a *p**P phase depending on the existence of φ-features on it. Moreover, we have another theoretical motivation for prepositional phases in this book; since we assumed that case is determined when transfer occurs in 3.5.2, the oblique case has to be assigned by some phase heads under the assumption. Thus, I claim that, following Matsubara (2000) referred to above, prepositional phrases constitute a strong-phase whose head is *p**.

6.1.2 A Weak-Phase *p*P

Once we assume that prepositional phrases form strong-phases, our interest is in whether or not weak-phases exist in prepositional phases as well. In this book, I claim that they do. I assume that it is determined by independency of a relevant prepositional phrase whether the prepositional phrase is a strong-phase or a weak-phase. Moreover, I claim that independency of prepositions is defined by selection by verbs. Based on these assumptions, independent prepositional phrases, namely, prepositional phrases which can exist without being selected by verbs as in (175a) (namely, adjunct PP) count as a strong-phase *p**P, whereas dependent prepositional phrases selected by verbs as shown in (175b) (that is, argument PP) serve as a weak-phase *p*P.

(175) a. I came here <u>at</u> 3:00. Strong-phase *p**P
b. I talked <u>to</u> Mary <u>about</u> that matter. Weak-phase *p*P

Based on this definition, in this chapter, I will explore explanatory possibilities of *p*P. Before moving on to the actual analysis, however, let us make theoretical considerations on adjunct islands, which are the main topic of this chapter.

6.2 Adjunct Islands

It is fair to say that adjunct islands are one of the most often-discussed phenomena in generative grammar. As can be seen in (176), it is agreed that elements within adjuncts cannot be extracted.

58 Of course, there is another possibility of "nominal phases" as Chomsky (2007) touches on in the last part of his paper. Unfortunately, I cannot extend explanations of Feature-Transcription to nominal weak-phases in this book and I will leave this possibility for future research.

(176) a.* Which vacation did John go to Hawaii during *t*?

(Takami (1992: 7))

b.* Which parent's wishes did John get married against *t*?

(Takami (1992: 15))

Of course, it is not that no element can be extracted from within prepositional phrases. It is only adjunct prepositional phrases that prohibit extraction.

(177) What did you talk about *t*? (Matsubara (2000: 155))

After Huang (1982), there have been a lot of discussions on this topic (e.g. Uriagereka (1999), Stepanov (2001, 2007) and Müller (2010)). In this section, we will take a look at Uriagereka (1999) as a representative of previous analyses within a relatively new framework because his approach is quite insightful and theoretically elegant. However, his analysis is not free from problems.

6.2.1 Previous Analysis

Uriagereka (1999) offers quite an interesting approach to adjunct islands. His claim is simple. He employs Kayne's (1994) Linear Correspondence Axiom (LCA) and claims that the linear order is determined based on asymmetric c-command relations. If a Spec has a complex internal structure, under the LCA, an asymmetric c-command relation cannot be established between the elements within the Spec and the complement. As is shown in (178a), YP in the Spec does not asymmetrically c-command the complement and their order cannot be decided. Therefore, he argues that Specs have to be spelled-out when they are merged into the derivation so as to be linearized properly, as in (178b).

(178)

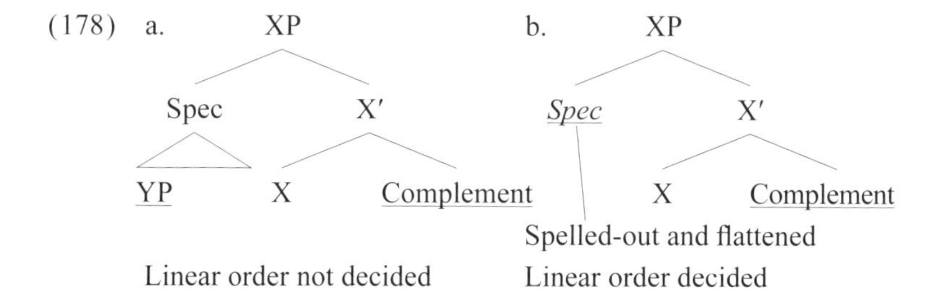

Under the assumption of "multiple spell-out," since they are already spelled-out, syntactic operations cannot access elements within Specs. In his framework, adjuncts are treated basically in the same way as Specs. Thus, subject islands (namely, the fact that elements within subjects cannot be extracted) and adjunct islands are explained in a parallel manner; extraction from them is impossible because they are already spelled-out and flattened when merged. Importantly, subjects and adjuncts themselves can be moved as a whole because they still exist in the derivation with a flat structure inside.

Nevertheless, his claim is too strong. We can easily find counter-examples to his approach.

(179) a. Who did you give [$_{DP}$ statues of *t*] [$_{PP}$ to all the season-ticket holders]? (Postal (1954: 195))
b. Who did you give [$_{DP}$ the book] [$_{PP}$ to *t*]?

If all extractions from within Specs and adjuncts are automatically ruled out due to multiple spell-out, the examples in (179) cannot be explained. Let us see the details of this discussion. In order to analyze (179a, b), we need to assume either of the two following structures.

(180)
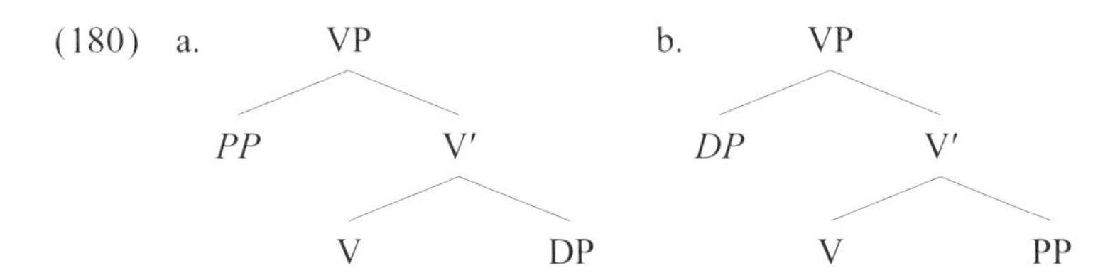

If we assume (180a) (which I employ later in this chapter), the DP is the complement of V and the *to* phrase is posited in the Spec of V (and the DP is moved before the *to* phrase and V raises to v^* later in the derivation to derive the proper word order). In this case, Uriagereka's (1999) framework wrongly expects that the *to* phrase is un-extractable contrary to the example in (179b), since this is in the Spec and is already flattened. To avoid this problem, we can assume the structure in (180b), where the *to* phrase is posited at the complement of V and the DP occupies Spec-VP. In this case, we can expect that the *to* phrase is extractable since this is the complement of V and not spelled-out yet. However, the DP is expected to disallow extraction despite the example in (179a) since this is posited in the Spec. Thus, Uriagereka's (1999) framework cannot explain the examples in (179).

Moreover, although Uriagereka (1999) attempts to derive adjunct islands (and subject islands) from an independent factor, namely, from spell-out, other previous research presupposes an assumption only in order to explain adjunct islands (e.g. late merger in Stepanov (2001, 2007) and additional assumptions in the Phase Theory in Müller (2010)). Thus, such approaches are no more theoretically valid than Uriagereka's (1999) approach because the fewer the apparatuses are, the more preferable the approach is in the MP.

In this book, I claim that adjunct islands are explained by interaction of multiple, independently required factors. Therefore, the approach here need not introduce apparatuses which are specifically designed to capture adjunct islands and thus it is agreeable in terms of economy. Now, in order to introduce the background of the claim, firstly, let us look at Chomsky's (2013) Labeling Algorithm in the next subsection.

6.2.2 The Labeling Algorithm

Chomsky (2013) further develops a theoretical framework of the MP and focuses on the Labeling Algorithm. He casts doubt on a concept which we have taken for granted: Specifiers. His argument starts by considering how labels on syntactic elements are determined. Thus far, we have assumed that if an element is merged with another element, the one that requires the merger operation projects the label of the resulted constituent (see Nunes (2013)). However, this process presupposes a stipulation of asymmetric merger operations, where an element causing the merger operation is somehow dominant. Chomsky (2013) claims that a simple merger operation should be symmetric in that there is no difference between A is merged with B and B is merged with A. Simply, A and B are merged. Then, the question of how the label of the resulted constituent of the merger operation is determined arises.

Chomsky (2013) proposes a detailed mechanism of the Labeling Algorithm. He suggests that the Labeling Algorithm is subject to the concept of the minimal computation. Therefore, if an element is merged with a syntactic constituent, the Labeling Algorithm starts and it determines the label of the new constituent based on the closest head in the constituent. As can be seen in (181), if X is merged with YP, the Labeling Algorithm selects X to be the label of the new element because it is the closest to the top than Y within YP. Hence, the constituent becomes XP.

(181)

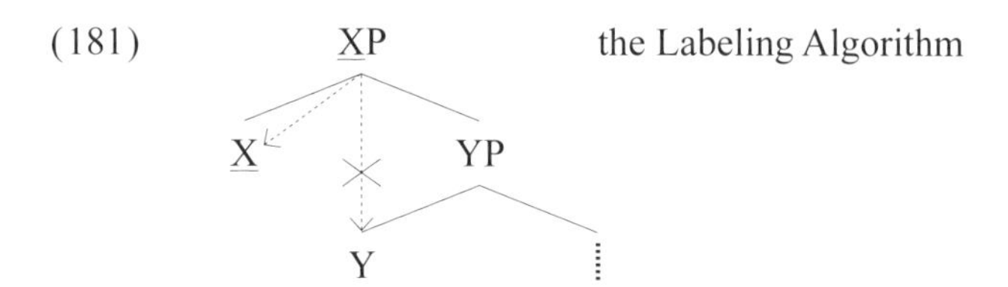

Now, the assumption of the Labeling Algorithm faces a problem under a certain situation. That is a situation where a merger operation concatenates XP and YP. Under the minimal computation, both heads are equally distant since they are both embedded in other projections. Thus, the Labeling Algorithm cannot determine the label of the new constituent. This is problematic because Chomsky (2013) argues that an element without a label cannot be read at the Interface.

(182)

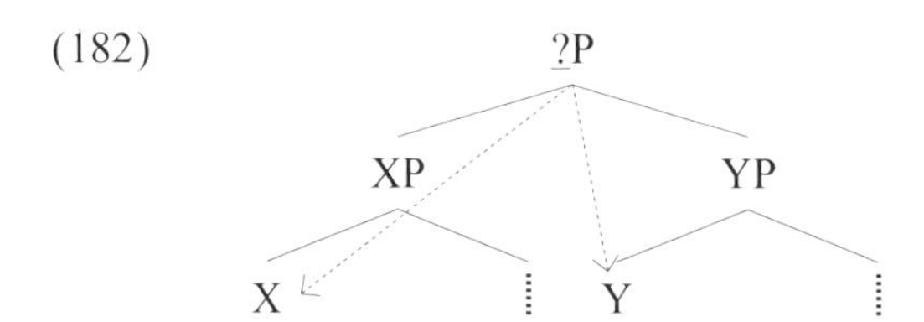

Then, he claims that there are three possibilities to circumvent this undesirable situation. Firstly, one of the two elements is moved. Although the XP-YP situation is problematic, if XP is moved, we have only YP in the domain. In this case, the Labeling Algorithm can determine the label of the new element as YP, for the Y head is the nearest head. Chomsky (2013) claims that this is the situation in which a constituent of the subject DP-*v**P results and thus the subject DP in Spec-*v**P in (183a) has to be moved in the later derivation.

(183) a.

b.

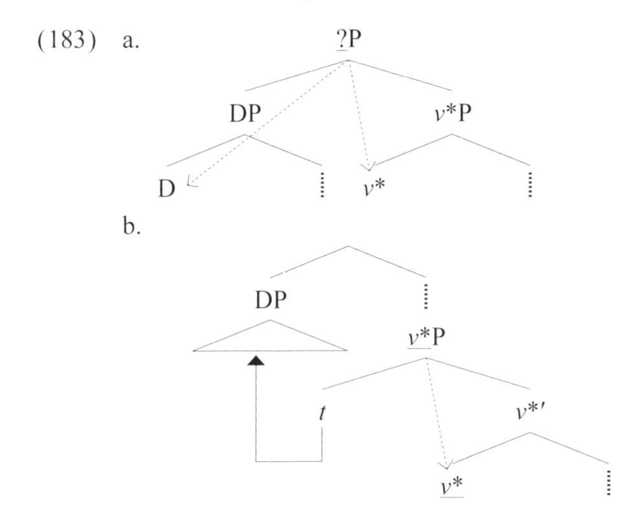

Another possibility is to find shared prominent features in both XP-YP. Note that in the assumption of Bare Phrase Structure, the label is considered as a set of features and thus features can be chosen as the label of an element. Let us exemplify this by observing how the label of TP with a DP in its "Spec" is determined. When the subject DP is moved to Spec-TP, another XP-YP situation is gained: DP-TP. However, in this case, these elements hold an Agree relation based on φ-features on them. In this way, they share prominent features, "φ." Thus, the label of DP-TP can be determined as "φ"P in this case.

(184)

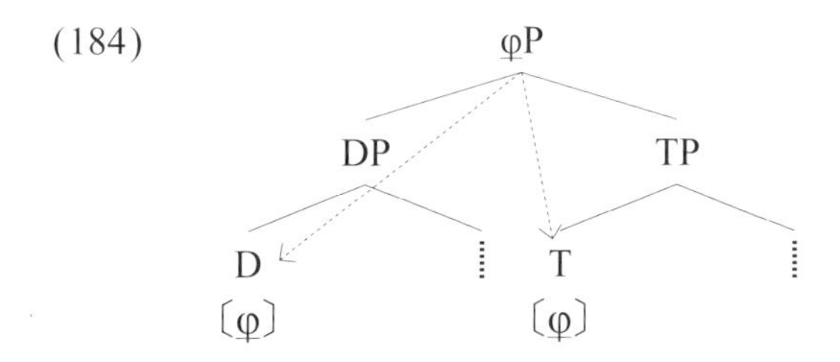

The last possibility is that one of the two elements gives up its standing as a candidate of labeling. If one of the projections cannot inherently be the label of the new constituent, the Labeling Algorithm can choose the other head to be the label. Chomsky (2013) argues that this is the situation found with conjunctions.

Although the three possibilities above are not directly related to the discussion on adjunct islands in this book, I will emphasize that the label of XP-YP cannot be determined since this plays an important role in the discussion. Now, let us move to another discussion as the background of the proposal, namely, how to ensure modification relations in syntax.

6.2.3 A Consideration on Modification Relations in Syntax

The discussion on adjunct islands in this book has much to do with modification relations in syntax. Firstly, we need clarification on the term, "modification relations." In this book, I refer to θ-role assignment from predicates to arguments and modification by adjuncts as "modification" in an extended sense. Both θ-roles and modification roles on adjuncts have to be "discharged" by merger with proper elements as in (185). As in (185a), θ-roles of predicates have to be discharged by merger with arguments (DP/PP), while a modification role on adjuncts needs to be discharged by merger with VP or TP.

(185) a. θ-role $\xrightarrow[\text{discharge}]{}$ DP/PP b. modification $\xrightarrow[\text{discharge}]{}$ VP/TP

In this subsection, let us consider how this "modification relation" is ensured in syntax under the framework in the MP. Namely, I attempt to unify the process of the "discharge" of θ-roles and modification roles on adjuncts in terms of a *Lexical Edge Feature*. To simplify the discussion, however, I concentrate on the mechanism of θ-role discharge for a moment.

6.2.3.1 Previous Analysis

How θ-role relations can be ensured in syntax has often been discussed in generative grammar. In the GB era, θ-roles were assigned based on the concept of "government" at the D-structure and if they are assigned, they are "saturated" in Stowell's (1981) terms. In addition, some assumptions or constraints were proposed to control semantic interpretation in that era (e.g. see the θ-criterion in Chomsky (1981) and the Uniformity of Theta-Assignment Hypothesis in Baker (1988)). In the MP, however, the θ-role assignment mechanism becomes unclear. Chomsky (2008: 140) simply assumes that "EM (External Merge) yields generalized argument structure." Therefore, probably, a θ-role is assigned when the relevant element undergoes external merge, but detailed mechanisms regarding how θ-roles are assigned are still controversial.

However, note that the θ-criterion suggested by Chomsky (1981) implies that discharge of θ-roles is obligatory. The θ-criterion indicates that "[e]ach argument bears one and only one θ-role, and each θ-role is assigned to one and only one argument (Chomsky (1981: 36))." This criterion consists of two parts summed up in (186).

(186) a. One DP has to receive one θ-role.
b. One θ-role has to be assigned to one DP.

It is fair to say that (186a) becomes controversial and some researchers (see, e.g. Hornstein (1999), Boeckx and Hornstein (2003), and Boeckx et al. (2010)) propose the Control as Movement approach, which presupposes a DP can receive two or more θ-roles. However, (186b) must survive so as to exclude the example in (187b) below.

(187) a. I expect there to be a man in the room.
b.* I forced there to be a man in the room.

(187b) is what is called the object control construction. Interestingly, the configurations in the examples in (187) are basically the same. Therefore, (187b) should be ruled out in terms of θ-roles; *force* cannot discharge its θ-role for object (say, "forcee"). This indicates that the ungrammaticality of (187b) is explained based on (186b) and thus (186b) should exist even in the recent framework.

Now, the simplest explanation in the MP, where uninterpretable features have much to do with syntactic operations, is to assume that θ-role assignments include uninterpretable feature checking and if the uninterpretable feature is not checked, the derivation crashes. Actually, some previous research attributes θ-role assignment to feature checking (see Bošković and Takahashi (1998), Hornstein (1999), Boeckx et al. (2010), and Kitada (2013)). However, if we attempt to derive (186b) in terms of uninterpretable feature checking, we are doomed to face a serious theoretical problem. Note that in Chomsky's (2001) (and his following) framework, feature checking is based on an Agree relation through an Agree operation. Then, given that an Agree operation occurs only when an uninterpretable feature c-commands its interpretable counterpart, the uninterpretable θ-feature on a *v** head (namely, u-Agent) cannot be checked by the subject DP in Spec-*v**P as in (188) under the normal assumption.

(188)

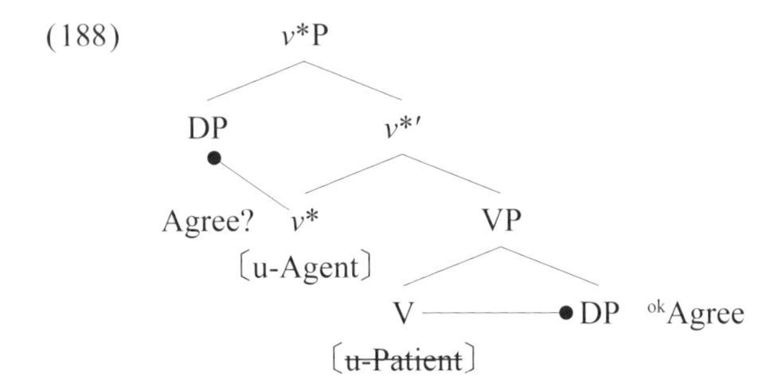

Of course, we can avoid this problem assuming that uninterpretable θ-features do not exist on a *v** head but rather on a DP, instead. Namely, we can suggest that a DP possesses an uninterpretable θ-feature (u-θ) and it has to be checked by its interpretable counterpart on a *v* head or a V head as in (189).

(189)

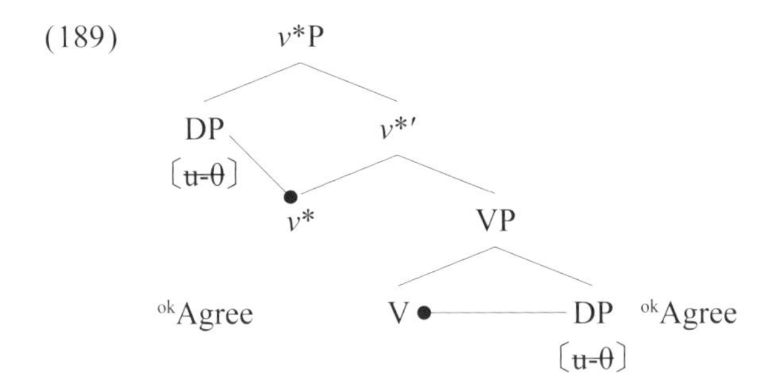

However, in that case, it is predicted that a verbal projection itself does not require checking at all. In other words, if there is no DP included in the derivation, no feature checking is necessary since features on a verbal projection are interpretable under the assumption that uninterpretable θ-features exist on DPs. This implies that θ-roles on a verbal projection need not be discharged and we wrongly expect that sentences such as in (190) can be generated. Therefore, the assumption that a DP owns an uninterpretable θ-feature causes over-generations.

(190) a.* Ate.
b.* Gave.

Thus, we face theoretical problems if we attempt to ensure θ-role relations in terms of "normal" feature checking. The same discussion holds in modification by adjuncts because we assumed that a modification role is also discharged by an external merger operation like checking of θ-features in 6.2.3.

6.2.3.2 Lexical Edge Features

However, notice that not all uninterpretable feature checking include Agree operations. There is one candidate for uninterpretable features that is checked without relying on Agree operations: Edge Features. Note that although Chomsky (2008) assumes that Edge Features are uninterpretable features, they are checked by external merge. For example, an external merger operation of a subject DP into Spec-*v**P is triggered by an Edge Feature on the *v** head under the recent framework. Then, given that c-command relations are never established between the root and the externally-merged element since the externally-merged element does not exist in the derivation before the external merge, this implies that an Edge Feature cannot be checked through a usual Agree operation based on c-command relations. Therefore, an Edge Feature must be checked without Agree operations through direct merge.

Recall that θ-role assignment is considered to be based on external merge as well. Therefore, it is reasonable to relate θ-role assignment to Edge Feature checking. If we assume this, the problem discussed in the last subsection does not occur. Namely, an Edge Feature related to a θ-role on *v** can be checked by merger of a DP without relying on c-command relations. Therefore, let us assume that θ-role assignment is related to checking of a special variety of Edge Features. I tentatively call the special Edge Features "Lexical" Edge Features.

I will return to detailed discussions on the nature of Lexical Edge Features later in 6.5. At this moment, let us tentatively assume that if there is a modification interpretation to be discharged on a syntactic element, the head possesses a Lexical Edge Feature and it must be checked by external merge of proper opponent. EF_{Lex} stands for *Lexical Edge Feature*.

(191) A $EF_{Lex[XP]}$ must be checked by a direct merger operation with XP.

For instance, *v** possesses "$EF_{Lex[DP]}$" and it must be checked by a merger operation with a DP. Moreover, I argue that this assumption is applied not only to θ-role relations but also to modification by adjuncts. Namely, verbal adjuncts have to possess $EF_{Lex[VP]}$ and sentential adjuncts, $EF_{Lex[TP]}$, both of which have to be checked by a merger operation with VP and TP, respectively.

Furthermore, note that an Edge Feature on *v** in general can trigger direct merger operation of *v**P and a DP as in (192a), not *v** and a DP as in (192b). If the Edge Feature exists on the *v** head, we expect that the Edge Feature concatenates *v** and a DP as in (192b), which violates the Extension Condition. This seems to indicate that the Edge Feature is posited on the label of the constituent, not on the head.[59]

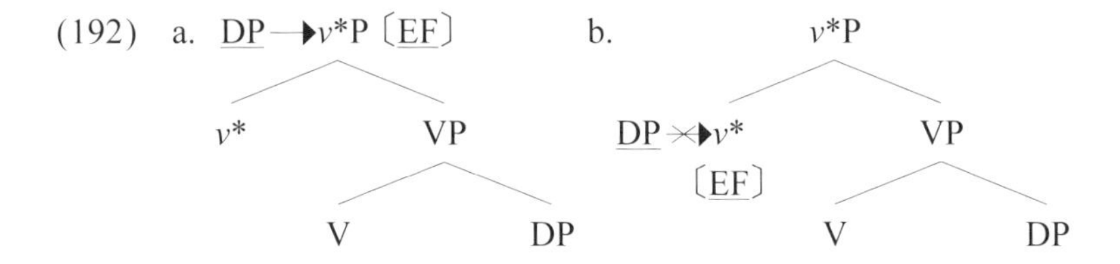

Now, keeping in mind the Labeling Algorithm and the assumption in (191), let us move back to the discussion on adjunct islands.

6.2.4 Adjunct Islands

Now, I will propose a new analysis of adjunct islands in this subsection. If an adjunct phrase forms a phase, the A-bar moved element must be once posited to the Spec of the adjunct phrase and constructs an XP-YP relation there so as to circumvent a PIC violation. In such case, the label of the con-

59 Given that Chomsky (2007: 22) notes that in Feature-Inheritance "P (phase head) assigns its inflectional features to *the label L of XP*, T or V," we may be able to generalize that all features including AF do not exist on a phase head but on its label. This is a desirable consequence in terms of Bare Phrase Structure, where the label of a syntactic element is not its category but the actual item itself serves as its own label.

stituent cannot be determined as we saw in 6.2.2. Then, I claim that the XP-YP situation prevents a direct merger operation of relevant elements and thus a Lexical Edge Feature cannot be checked, based on (191), when extraction from an adjunct occurs.[60] Let us assume that adjunct phrase constitutes *p**P and exemplify this in (193) and (194).[61]

(193) John went to Hawaii during the winter vacation.

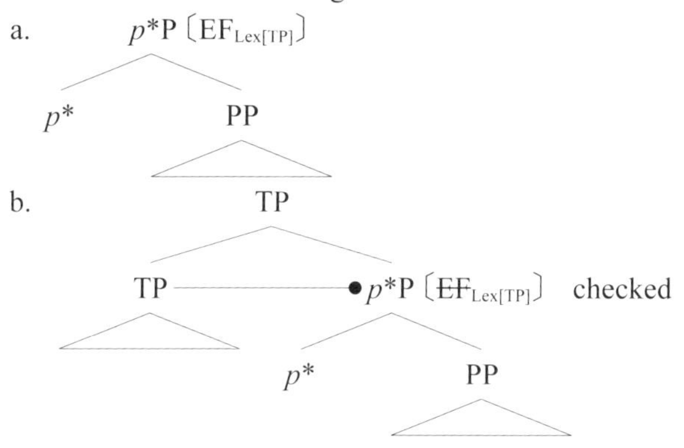

(193) indicates a convergent derivation without extraction. As can be seen in (193a), a Lexical Edge Feature is posited on the position of the label "*p**P." Then, it can be checked by direct merger based on (191).

60 Interestingly, Kurogi (2014) claims that the XP-YP constituent cannot be involved in internal merge and solves abundant problems related to Parasitic Gaps based on this assumption. Considering that internal merge includes valuing of a(n uninterpretable) feature, the impossibility of Lexical Edge Feature checking here can be generalized as "a XP-YP situation prevents feature valuing." If so, the Lexical Edge Feature cannot be checked not because of the impossibility of direct merge, but due to the impossibility of valuing. I will leave this possibility open in this book.

61 Although the approach here does not structurally distinguish adjuncts and arguments, this approach raises a problem concerning the label of the constituent of TP-*p**P in (193b) and (194b) under the Labeling Algorithm. Obviously, in these cases, the adjunct *p**P cannot be the label of this constituent somehow and TP must be the label. In this way, the distinction between adjuncts and arguments has to remain (and hence Chomsky (2004) assumes Pair-Merge). I will leave this problem on the nature of the label of adjuncts for future research.

(194) *Which vacation did John go to Hawaii during *t*? (=(176a))

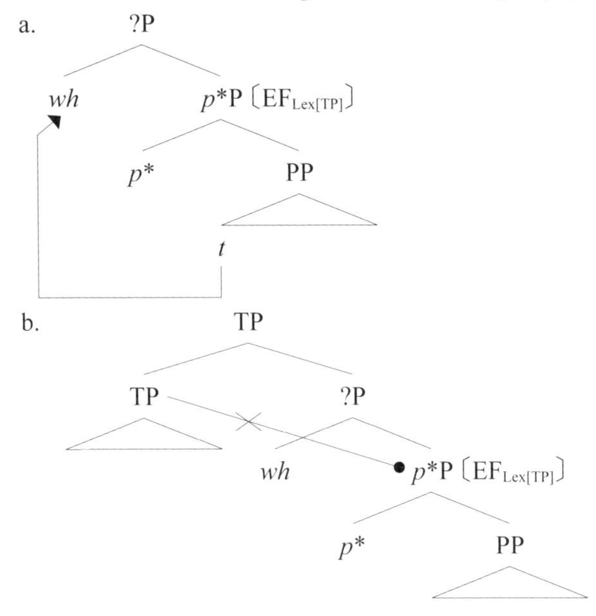

In (194) in turn, in order for the *wh*-element to be moved into the main clause, the PIC forces the element to be moved to the Spec of *p**P. Then, the A-bar movement of the *wh*-phrase to the Spec-*p**P produces a XP-YP situation, whose label cannot be determined. Thus, even though the Lexical Edge Feature is posited on *p**P, it cannot be checked since *p**P is not directly merged with TP in (194b).[62, 63] Therefore, $EF_{Lex[TP]}$ remains unchecked and the derivation crashes. Hence, no derivation converges if the extraction occurs from within *p**P.

If we assume that adjuncts project *p**P in general, we can extend the approach to all of the adjunct islands, not only to prepositional adjuncts. Thus, we need not postulate a special status for adjuncts; they are simply

62 Here, I have to assume that the merge of TP and *p*P in (194b) is not triggered by the Lexical Edge Feature on *p*P but a reused "normal" Edge Feature on T based on some requirement of the T head.

63 Here, note that the checking process is quite "derivational" in that even after the *wh*-phrase moves out and the XP-YP situation disappears, it is too late to check the Lexical Edge Feature. Note, again, that this book does not follow Chomsky's (2015) "representational" approach based on free merger (see footnote 1).

strong-phases. Moreover, under this approach, there is a loophole. That is, if a strong-phase *p**P is not included in the derivation, extraction is allowed, which is the topic of the next section.

6.3 Preposition-Stranding/Pied-Piping

Let us move to concrete data in this section. As can be seen in (195), a preposition in English can be stranded or pied-piped when it is involved in movement.

(195) a. Who did you give the book to?
      b. To whom did you give the book?

As far as I can see, there is no semantic difference between (195a, b) and I claim that this fact should be explained from a purely syntactic perspective.[64] There are many researchers who attempt to explain this fact. For instance, Hornstein and Weinberg (1981) try to account for preposition-stranding based on "reanalysis," which connects a verb and a preposition into one large verbal projection. In recent framework, Abels (2003) attempts to capture preposition-pied-piping based on PP-phases. Moreover, Drummond et al. (2010) points out that although preposition-pied-piping is obligatory in rightward movement (a problem to which we will return soon), it is optional in leftward movement. However, their approaches do not offer an explanation to the motivation for the optionality, or they presume special optional operations only to derive the optionality in preposition-stranding/pied-piping although the reasoning lacks sufficient motivation.[65]

In the last section, I derived adjunct islands based on the Labeling Algorithm and the Phase Theory. Shortly put, if a derivation includes a strong-phase *p**P and an element moves out of *p**P, an XP-YP situation is derived and a Lexical Edge Feature on *p**P cannot be checked. However, as was already

64 Sometimes it is said that preposition-pied-piping in (195b) is more formal and it is not natural in usual oral conversations. However, I claim that this is due to some pragmatic reasons and I will put aside discussions on this problem in this book.

65 For example, Hornstein and Weinberg (1981) claims that "reanalysis" is an optional operation and Abels (2003) claims that prepositional phrases in English optionally constitute a phase.

noted, it is expected that if a strong-phase p*P is not involved, extraction is applicable, since an XP-YP situation need not derived. I claim that this is the case when weak-phase pP is involved. Moreover, I argue that when weak-phase pP is included, the two possibilities of derivation in 3.5.1 derive an optionality of preposition-stranding/pied-piping in English, which cannot be explained in previous research.

Now, let us firstly observe how a case of preposition-stranding is derived. I argue that Individual-derivation produces preposition-stranding.

(196) Who did you give the book to? (=(195a))

(197)

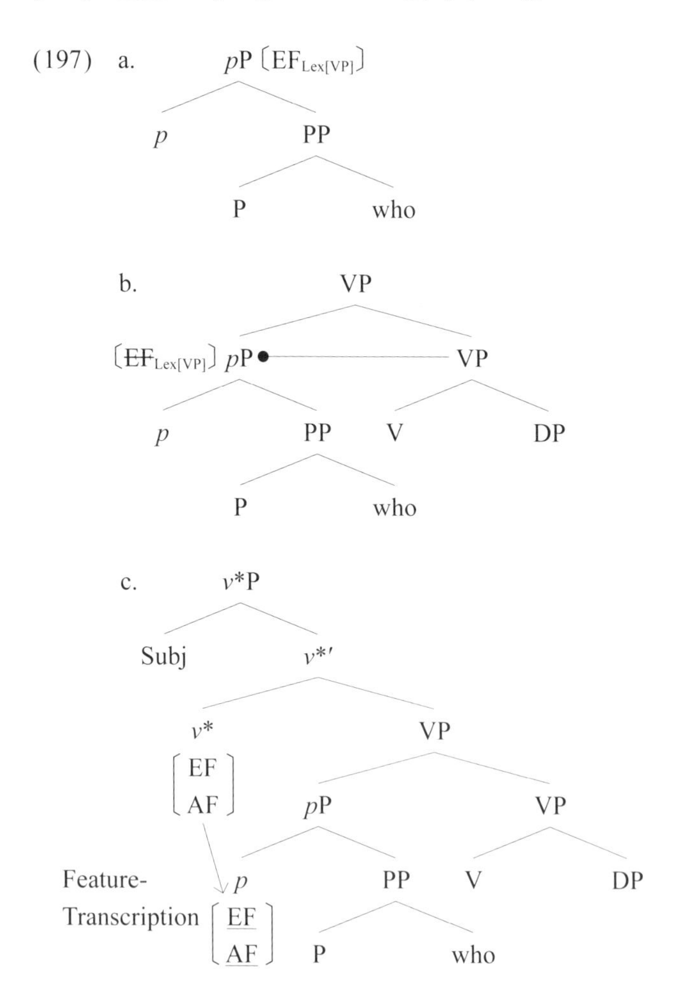

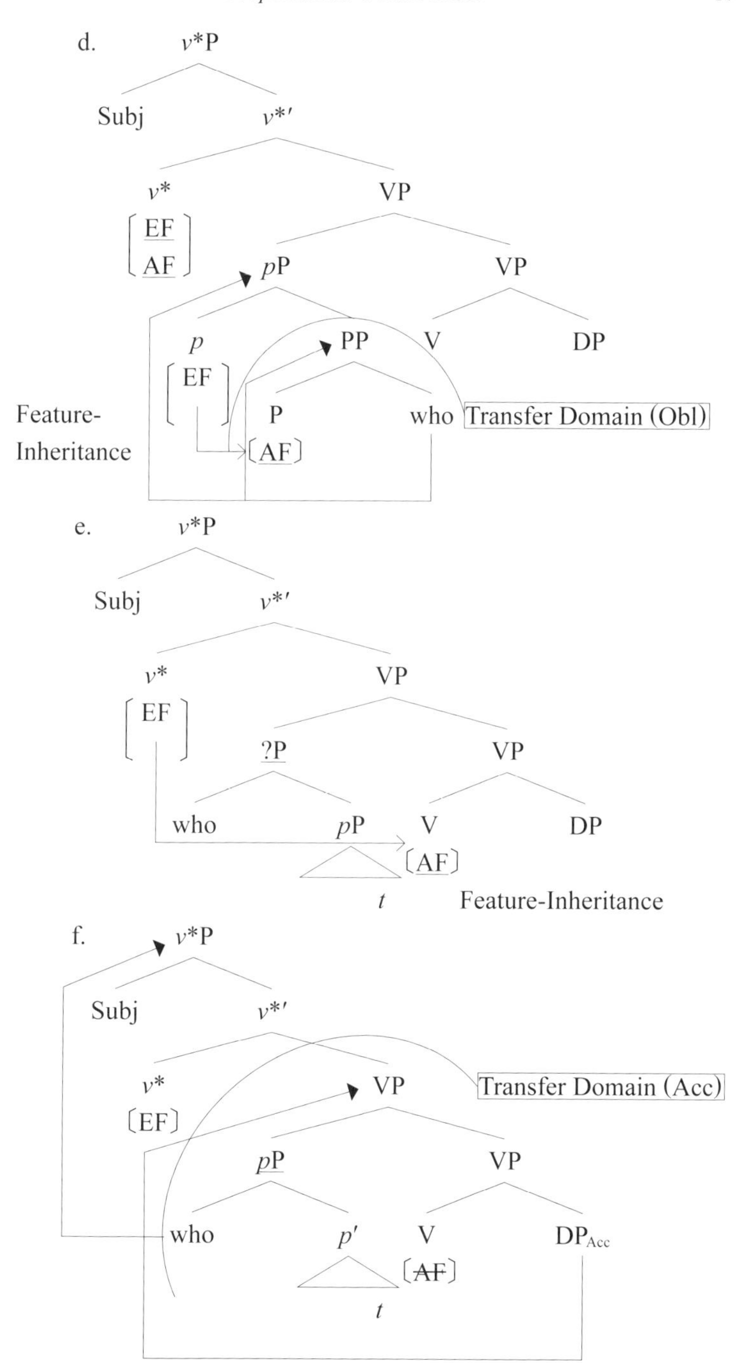
d.
v*P
Subj
v*′
v*
EF
AF
VP
pP
VP
p
EF
PP
V
DP
Feature-
Inheritance
P
who
Transfer Domain (Obl)
AF
e.
v*P
Subj
v*′
v*
EF
VP
?P
VP
who
pP
V
DP
AF
t
Feature-Inheritance
f.
v*P
Subj
v*′
v*
EF
VP
Transfer Domain (Acc)
pP
VP
who
p′
V
DPAcc
AF
t

Following Takano (1998), I assume that the prepositional phrase exists in the Spec of VP. As can be seen in (197a), *p*P is formed by merger operations of *who*, P, and *p*. Here, although I suggest that a weak-phase head cannot possess an Edge Feature and an Agree Feature, which only a strong-phase head can possess, a Lexical Edge Feature can exist on the *p* head since it is a feature a normal syntactic item can possess so as to ensure a modification relation. In this derivation, importantly, *p*P is merged with VP before the movement of *who* to the Spec of *p*P occurs as in (197b) since the weak-phase head *p* cannot trigger its syntactic operations before Feature-Transcription, except for external merge. Thus, $EF_{Lex[VP]}$ is checked by the merger of *p*P and VP, unlike what we saw in the last section. Then, when *v**P is formed, Feature-Transcription from *v** to *p* is triggered as in (197c).

Since we are considering individual-derivation here, *p* starts its operations before *v** and it transmits its Agree Feature to P. After the inheritance, the Edge Feature on *p* attracts *who* to its Spec and the XP-YP situation is generated as in (197d). Let me emphasize that when the movement occurs, the $EF_{Lex[VP]}$ has already been checked and thus no problem occurs. Now, since *who-p*P is in a XP-YP situation and cannot be labeled as we saw in 6.2.2, it should be modified somehow. Hence, I claim that *v** has to attract *who*, not *who-p*P as a whole as we witnessed in the case of the DOC in 4.4.4.2.1, when *v** starts its syntactic operations. Thus, after Feature-Inheritance from *v** to V in (197e), the Edge Feature on *v** moves *who* to its Spec, while the Agree Feature on V attracts the DP to the outer Spec of VP. As a consequence, therefore, preposition-stranding as in (196) is derived.

Once we observe the case of individual-derivation, we have to consider what occurs in a simultaneous-derivation manner. I argue that simultaneous-derivation produces preposition-pied-piping. Let us observe the derivation.

(198) To whom did you give the book? (=(195b))

(199) a.

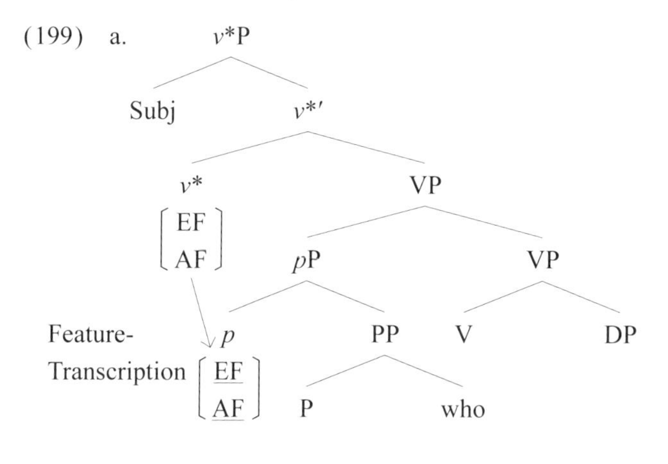
v*P
Subj
v*′
v*
EF
AF
VP
pP
VP
Feature-
Transcription
p
EF
AF
PP
V
DP
P
who

b.

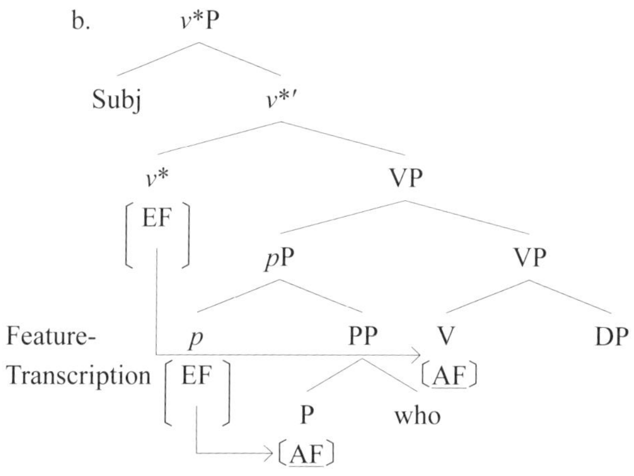
v*P
Subj
v*′
v*
EF
VP
pP
VP
Feature-
Transcription
p
EF
PP
V
DP
AF
P
who
AF

c.

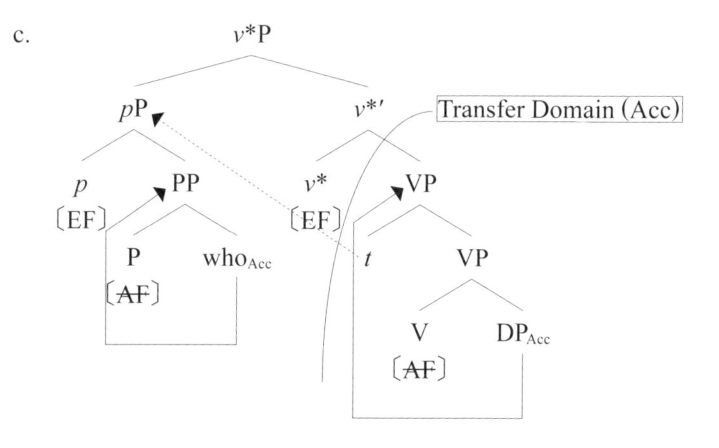
v*P
pP
v*′
Transfer Domain (Acc)
p
EF
PP
v*
EF
VP
P
AF
whoAcc
t
VP
V
AF
DPAcc

I omit the derivation before Feature-Transcription because this is equivalent to that in (197a-b). After Feature-Transcription, syntactic operations in *v**P and *p*P occur simultaneously in simultaneous-derivation, as can be seen in (199b). Feature-Inheritance occurs from *v** and *p* to V and P, respectively, as in (199b). Following the inheritance, the transmitted AFs on V and P hold an Agree relation with the DP and *who*, respectively as in (199c).[66] Simultaneously, the Edge Feature on *v** attracts *p*P as a whole as is expressed by the broken line in (199c). Recall the discussion in 4.4.4.2.1. Let us assume that because of some kind of a percolation operation, both *wh*-phrase and *p*P possess a *wh*-feature. Then, under the default situation, preposition-pied-piping is more economical in that preposition-stranding always requires longer movement than preposition-pied-piping. Therefore, *v** must raise *p*P as a whole, instead of *who* only, to its Spec in this case. Hence, the derivation here produces preposition-pied-piping. Furthermore, notice that if *p* attracts *who* in this case, there is no way to rescue the XP-YP situation of moved *who*-*p*P in the later derivation. Thus, only the derivation, where *p* does not attract *wh*-element, converges.

Let me emphasize that the two possibilities above, namely, individual-derivation and simultaneous-derivation are always optional when a weak-phase is involved. Therefore, the optionality of preposition-stranding/pied-piping, which has not been adequately accounted for in previous research as far as I know, is readily explained. In this section, I have explored the explanatory possibilities of Feature-Transcription in preposition-stranding/pied-piping. In the next section, we will move to a related but more complicated phenomenon, namely, the impossibility of preposition-stranding in rightward movement.

---

66 Here, the DP receives the accusative case since it is transferred by *v**. But I claim that *who* is also assigned the accusative case in this case. The reasoning is following: adopting Obata and Epstein's (2008) feature-splitting, I assume that a u-case feature on *who* remains on the copy of it within VP, and the u-case feature is assigned the accusative value based on the transfer-based case assignment mechanism, since it is transferred by *v**. Note that because *who* is finally pronounced outside the transfer domain of *v**, this process does not violate the Distinctness Condition in 4.4.3.3, which is a condition at the phonological component. Moreover, importantly, there is no difference in phonetic forms of the accusative case and the oblique case in English. This fact that the case manifestation pattern of the accusative case is the same as that of the oblique case may have something to do with whether the language permits preposition-stranding or not, but I will leave this possibility open in this book.

6.4 Preposition-Stranding in Rightward Movement

In this section, we will investigate the impossibility of preposition-stranding in rightward movement, which has not been given proper explanations in previous research. Concerning leftward movement, both preposition-stranding and pied-piping are optional, as we already saw in the last section. However, when it comes to rightward movement, there is no extracting from within prepositional phrases, namely, no preposition-stranding is observed as in (199b).

(200) a. I gave the book to a man with long hair yesterday.
b.* I gave the book to yesterday a man with long hair. (stranding)
c. I gave the book yesterday to a man with long hair. (pied-piping)

Drummond et al. (2010) imply that this problem can be solved if a prepositional phrase is a phase and its escape hatch is found only on its left, not on its right. Thus, preposition-stranding is observed only in leftward movement via the leftward escape hatch. However, their discussion is quite unclear, leaving the details of the mechanism unexplained.

In this section, I will claim that the Feature-Transcription framework can deal with this problem. Concerning rightward movement, I adopt Tanaka's (2011) "Edge Feature-Inheritance" framework. Let us briefly look at his main point.

Tanaka (2011) claims that rightward movement such as "extra-position from NP" occurs when triggered by an Edge Feature which is not posited on the phase head as in the normal case, but is transmitted to its complement via Edge Feature-Inheritance (see a discussion in 6.5.4 as well). Thus, the sentence in (201) is derived as in (202).

(201) John read [a paper *t*] over the summer **of Chomsky's**.
(Tanaka (2011: 176))

(202) a.

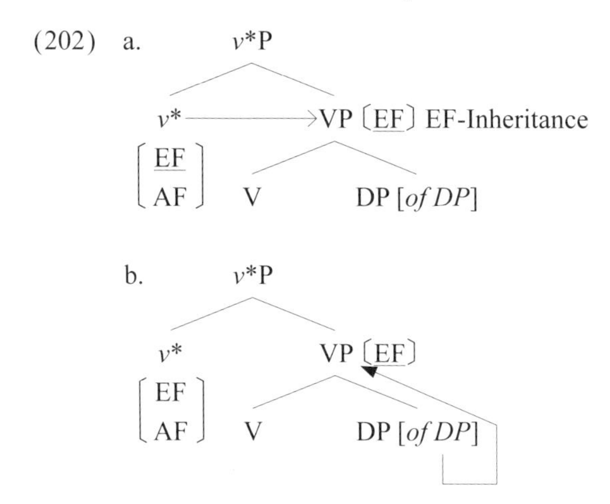

As can be seen in (202), when rightward movement occurs, the phase head *v** transmits its Edge Feature to its complement. Since I assume that an Edge Feature is always posited on the label in this book, I claim that the transmitted Edge Feature is directly passed to the label of VP as in (202a). Then, the Edge Feature attracts the *of* phrase to its right. In this process, rightward movement is explained.

Adopting Tanaka's (2011) Edge Feature-Inheritance, I claim that rightward preposition-stranding cannot be generated. Firstly, let us consider the case of preposition-stranding involving a strong-phase *p**P. This case is quite easy: If an element is extracted from within *p**P via rightward movement, when the element is moved rightward directly, it violates the PIC as in (203a), whereas when the element is firstly posited on escape hatch of Spec-*p**P as in (203b), it is ruled out as a case of adjunct islands due to the reason shown in the last section. Namely, if the DP is moved to the phase edge, it constitutes the XP-YP situation and leaves the Lexical Edge Feature unchecked, causing the derivation to crash.

(203)

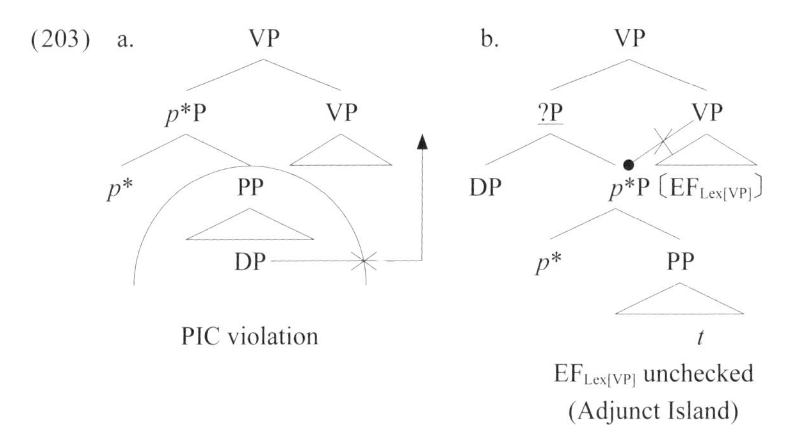

When weak-phase *p*P is involved in rightward movement, the situation becomes a little confusing since the weak-phase offers us two derivational possibilities. In what follows, I will show that rightward preposition-stranding is excluded even in simultaneous-derivation as well as in individual-derivation under the Feature-Transcription framework. Let us see the possible derivational patterns in sequence. Firstly, I will present the derivation under simultaneous-derivation. For simplicity, I omit Agree Feature-related operations in (205) (also for expository purposes, DPs which undergo rightward movement are expressed in italic "*DP*").

(204) *I gave [$_{DP1}$ the book] to yesterday [$_{DP2}$ a man with long hair]. (=(199b))

(205)

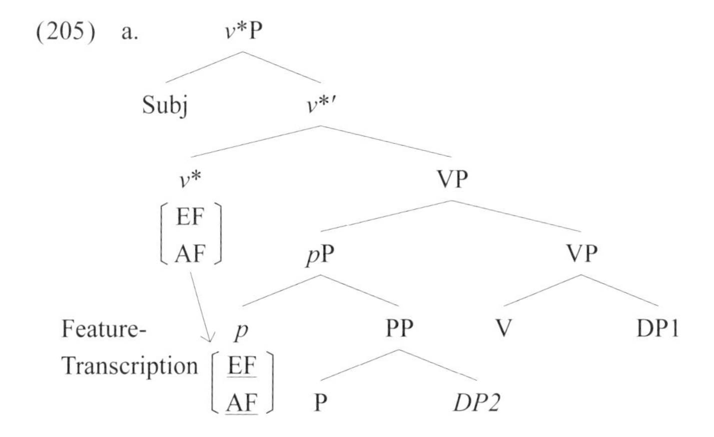

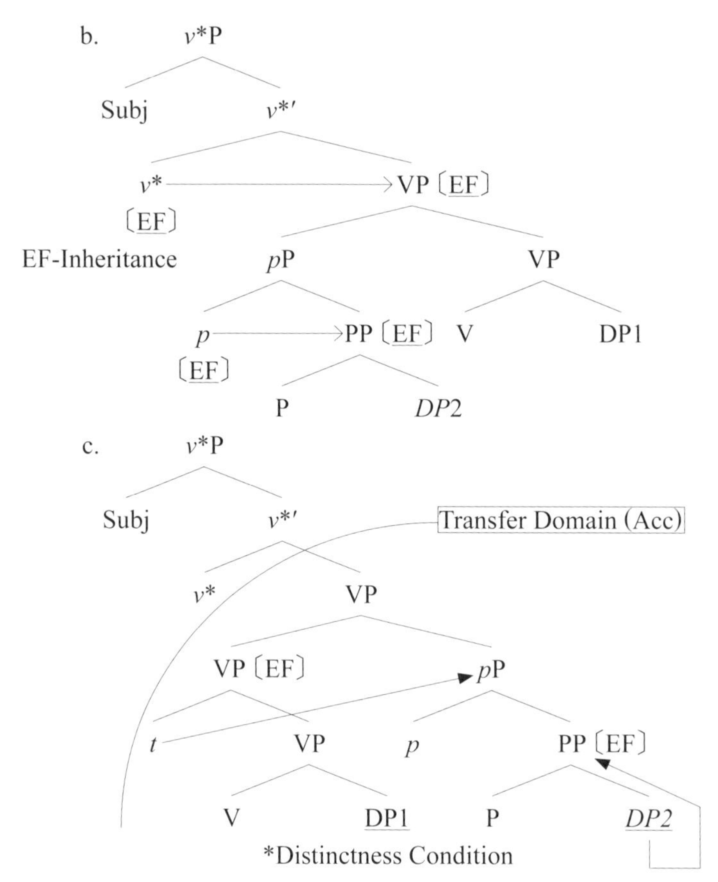

As can be seen in (205a), Feature-Transcription occurs from *v** to *p*. Then, they start their syntactic operations simultaneously. Now, recall that as was discussed in 4.4.4.2.1 and in the last section, preposition-pied-piping is preferred to stranding in simultaneous-derivation when A-bar movement occurs under the default situation. Thus, *p*P as a whole is moved as in (205c). Moreover, in this case, note that the resulted structure violates the Distinctness Condition seen in 4.4.3.3 as is shown in (205c). Thus, not only is preposition-stranding rightward movement not allowed, but simultaneous-derivation also does not produce convergent derivations whether the preposition is stranded or pied-piped. Note that the linear order does not change whether or not the Edge Feature on P attracts the heavy DP to the right adjunct position of PP in (205c).

Now, let us move to individual-derivation. The example is the same as in (204) above. Under individual-derivation, two different derivational possibilities are observed depending on whether Edge Feature-Inheritance occurs within *p*P or not. Firstly, if Edge Feature-Inheritance occurs in *p*P, the heavy DP is moved to the right adjunct position of PP and remains that position as in (206a). Then, after the transfer by *p*, the inherited Edge Feature on V cannot attract the DP since it is already transferred as in (206b). Thus, *p*P as a whole must be moved and preposition-stranding cannot be derived again.

(206) a.

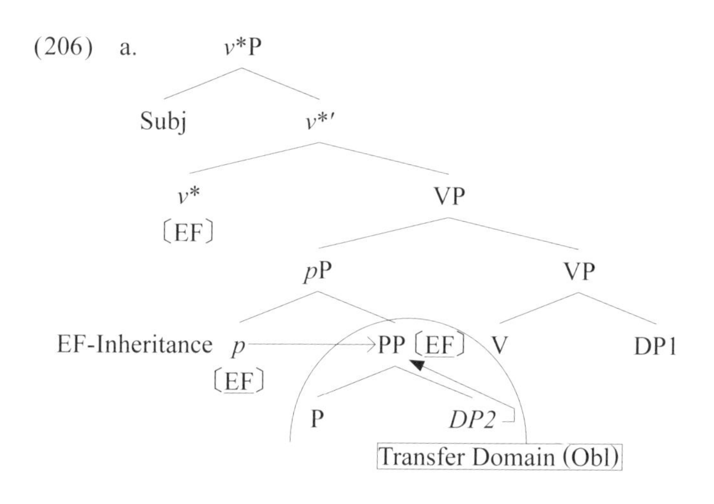

b.

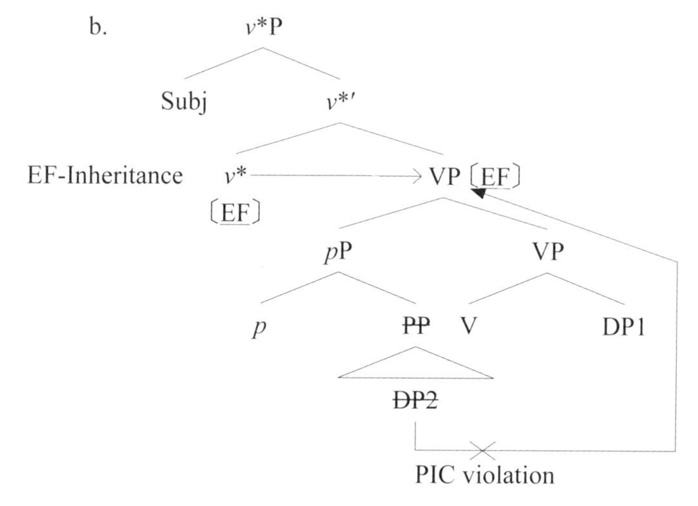

Importantly, if we assume that Edge Feature-Inheritance occurs optionally and the heavy DP is moved once to Spec-*p*P, the PIC violation can be avoided as in (207a). Notice that since this is weak-phase *p*P, the problem of adjunct islands noted above does not occur (since a Lexical Edge Feature on *p*P is already checked when *p*P starts its syntactic operations). However, even though the rightward movement of the heavy DP itself is allowed in this case, the escaped heavy DP remains in the transfer domain of *v**, namely within VP. Then, the Distinctness Condition is violated again, since the two DPs exist within the same transfer domain as in (207b).

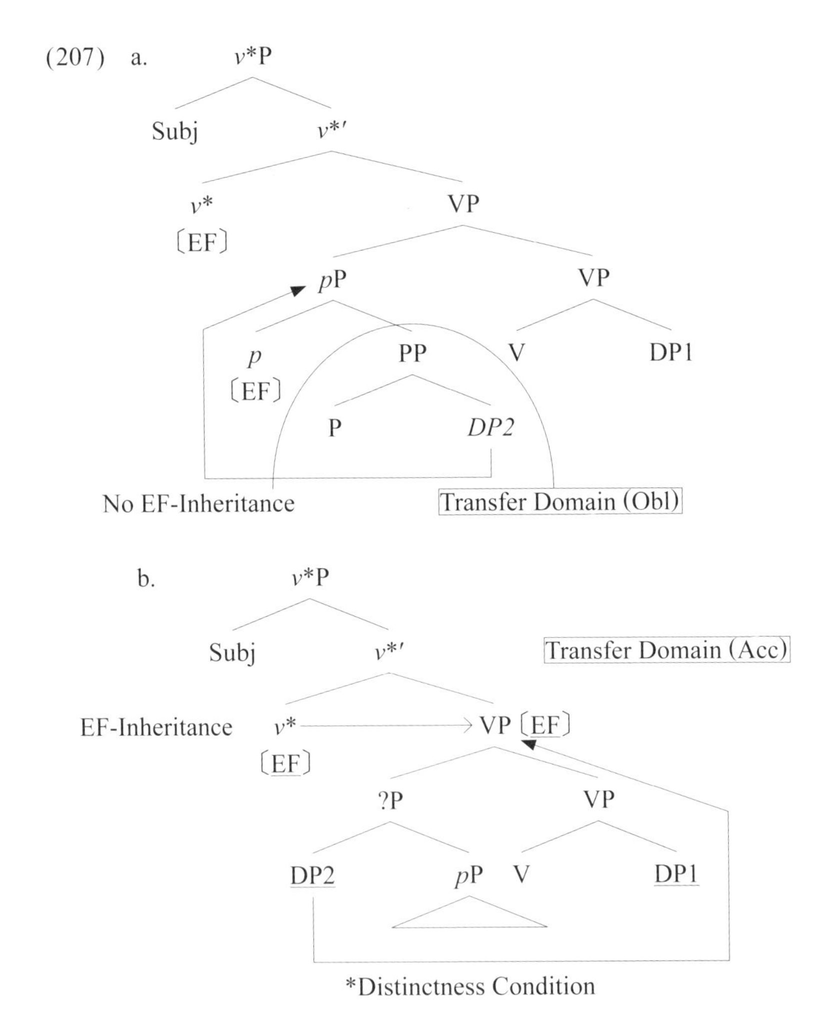

The discussion above predicts that if only one DP is included in preposition-stranding in rightward movement, the sentence may be grammatical. This expectation is borne out by the following examples pointed out by Rochemont and Culicover (1990).

(208) a.? We slept in when we were in Connecticut a marvelous bed that had belonged to George Washington.
b.? We looked at last night a wonderful film about New York that had been made during the Depression.
(Rochemont and Culicover (1990: 191))

In sum, I have claimed that under the Feature-Transcription framework, no derivation which produces preposition-stranding in rightward movement converges. Moreover, I have shown that even its exception of "one DP included" rightward preposition-stranding in (208) can be captured as well.

6.5 A Consideration on Edge Features

In the last section of this book, I will consider the nature of Edge Features. More specifically, since I have tentatively proposed a new kind of Edge Features, namely Lexical Edge Features, I have to consider their characteristics. Firstly, let us consider the nature of both "normal" Edge Features and Lexical Edge Features in sequence. After this consideration, I will claim that Lexical Edge Features can be derived in terms of θ-role features. Furthermore, I will consider the nature of an Edge Feature which only a phase head possesses (I refer to it as a Phasal Edge Feature) and sum up the whole picture of the framework of this book concerning Edge Features.

6.5.1 The Nature of "Normal" Edge Features

The concept of Edge Features is introduced by Chomsky (2008). As has already been pointed out, "normal" Edge Features are unique in that they can be checked even by external merge (without c-command relations). Concerning the nature of "normal" Edge Features, Chomsky (2007: 11) says "Empirical evidence reveals that SPECs exists, that is, that EF is undeletable." Moreover, in his footnotes, he notes "As an uninterpretable feature, EF cannot reach the interface, so presumably deletion of EF is an automatic part of the operations of transfer (Chomsky (2007: 11))." Thus, "normal" Edge Features seem to have the following three characteristics.

(209) a. A "normal" Edge Feature is an uninterpretable feature.
b. A "normal" Edge Feature cannot be deleted even if it is checked.
c. A "normal" Edge Feature is automatically eliminated at transfer.

The assumption in (209c) derives an interesting consequence; checking of a "normal" Edge Feature is optional. This is because even if it is not checked, still it can be gotten rid of when transfer occurs following (209c) and no problem occurs in the C-I Interface. Moreover, even if a "normal" Edge Feature does not receive a syntactic value via checking, it raises no problem in the SM Interface, either, because the "normal" Edge Feature has no contribution to pronunciations and thus is not sent to the SM Interface.[67] Thus, optional checking of Edge Features is theoretically derived.

In addition, if it receives a syntactic value by checking, the "normal" Edge Feature cannot be involved in feature checking anymore and (209b) is not expected. Thus, to derive (209b), (210) should be assumed.

(210) A "normal" Edge Feature cannot receive a syntactic value even if it is checked.

Based on (210), even if a "normal" Edge Feature is checked by a merger operation with an element, it cannot be valued and still lacks its value. Thus, the once checked "normal" Edge Feature can be reused to trigger another external merger operation.

6.5.2 The Nature of Lexical Edge Features

Now, what are Lexical Edge Features? The discussion in the last section concerning adjunct islands and preposition-stranding/pied-piping leads us to the following assumption.

67 Therefore, "normal" Edge Features are quite syntax-specific features without contribution to the C-I/SM Interfaces. They exist only so as to trigger merge in syntax.

(211) A Lexical Edge Feature has to be valued via direct merger with a proper item.

However, assumption (211) raises one serious theoretical problem: if a Lexical Edge Feature is valued, how can the simultaneity problem in 2.3.2 be avoided? For instance, when a Lexical Edge Feature on V is checked (valued) as in (212a), the checked (valued) Lexical Edge Feature remains in the derivation until *v**P is formed and VP is transferred as in (212b). Thus, if a Lexical Edge Feature is an uninterpretable feature and needs to be valued, the simultaneity problem arises because it cannot be transferred simultaneously with the valuation.

(212)

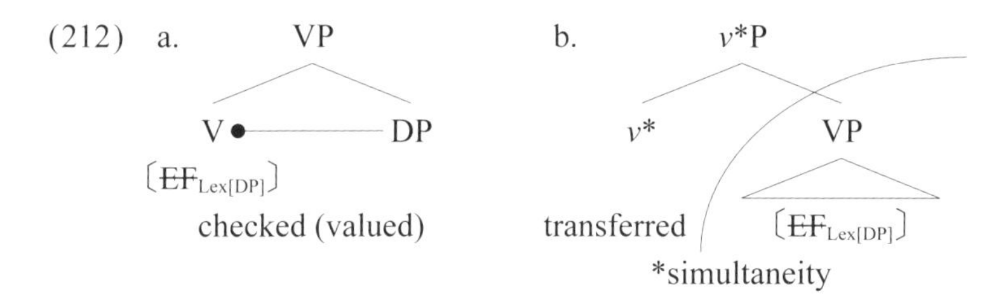

Since Feature-Inheritance is suggested in order to solve the simultaneity problem, the situation shown in (212) is seriously problematic under the present framework, which is based on the assumption of Feature-Inheritance.

Interestingly, a possible solution to the problem above is to assume that a Lexical Edge Feature is an *interpretable feature without a syntactic value*. If a Lexical Edge Feature is an interpretable feature, it need not (or even *cannot*) be removed from the derivation so as to reach the C-I Interface and thus the simultaneity problem does not arise. At first sight, the assumption that a Lexical Edge Feature is an unvalued interpretable feature seems theoretically inadequate. This is because Chomsky (2001) assumes that an uninterpretable feature is a feature without a syntactic value. However, notice that this is just an assumption. Actually, Pesetsky and Torrego (2007) claim that the four possibilities in (213) should exist and propose an analysis based on this assumption (although I will not present the detail of their discussion). Given that we have two pairs of two possibilities for features, namely, interpretable/uninterpretable, and valued/unvalued, the logical possibilities should be the following four in (213).

(213) a. An Interpretable Feature with a Value
b. An Interpretable Feature without a Value
c. An Uninterpretable Feature with a Value[68]
d. An Uninterpretable Feature without a Value

Therefore, it is not unreasonable to claim that the four possibilities in (213) are valid and a Lexical Edge Feature is a case of (213b). If we assume that a Lexical Edge Feature is an unvalued interpretable feature, any syntactic item can possess it theoretically, since the simultaneous problem never occurs. Namely, even if V has a Lexical Edge Feature and it is checked (valued) when V and a DP merge, the Lexical Edge Feature is sent to the C-I Interface and thus need not be distinguished from other normal interpretable features. Thus, the derivation can put off the transfer of the checked (valued) Lexical Edge Feature until *v**P is formed. However, we expect that if it is not checked (valued), it causes a problem at the C-I Interface because although it can be interpreted, the interpretation is "gibberish" (see the next subsection for detail).

Nevertheless, a large question remains; what is an unvalued interpretable feature? Moreover, if a Lexical Edge Feature is interpretable, what interpretation does it contribute to? These are the topics of the next subsection.

6.5.3 Deriving Lexical Edge Features from θ-Role Features

In this chapter, we have tentatively assumed Lexical Edge Features. The introduction of Lexical Edge Features was based on the consideration that if we analyze θ-role assignment in terms of feature checking, the problem concerning c-command relations arises and this problem is circumvented if θ-role assignment is related to Edge Features (see 6.2.3 for detail). Then, I have derived adjunct islands and related phenomena including preposition-stranding and pied-piping based on the assumption of Lexical Edge Features. Therefore, I have shown that the introduction of Lexical Edge Features gains empirical support through the explanation to those phenomena. However, a

68 The concept of an uninterpretable feature with a value seems to me to be problematic because if the feature has a value, the value can be interpreted and thus it should be interpretable. Thus, only the remaining three possibilities may survive; uninterpretable features without a value and interpretable with or without a value. I will put aside the detailed discussion of the validity of uninterpretable features with a value for future research.

Lexical Edge Feature is a brand-new apparatus and its theoretical validity has not been considered in enough detail. Ideally, Lexical Edge Features should be derived from more fundamental mechanisms. Moreover, even though I introduced Lexical Edge Features as some kinds of helpers for θ-role assignment, it is unclear what roles Lexical Edge Features can play in θ-role assignment and how they can carry out the roles. In this subsection, I consider the nature of θ-role assignment and conclude that a Lexical Edge Feature is a ("normal") Edge Feature plus a θ-role feature.

Now, let us put aside the discussion of Lexical Edge Features for a moment and move back to θ-role assignment in the MP. Recall that we have attempted to reframe θ-role assignment in terms of feature checking so as to derive the latter half of the θ-criterion in (214) to exclude the example in (215b). In this approach, we assume that there exist Agent, Theme, and other features in the derivation and they have to be checked by proper elements.

(214) One θ-role has to be assigned to one DP. (=(186b))

(215) a. I expect there to be a man in the room. (=(187))
b.* I forced there to be a man in the room.

However, if we keep on considering a feature checking version of θ-role assignment, a problem occurs. If we capture θ-role assignment in terms of feature checking, we cannot derive optional assignment. It is obvious that some kinds of θ-roles are optionally assigned as are exemplified in (216).

(216) a. John talked to Mary about that matter.
b. John talked to Mary.
c. John talked about that matter.

The example in (216a) includes a Goal *to Mary* and a Theme *about that matter*. However, in (216b), only *to Mary* appears and in (216c) only *about that matter* can be found. Then, a question is what happens to the Theme feature in (216b) and the Goal feature in (216c). We cannot assume that θ-role features are checked optionally, because we cannot presume optional feature checking under Chomsky's feature checking framework (except for "normal" Edge Features).

One can claim that this problem is solved if we assume that a verbal head can have different sets of theta-role features depending on the specifics of the situation. Namely, in one case, the verb *talk* has an Agent feature only, but in other case *talk* has some other features. However, this assumption is almost the same as assuming many kinds of *talk* heads as in (217). The assumption of so many kinds of *talk* heads is an ad hoc stipulation and thus this is not a principled explanation.

(217) talk A [Agent]
talk B [Agent, Theme]
talk C [Agent, Theme, Goal]
⋮

Now, note that the problem thus far arises because we suggest that θ-role features originally exist on a verbal head. Hence, one possible solution to this problem of optional θ-role assignment is to assume that θ-role features exist outside of the verbal head, namely, on other projections separately. In the recent framework, it is assumed that a Theme role is assigned to a DP by a V head, but an Agent role is assigned to a DP by a *v** head. Then, under the feature checking framework for θ-role assignment, it is possible to assume that the Agent feature is not transmitted from a V head to *v** but is originally posited on *v** as in (218b). In a similar vein, Goal or other roles are also not placed on the V head but on other heads (probably Voice or Asp, although I will not discuss what heads they are in this book) and such heads can be introduced within the layers of the verbal projection when necessary as in (218c).

(218) a. V [Theme]
b. *v** [Agent] + V [Theme]
c. *v** [Agent] + X [Goal] + V [Theme]

In this way, we can account for the problem of optional θ-role assignment as follows: an Agent feature must be obligatorily checked because it is necessarily introduced in the derivation since it is posited on *v** and *v** is an essential projection to finish the derivation successfully (except for passive or unaccusative sentences). Moreover, assuming that a Theme feature exists on transitive or unaccusative V heads, the Theme feature is necessarily introduced and thus necessarily checked, given that the derivation cannot converge without the verbal heads.[69] On the other hand, Goal or other roles exist on a head which is optionally introduced in the derivation and thus they sometimes do not appear in the derivation.

Under this assumption, θ-roles are not assigned directly from a verbal head to an argument, but a θ-role feature acts as a kind of a bridge between an argument and a specific semantic interpretation of a verb. I assume that the verbal head *eat*, for example, possesses more specific roles of *eater*, *food*, *manner*, *location*, or etc. Then, syntactic derivation determines how much information is encoded in the sentence. If the syntactic derivation includes *v** with an Agent feature as in the active sentence *John ate the sushi*, the Agent feature on *v** has to be checked by merger with the subject *John* and the Theme on V, with *the sushi*, and the θ-role relation in (219a) is derived. Then, the Agent feature and the Theme feature act as bridges between the subject *John* and the object *the sushi* and the specific interpretation *eater* and *food* on the verb, respectively, at the C-I Interface. In a similar vein, in the passive sentence *The sushi was eaten*, *v* without an Agent feature is introduced and only a Theme feature exists as in (219b). Then, the DP *the sushi*, which has checked the Theme role feature, is associated with the specific interpretation of *food* on the verb as in (219b).

(219) a. John ate the sushi.

Checkers	[John, the sushi]	
	| \	feature checking relation
θ-roles	[Agent, Theme]	
	| /	association at the C-I Interface
Roles on *eat*	[eater, food, place...]	

b. The sushi was eaten.

Checkers	[the sushi]	
	|	feature checking relation
θ-roles	[Theme]	
	\	association at the C-I Interface
Roles on *eat*	[eater, food, place...]	

69 I suggest that an unergative verb does not possess a Theme feature.

Now, it is derived that a θ-role feature exists on a projection which introduces a DP (or a prepositional phrase) in order to check the θ-role feature. In other words, the θ-role feature is posited on the projection with which the DP is externally merged. Recall that a Lexical Edge Feature triggers external merge with an argument. Then, the distribution of θ-role features is exactly the same as that of Lexical Edge Features. At first, I tentatively proposed Lexical Edge Features as something related to θ-role assignment, but now we can derive that a Lexical Edge Feature is not a helper for θ-role assignment, but it is exactly a θ-role feature itself. We can derive Lexical Edge Features as follows:

(220) Lexical Edge Feature = "normal" Edge Feature + θ-role feature

Thus, I claim that the checking of θ-role features occurs through first Edge Feature checking when an element is externally merged. Recall that Edge Features can be reused as we saw in 6.5.1. Thus, after checking of a θ-role feature, an Edge Feature can still act as a trigger for internal merge if some motivation exits.

As we assumed that Lexical Edge Features are not only related to θ-roles but also to modification by adjuncts, we have to extend the assumption in (220) to adjuncts as well. Clearly, adjuncts should possess Manner or Frequency features and we can assume that such features have to be checked via merger with VP or TP. In this way, we can incorporate modification roles on adjuncts in (220) by assuming that modification role features of Manner or Frequency are included in θ-role features in an extended sense.

Now, the final question is what kind of operation the checking of θ-role features is. What values are θ-role (and modification) features assigned? Recall that I argued that Lexical Edge Features are *unvalued interpretable* features in this subsection. Then, if a Lexical Edge Feature is a "normal" Edge Feature plus a θ-role feature, this should be the status of the θ-role feature; θ-role features are *unvalued interpretable* features. Here we can observe the nature of unvalued interpretable features. Imagine an Agent feature. The concept of Agent is interpretable as an "[e]ntity instigating some action (Radford (2009: 202))." However, Agent itself does not have any concrete meaning. In order to be fully interpreted at the C-I Interface, more information is needed such as [+/−human] or [+/−animate]. In this way, an

Agent feature is an interpretable feature but it lacks values. In a similar vein, I suggest that modification features on adjuncts such as Manner or Frequency need specification concerning the status of its modifying event such as [+/−stative] or [+/−teric]. Therefore, the checking of θ-role and modification features is an operation to copy such feature values on an argument or VP/TP onto the θ-role or the modification features, respectively. Given that a lexical item is considered to be a bundle of features in the MP, probably, all the relevant feature values on a merged item are copied on a θ-role (or modification) feature through the valuation. Therefore, after the derivation, the θ-role features in (219) should be more specific as in (221). Hence, I claim that due to the copy of values, the association process at the C-I Interface need not look back at the checking operation between the DP and the θ-role feature, but need only see the value on the θ-role feature as in (221). In this way, the computational burden of the association operation is reduced.

(221) a. John ate the sushi.
θ-roles [$\text{Agent}_{[\text{John}]}$, $\text{Theme}_{[\text{the sushi}]}$]
association at the C-I Interface
Roles on *eat* [eater, food, place…]
b. The sushi was eaten.
θ-roles [$\text{Theme}_{[\text{the sushi}]}$]
association at the C-I Interface
Roles on *eat* [eater, food, place…]

Finally let us consider how the feature checking framework for θ-role assignment above excludes inappropriate examples. There are two logical possibilities of inappropriate examples: those lacking sufficient arguments or those involving superfluous arguments. Firstly, the example lacking a sufficient argument in (222) is excluded as follows:

(222) *John gave Mary.

The sentence in (222) includes a Theme role which is not "discharged," in traditional terms. This sentence is ruled out because although the DOC includes three θ-role features of Agent on *v**, Recipient on Asp, and Theme on V (recall the discussions in 4.4.3.2), the Theme feature is not checked.

Thus, since the Theme feature is not valued, the interpretation of that feature at the C-I interface fails.

Secondly, a sentence including a superfluous argument as in (223) is excluded as is discussed below.

(223) *John hit Mary Ken.

In order to derive (223), there are two possibilities. One possibility is that the derivation includes *Mary*, which is adjoined to VP or *v**P without checking any θ-role features. In this case, the sentence results in including an argument which does not contribute to any interpretation for the argument structure. Note that adjuncts still have to possess some modification features such as Manner and the features should be checked under the assumption here. Thus the DP *Mary* even cannot be treated as an adjunct. Thus, I claim that the existence of the DP violates the full interpretation principle in a broad sense since although the features on the DP themselves are interpretable, the DP itself cannot be interpreted as a member involved in the event expressed by the sentence.

The other possibility is that the derivation includes the structure in the DOC with Agent, Recipient, and Theme features. Namely, if the derivation includes Asp, Appl and *v** heads as in 4.4.3.2, the syntax can produce the example in (223). However, the θ-role relations that are gained cannot be associated with the interpretation on *hit* and thus the association results in failure as in (224). In this way, (223) is ruled out at the C-I Interface.

(224) *John hit Mary Ken.

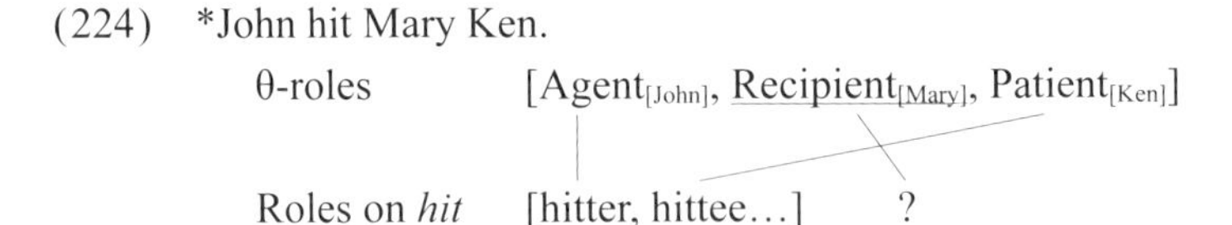

Interestingly, some unusual verbs can be found in DOC structures in a proper context as in (225). This indicates that the unusual association is possible if there is a possible interpretation on the verb. Therefore, (223) should not be completely ruled out in syntax, but should be excluded at the C-I Interface.

(225) She kicked him a ball. (Goldberg (2006: 42))

6.5.4 On Phasal Edge Features and the Whole Framework in this Book

Thus far, we have considered the natures of a "normal" Edge Feature and its variant, a Lexical Edge Feature, which are finally reduced to a "normal" Edge Feature plus a θ-feature. However, we still have one special case of Edge Features; that is, an Edge Feature which a strong-phase head possesses and transcribed onto a weak-phase head through Feature-Transcription, or transmitted to the complement head through EF-Inheritance (see 6.4). Let us call this variant of an Edge Feature a Phasal Edge Feature. As anonymous reviewer points out, obviously, its behavior is different from that of a "normal" Edge Feature.

Recall that a Phasal Edge Feature triggers movement of discourse-related items such as *wh*/Topic/Focus elements to the phase edge. Then, a straightforward expectation is that a Phasal Edge Feature is a "normal" Edge Feature plus a discourse-related feature. Therefore, although I have argued that an Edge Feature is copied through Feature-Transcription and it is passed to a complement head in EF-Inheritance (see 6.4), strictly speaking, it is this discourse-related feature that is copied or passed via these processes.

Finally, the whole picture of the framework in this book concerning Edge Features emerges: although checking of an Edge Feature is optional, it requires some additional requirement, e.g., φ-feature checking, θ-feature checking, or discourse-related feature checking. To be more specific, external merge is triggered by an Edge Feature motivated by a θ-feature (or in some cases such as external merge of T and *v**P, probably, motivated by a selection feature). On the other hand, internal merge occurs in terms of an Edge Feature motivated by φ-features (a case of A-movement) or a discourse-related feature (when it comes to A-bar movement). In any case, an Edge Feature cannot trigger merge on its own without additional motivations. This is consistent with Chomsky's (2001: 34) assumption in (226).

(226) Optional operations can apply only if they have an effect on outcome.

Thus, I conclude that every syntactic operation occurs as a Last Resort, as has been assumed within the Minimalist framework.

6.6 Summary

In this chapter, we have observed how adjunct islands are derived from the Labeling Algorithm and the Phase Theory, under the Feature-Transcription framework. What plays an important role under the claim is the assumption of a Lexical Edge Feature, which is a variant of a "normal" Edge Feature. Based on the Labeling Algorithm, the XP-YP situation prevents checking of a Lexical Edge Feature and thus adjunct islands are ruled out. Moreover, I have shown that if we assume prepositional weak-phases, namely, *p*P, the optionality of preposition-stranding/pied-piping is captured and the discussion can be extended to the impossibility of preposition-stranding in rightward movement. Furthermore, I have shown a detailed consideration on the nature of "normal" Edge Features, Lexical Edge Features, and Phasal Edge Features, concluding that Edge Feature checking requires some additional motivation such as checking of φ-features, a θ-role feature, a discourse-related feature and so on.

7

Concluding Remarks

In this book, I have claimed that although Chomsky's (2007, 2008, 2013) Feature-Inheritance framework is theoretically elegant and also gains empirical support, a problem concerning weak-phases arises. This problem can be summed up as in (227) as the paradox of weak-phases.

(227) The paradox of weak-phases
  a. Concerning A-movement, a weak-phase serves **as a non-phase**.
  b. Concerning A-bar movement, a weak-phase serves **as a phase**.

The main claim of this book is that the paradox of weak-phases is readily solved based on (228) and this is derived under the assumption of an extended version of Feature-Inheritance, namely, Feature-Transcription in (229).

(228) A solution to the paradox of weak-phases:
  The operations in a weak-phase must occur **at the next strong-phase level**.

(229) Feature-Transcription

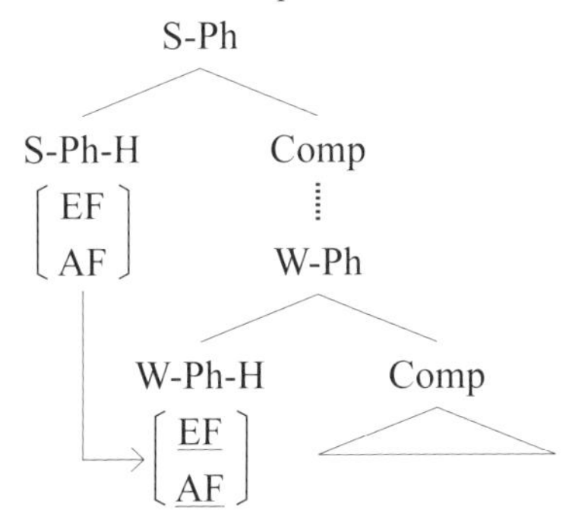

In this way, this book has contributed to Chomsky's Feature-Inheritance framework by sorting out tangles in the theory.

Furthermore, the discussion in this book has derived an important consequence of optional derivations, which is a blind side in the MP: Under the MP, every operation is evaluated in terms of economy and thus optional operations are a difficult to derive theoretically. However, under the Feature-Transcription framework, the two kinds of economy, namely, the size of transfer operations and the number of transfer operations counterbalance each other and in this way the optionality of the two derivational patterns below is derived.

(230) Simultaneous-derivation

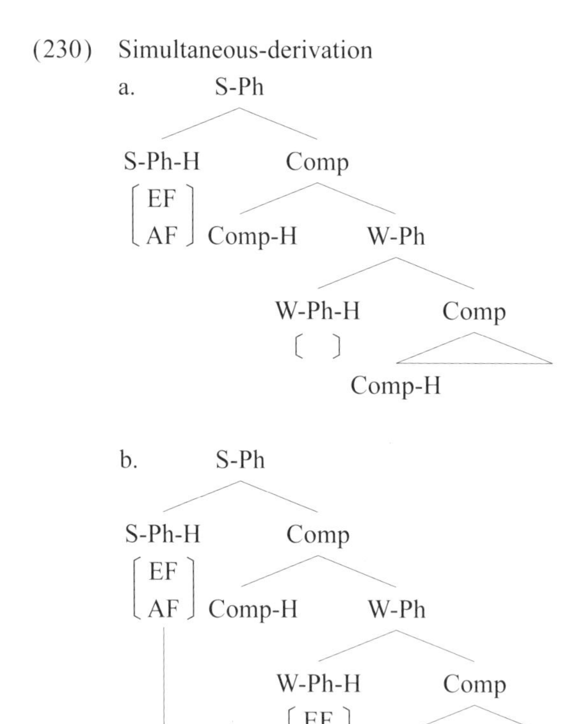

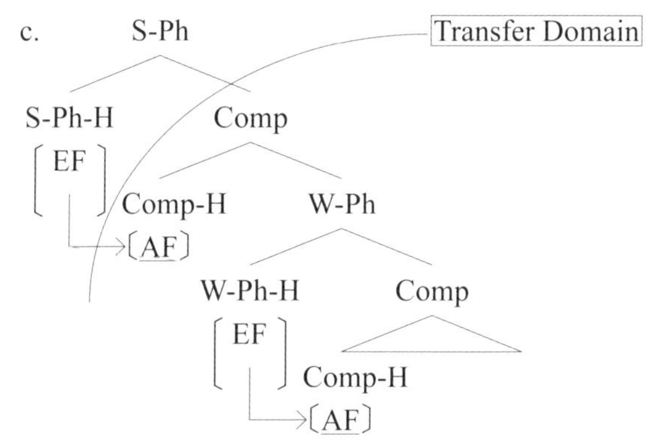

(231) Individual-derivation

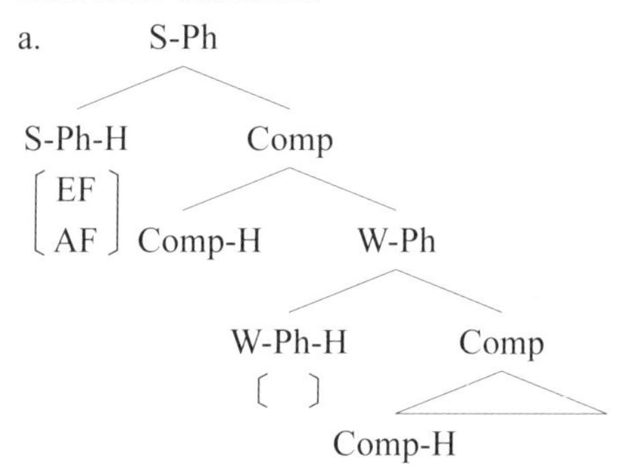

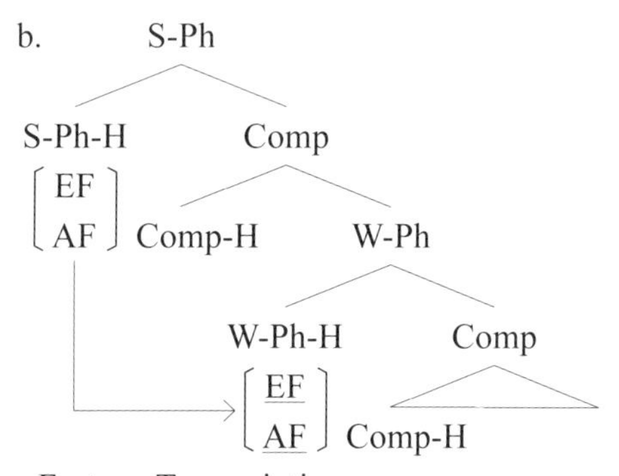

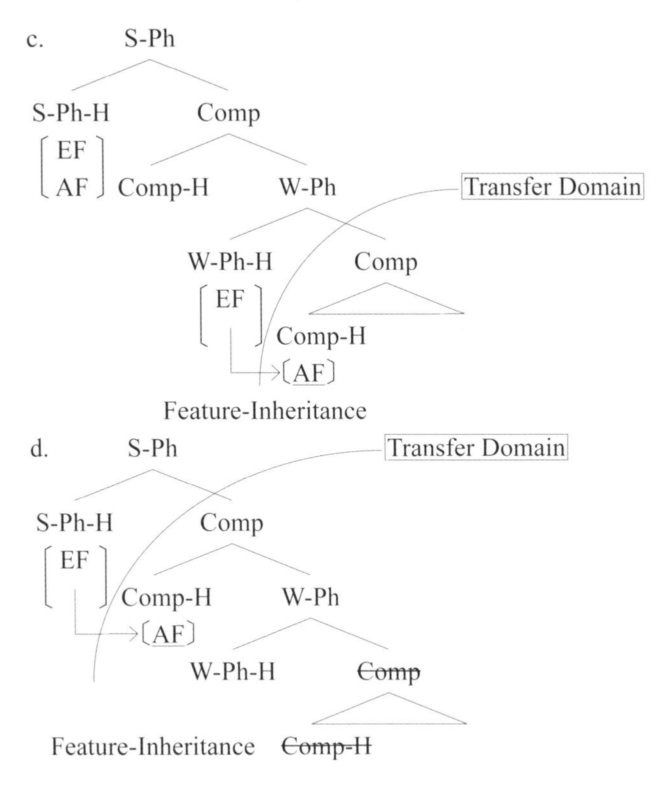

Thus, based on these two possibilities, the Feature-Transcription framework can explain optional phenomena in human languages. The important assumption concerning the two possibilities is the following transfer-based case assignment mechanism.

(232) A phase head determines a DP's case within its domain, when it triggers Transfer.

Based on these assumptions, I have explicated many phenomena concerning weak-phases. In chapter 4, I have explained phenomena related to verbal weak-phases including the inflection-movement connection in Scandinavian languages, the Th/Ex construction in English, the nominative/accusative case conversion in Japanese, and the DOC in English. In chapter 5, I have extended the research to clausal weak-phases including the ECM construction in the Irish dialect of English, the Japanese Raising-to-Object Construction, and complementizer agreement in West Flemish. In the last chapter, I have explicated adjunct islands based on the Labeling Algorithm and Lexical Edge Features under the Feature-Transcription framework. The phenomena investigated in this chapter included preposition-stranding/pied-piping in leftward and rightward movement in English. In this way, I hope to have shown enough empirical evidence to warrant the assumption of Feature-Transcription.

To wrap up, I have shown that Feature-Transcription not only solves the theoretical problem under Chomsky's Feature-Inheritance framework but also enable the recent framework to accommodate challenging examples of optionality. In this way, this book contributes to the further development of the MP and generative grammar. Finally, I strongly believe that the enterprise of generative grammar will someday reach the glorious terminal point of clarifying the language faculty of human beings.

Before ending the discussion in this book, one question remains: whether Feature-Transcription is actually an extended version of Feature-Inheritance or it is an independent, different operation. Although this book has assumed that it is an extended case of Feature-Inheritance, the differences discussed in 3.4.2 should not be ignored. Further research may reveal that Feature-Transcription is derivable from some other mechanisms. At any rate, in order to explain the characteristics of weak-phases, we need some activation mechanism between strong/weak-phase heads and a contribution this book has hopefully made is to clarify that point. I believe that development of the framework will crystallize the true answer to the remaining question.

References

Abels, Klaus (2003) *Successive Cyclicity, Anti-Locality, and Adposition Stranding*, Doctoral dissertation, University of Connecticut.

Ackema, Peter and Ad Neeleman (2004) *Beyond Morphology: Interface Conditions on Word Formation*, Oxford University Press, Oxford.

Amano, Masachiyo (1998) *Eigo Niju Mokutekigo no Togo Kozo ni kansuru Seisei Rironteki Kenkyu* (A Generative Approach to the Syntactic Structure of the Double Object Construction in English), Eichosha, Tokyo.

Baker, Mark C. (1988) *Incorporation: A Theory of Grammatical Function Changing,* University of Chicago Press, Chicago.

Baker, Mark C. (1997) "Thematic Roles and Syntactic Structure," *Elements of Grammar*, ed. by Lilian Haegeman, 73–137, Kluwer, Dordrecht.

Baker, Mark C. (2012) "On the Relationship of Object Agreement and Accusative Case: Evidence from Amharic," *Linguistic Inquiry* 43, 255–274.

Barss, Andrew and Howard Lasnik (1986) "A Note on Anaphora and Double Objects," *Linguistic Inquiry* 17, 347–354.

Beck, Sigrid and Kyle Johnson (2004) "Double Objects Again," *Linguistic Inquiry* 35, 97–123.

Blight, Ralph C. (1999) "Verb Positions and the Auxiliary *Be*," ms., University of Texas.

Boeckx, Cedric (2008) *Understanding Minimalist Syntax: Lessons from Locality in Long-Distance Dependencies*, Blackwell, Malden, MA.

Boeckx, Cedric and Norbert Hornstein (2003) "Reply to 'Control Is Not Movement,'" *Linguistic Inquiry* 35, 431–452.

Boeckx, Cedric, Norbert Hornstein and Jairo Nunes (2010) *Control as Movement*, Cambridge University Press, Cambridge.

Boeckx, Cedric and Fumikazu Niinuma (2004) "Conditions on Agreement in Japanese," *Natural Language and Linguistic Theory* 22, 453–480.

Bošković, Želiko and Daiko Takahashi (1998) "Scrambling and Last Resort," *Linguistic Inquiry* 20, 219–251.

Bowers, John (1993) "The Syntax of Predication," *Linguistic Inquiry* 24, 591–656.

Bresnan, Joan, Anna Cueni, Tatiana Nikitina and Harald Baayen (2007) "Predicting the Dative Alternation," *Cognitive Foundations of Interpretation*, ed. by Gerlof Boume, Irene Krämer and Joost Zwarts, 69–94, Royal Netherlands Academy of Science, Amsterdam.

Bresnan, Joan and Tatiana Nikitina (2010) "The Gradience of the Dative Alternation," *Reality Exploration and Discovery: Pattern Interaction in Language and Life*, ed. by Linda Uyechi and Lian Hee Wee, CSLI Publications, Stanford, CA.

Bruenning, Benjamin (2010a) "Double Object Constructions Disguised as Prepositional Datives," *Linguistic Inquiry* 41, 287–305.

Bruenning, Benjamin (2010b) "Ditransitive Asymmetries and a Theory of Idiom Formation," *Linguistic Inquiry* 41, 519–562.

Caponigro, Ivano and Carson T. Schütze (2003) "Parameterizing Passive Participle Movement," *Linguistic Inquiry* 34, 293–307.

Chomsky, Noam (1981) *Lectures on Government and Binding*, Foris, Dordrecht.

Chomsky, Noam (1995) *The Minimalist Program*, MIT Press, Cambridge, MA.

Chomsky, Noam (2000) "Minimalist Inquiries: The Framework," *Step by Step: Essays on Minimalist Syntax in Honor of Howard Lasnik*, ed. by Roger Martin, David Michaels and Juan Uriagereka, 89–155, MIT Press, Cambridge, MA.

Chomsky, Noam (2001) "Derivation by Phase," *Ken Hale: A Life in Language*, ed. by Michael Kenstowicz, 1–52, MIT Press, Cambridge, MA.

Chomsky, Noam (2004) "Beyond Explanatory Adequacy," *Structures and Beyond: The Cartography of Syntactic Structures*, Vol.3, ed. by Adriana Belletti, 104–131, Oxford University Press, Oxford.

Chomsky, Noam (2007) "Approaching UG from Below," *Interfaces + Recursion = Language?*, ed. by Uli Sauerland and Hans-Martin Gärtner, 1–29, Mouton de Gruyter, Berlin.

Chomsky, Noam (2008) "On Phases," *Foundational Issues in Linguistic Theory*, ed. by Robert Freidin, Carlos P. Otero and Maria L. Zubizarreta, 133–166, MIT Press, Cambridge, MA.

Chomsky, Noam (2013) "Problems of Projection," *Lingua* 130, 33–49.

Chomsky, Noam (2015) "Problems of Projection: Extensions," *Structures, Strategies and Beyond: Studies in Honour of Adriana Belletti*, ed. by Elisa Di Domenico, Cornelia Hamann and Simona Matteini, 3–16, John Benjamins, Amsterdam.

Chomsky, Noam and Howard Lasnik (1993) "The Theory of Principles and Parameters," *Syntax: An International Handbook of Contemporary Research*, ed. by Joachim Jacobs, Arnim von Stechow, Wolfgang Sternefeld and Theo Vennemann, 506–569, Walter de Gruyter, Berlin.

Citko, Barbara (2011) *Symmetry in Syntax*, Cambridge University Press, Cambridge.

Drummond, Alex, Norbert Hornstein and Howard Lasnik (2010) "A Puzzle about P-Stranding and a Possible Solution," *Linguistic Inquiry* 41, 689–692.

Epstein, Samuel David, Eric M. Groat, Ruriko Kawashima and Hisatsugu Kitahara (1998) *A Derivational Approach to Syntactic Relations*, Oxford University Press, Oxford.

Epstein, Samuel David and T. Daniel Seely (2002) "Rule Applications as Cycles in a Level-Free Syntax," *Derivation and Explanation in the Minimalist Program*, ed. by Samuel David Epstein and T. Daniel Seely, 65–90, Blackwell Publishers Ltd, Malden, MA.

Fox, Danny (1995) "Condition C and ACD," *Papers on Minimalist Syntax, MIT Working Papers in Linguistics* 27, ed. by Rob Pensalfini and Hiroyuki Ura, 105–119, MIT Press, Cambridge, MA.

Fox, Danny (2000) *Economy and Semantic Interpretation*, MIT Press, Cambridge, MA.

Fukui, Naoki (1993) "A Note on Improper Movement," *The Linguistic Review* 10, 111–126.

Goldberg, Adele Eva (2006) *Constructions at Work*, Oxford University Press, Oxford, New York.

Haegeman, Lilian and Marjo van Koppen (2012) "Complementizer Agreement and the Relation C^0 and T^0," *Linguistic Inquiry* 43, 441–454.

Hasegawa, Nobuko (2005) "Honorifics," *The Blackwell Companion to Syntax* 2, ed. by Martin Everaert and Henk Van Riemsdijk, 493–543, Blackwell, Oxford.

Hiraiwa, Ken (2005) *Dimensions of Symmetry in Syntax: Agreement and Clausal Architecture*, Doctoral dissertation, MIT.

Holmberg, Anders (2002) "Expletives and Agreement in Scandinavian Passive," *Journal of Comparative Germanic Linguistics* 4, 85–128.

Hornstein, Norbert (1999) "Movement and Control," *Linguistic Inquiry* 30, 69–96.

Hornstein, Norbert (2009) *A Theory of Syntax: Minimal Operations and Universal Grammar*, Cambridge University Press, Cambridge.

Hornstein, Norbert and Amy Weinberg (1981) "Case Theory and Preposition Stranding," *Linguistic Inquiry* 12, 55–92.

Huang, C.-T. James (1982) *Logical Relations in Chinese and the Theory of Grammar*, Doctoral dissertation, MIT.

Kanno, Satoru (2008) "On the Phasehood and Non-Phasehood of CP," *English Linguistics* 25, 21–55.

Kayne, Richard (1994) *The Antisymmetry of Syntax*, MIT Press, Cambridge, MA.

Kishimoto, Hideki (1996) "Agr and Agreement in Japanese," *Formal Approaches to Japanese Linguistics 2, MIT Working Papers in Linguistics* 29, ed. by Masatoshi Koizumi, Masayuki Oishi and Uli Sauerland, 41–60, Cambridge, MA.

Kitada, Shin-Ichi (2013) "Feature Inheritance and Four Types of Argument Structure," *JELS* 30, 97–103.

Koizumi, Masatoshi (1994) "Nominative Objects: The Role of TP in Japanese," *Formal Approaches to Japanese Linguistics* 1, *MIT Working Papers in Linguistics* 24, ed. by Masatoshi Koizumi and Hiroyuki Ura, 211–230, MIT Press, Cambridge, MA.

Kuno, Susumu (1973) *The Structure of the Japanese Language*, MIT Press, Cambridge, MA.

Kurogi, Takayoshi (2014) *Two Approaches to the Parasitic Gap Construction in English*, Doctoral dissertation, Kyushu University.

Larson, Richard K. (1988) "On the Double Object Construction," *Linguistic Inquiry* 19, 335–391.

Legate, Julie Anne (2003) "Some Interface Properties of the Phase," *Linguistic Inquiry* 34, 506–516.

Maeda, Masako (2013) *Derivational Feature-Based Relativized Minimality*, Doctoral dissertation, Kyushu University. [Published by Kyushu University Press, Fukuoka, 2014]

Marantz, Alec (1993) "Implications of Asymmetries in Double Object Constructions," *Theoretical Aspects of Bantu Grammar*, ed. by Sam A. Mchombo, 113–150, CSLI Publications, Stanford, CA.

Matsubara, Fuminori (2000) "p*P Phases," *Linguistic Analysis* 30, 127–161.

May, Robert (1979) "Must COMP-to-COMP Movement Be Stipulated?," *Linguistic Inquiry* 10, 719–725.

McCloskey, James (2000) "Quantifier Float and *Wh*-Movement in an Irish English," *Linguistic Inquiry* 31, 57–84.

Mikami, Akira (1970) "Keigoho Naigai (The Honorifics within or outside of Japan)," *Bunpo Shoronshu* (A Collection of Short Papers in Grammar), 88–112, Kurosio, Tokyo.

Milsark, Gary Lee (1994) *Existential Sentences in English*, Doctoral dissertation, MIT. [Published by Garland, New York, 1979]

Miyagawa, Shigeru (2010) *Why Agree? Why Move?: Unifying Agreement- Based and Discourse-Configurational Languages*, MIT Press, Cambridge, MA.

Müller, Gereon (2010) "On Deriving CED Effects from the PIC," *Linguistic Inquiry* 41, 35–82.

Nishimura, Megumi (2013) *A Derivational Approach to Multiple Wh-Questions in English*, Doctoral dissertation, Kyushu University.

Nissenbaum, Jon (1998) "Movement and Derived Predicates: Evidence from Parasitic Gaps," *The Interpretive Tract, MIT Working Papers in Linguistics* 25, ed. by Uli Sauerland and Orin Percus, 247–295, MIT Press, Cambridge, MA.

Nunes, Jairo (2013) "X′-Structure and Minimalism," *The Bloomsbury Companion to Syntax*, ed. by Silvia Luraghi and Claudia Parodi, 76–87, Bloomsbury Publishing, NY.

Oba, Yukio (2005) "The Double Object Construction and Thematization/ Extraction," *English Linguistics* 22, 56–81.

Obata, Miki (2010) *Root, Successive-Cyclic and Feature-Splitting Internal Merge: Implications for Feature-Inheritance and Transfer*, Doctoral dissertation, The University of Michigan.

Obata, Miki (2012) "Feature-Splitting Internal Merge and its Implications for the Elimination of A/A′-Position Types," *Phases: Developing the Framework*, ed. by Ángel J. Gallego, 173–194, De Gruyter Mouton, Boston, MA.

Obata, Miki and Samuel David Epstein (2008) "Deducing Improper Movement from Phase-Based C-to-T Phi Transfer: Feature-Splitting Internal Merge," *Proceedings of the 27th West Coast Conference on Formal Linguistics*, 353–360.

Oka, Toshifusa (1988) "Abstract Case and Empty Pronouns," *Tsukuba English Studies* 7, 187–227.

Otsuka, Tomonori (2014) "An Extension of Feature-Inheritance," *English Linguistics* 31, 509–544.

Pesetsky, David (1995) *Zero Syntax: Experiencers and Cascades*, MIT Press, Cambridge, MA.

Pesetsky, David and Esther Torrego (2007) "The Syntax of Valuation and the Interpretability of Features," *Phrasal and Clausal Architecture: Syntactic Derivation and Interpretation*, ed. by Simin Karimi, Vida Samiian and Wendy K. Wilkins, 262–294, John Benjamins, Amsterdam.

Pollock, Jean-Yves (1989) "Verb Movement, Universal Grammar, and the Structure of IP," *Linguistic Inquiry* 20, 365–424.

Postal (1974) *On Raising: One Rule of English Grammar and its Theoretical Implications,* MIT Press, Cambridge, MA.

Pylkkänen, Liina (2008) *Introducing Arguments*, MIT Press, Cambridge, MA.

Radford, Andrew (2009) *An Introduction to English Sentence Structure*, Cambridge University Press, Cambridge.

Richards, Marc D. (2007) "On Feature Inheritance: An Argument from the Phase Impenetrability Condition," *Linguistic Inquiry* 38, 563–572.

Richards, Marc D. (2012) "On Feature Inheritance, Defective Phases, and the Movement-Morphology Connection," *Phases: Developing the Framework*, ed. by Ángel J. Gallego, 195–232, De Gruyter Mouton, Boston, MA.

Richards, Norvin (2001) "An Idiomatic Argument for Lexical Decomposition," *Linguistic Inquiry* 32, 183–192.

Richards, Norvin (2010) *Uttering Trees*, MIT Press, Cambridge, MA.

Rizzi, Luigi (1997) "The Fine Structure of the Left Periphery," *Elements of Grammar*, ed. by Lilian Haegeman, 281–337, Kluwer, Dordrecht.

Rochemont, Michael S. and Peter W. Culicover (1990) *English Focus Constructions and the Theory of Grammar*, Cambridge University Press, Cambridge.

Saito, Mamoru (1985) *Some Asymmetries in Japanese and their Theoretical Implications*, Doctoral dissertation, MIT.

Sakai, Hiromu (1998) "Raising Asymmetry and Improper Movement," *Japanese/Korean Linguistics* 7, ed. by Noriko Akatsuka, Hajime Hoji, Shoichi Iwasaki, Sung-Ock Sohn and Susan Strauss, 481–497, CSLI Publications, Stanford, CA.

Sigurðsson, Halldór Ármann (2006) "The Nominative Puzzle and the Low Nominative Hypothesis," *Linguistic Inquiry* 37, 289–308.

Stepanov, Arthur (2001) "Late Adjunction and Minimalist Phrase Structure," *Syntax* 4, 94–125.

Stepanov, Arthur (2007) "The End of CED? Minimalism and Extraction Domains," *Syntax* 10, 80–126.

Stowell, Timothy (1981) *Origins of Phrase Structure*, Doctoral dissertation, MIT.

Svenonius, Peter (2001) "Impersonal Passives: A Phase-Based Analysis," *Proceedings of the 18th Scandinavian Conference of Linguistics*, 109–125.

Tada, Hiroaki (1992) "Nominative Objects in Japanese," *Journal of Japanese Linguistics* 14, 91–108.

Takahashi, Masahiko (2011) "Case-Valuation, Phasehood, and Nominative/Accusative Conversion in Japanese," *Proceedings of the 39th Conference of NELS*, 759–770.

Takami, Ken-ichi (1992) *Preposition Stranding: From Syntactic to Functional Analyses*, Mouton de Gruyter, NY.

Takano, Yuji (1998) "Object Shift and Scrambling," *Natural Language and Linguistic Theory* 16, 817–889.

Takano, Yuji (2000) "Illicit Remnant Movement: An Argument for Feature-Driven Movement," *Linguistic Inquiry* 31, 141–156.

Takano, Yuji (2003) "Nominative Objects in Japanese Complex Predicate Constructions: A Prolepsis Analysis," *Natural Language and Linguistic Theory* 21, 779–834.

Takeuchi, Hajime (2010) "Exceptional Case Marking in Japanese and Optional Feature Transmission," *Nanzan Linguistics* 6, 101–128.

Tanaka, Hidekazu (2002) "Raising to Object out of CP," *Linguistic Inquiry* 33, 637–657.

Tanaka, Hiroyoshi (2011) "On Extraposition from NP Constructions: A Phase-Based Account," *English Linguistics* 28, 173–205.

Toribio, Almeida Jacqueline (1990) "Specifier-Head Agreement in Japanese," *WCCFL* 9, 535–548.

Travis, Lisa deMena (2010) *Inner Aspect: The Articulation of VP*, Springer, Dordrecht.

Ura, Hiroyuki (1996) *Multiple-Feature Checking: A Theory of Grammatical Function Splitting*, Doctoral dissertation, MIT.

Ura, Hiroyuki (2007) "Long-Distance Case-Assignment in Japanese and its Dialectal Variation," *Gengo Kenkyu* 131, 1–43.

Uriagereka, Juan (1999) "Multiple Spell-Out," *Working Minimalism: Current Studies in Linguistics*, ed. by Samuel David Epstein and Norbert Hornstein, 251–282, MIT Press, Cambridge, MA.

Zwart, Jan-Wouter (1994) "On Holmberg's Generalization," *Language and Cognition* 4, 229–242.

Index

Studies in the Humanities

The Faculty of Humanities, Kyushu University, as a center of research in and education on the Humanities, has set up a fund to publish the results of its academic research under the series title *Studies in the Humanities*, to promote its research activities and share the outcomes with a wide audience.

Already published in the series:

1 王昭君から文成公主へ――中国古代の国際結婚――
藤野月子(九州大学大学院人文科学研究院・専門研究員)

2 水の女――トポスへの船路――
小黒康正(九州大学大学院人文科学研究院・教授)

3 小林方言とトルコ語のプロソディー
――一型アクセント言語の共通点――
佐藤久美子(長崎外国語大学外国語学部・講師)

4 背表紙キャサリン・アーンショー
――イギリス小説における自己と外部――
鵜飼信光(九州大学大学院人文科学研究院・准教授)

5 朝鮮中近世の公文書と国家――変革期の任命文書をめぐって――
川西裕也(日本学術振興会特別研究員 PD) 〈第4回三島海雲学術賞受賞〉

6 始めから考える――ハイデッガーとニーチェ――
菊地惠善(九州大学大学院人文科学研究院・教授)

7 日本の出版物流通システム――取次と書店の関係から読み解く――
秦　洋二(流通科学大学商学部・准教授) 〈第7回地理空間学会賞学術賞受賞〉

8 御津の浜松一言抄――『浜松中納言物語』を最終巻から読み解く――
辛島正雄(九州大学大学院人文科学研究院・教授)

9 南宋の文人と出版文化――王十朋と陸游をめぐって――
甲斐雄一(日本学術振興会特別研究員 PD)

10 戦争と平和，そして革命の時代のインタナショナル
山内昭人(九州大学大学院人文科学研究院・教授)

11 On Weak-Phases: An Extension of Feature-Inheritance
Tomonori Otsuka (Lecturer of English Linguistics, Kyushu Kyoritsu University)

12 A Grammar of Irabu, A Southern Ryukyuan Language
Michinori Shimoji (Associate Professor of Linguistics, Kyushu University)

(著者の所属等は刊行時のもの)